3/13

D1578803

Athens

GREENWICH LIBRARIES

3 8028 01616466 4

Cities of the Imagination

Cities of the Imagination

Athens

A cultural and literary history

Michael Llewellyn Smith

Signal Books
Oxford

L B OF GREENWICH LIBRARIES	
016164664	
Cypher	12.07.04
949.512	£12.00

© Michael Llewellyn Smith, 2004
Foreword © Roderick Beaton, 2004

The right of Michael Llewellyn Smith to be identified as the author of this work has
been asserted by him in accordance with the Copyright, Design
and Patents Act, 1988.

All rights reserved. The whole of this work, including all text and illustrations, is
protected by copyright. No parts of this work may be loaded, stored, manipulated,
reproduced or transmitted in any form or by any means, electronic or mechanical,
including photocopying and recording, or by any information, storage and retrieval
system without prior written permission from the publisher, on behalf of the
copyright owner.

A catalogue record for this book is available from the British Library

ISBN 1-902669-80-0 Cloth
ISBN 1-902669-81-9 Paper

Drawings by Wendy Skinner Smith

Cover Design: Baseline Arts
Typesetting: Devdan Sen
Cover Images: Michael Llewellyn Smith; Baseline Arts; Byron © Queen's Printer and
Controller of HMSO, 2003. UK Government Art Collection

Printed in Canada by Webcom

Contents

CHAPTER FOUR
LANDSCAPING THE ACROPOLIS

CHAPTER FIVE
THE AGORA AND THE CLASSICAL CITY

CHAPTER SIX
THE ATHENIAN WAY OF DEATH

CHAPTER SEVEN
BYZANTINES, FRANKS, CATALANS AND FLORENTINES

CHAPTER EIGHT
THE TURKISH TOWN

CHAPTER NINE
ATHENS REVIVED

CHAPTER TEN
ATHENS CAPITAL CITY

Foreword

Athens is famous among cities for being *old*. Home of the most ancient civilisation in Europe, the brilliant white marble monuments of the Acropolis provoked from Edward Lear the astonished cry: "Poor old scrubby Rome sinks into nothing by the side of such beautiful magnificence." And yet, for all the splendours of the ruins at its heart, Athens is not an old city in the way that Rome is, or Istanbul (Constantinople), or even Greece's second city, Thessaloniki. These have always been cities, ever since their founding more than two thousand years ago. Not so Athens.

After the coming of Christianity in the fourth century of our era, after the closing of the theatres and the schools of philosophy a century later, and after long periods of instability during the Middle Ages, by the twelfth century Athens had declined to little more than a large village. When Byron arrived in 1809, to fall in love with the "Maid of Athens", some 12,000 people lived in a smallish cluster of houses round the foot of the Acropolis. A few years later, many of those would be destroyed or badly damaged during the fighting for Greek independence, from 1821 to 1827. When the first king of Greece arrived (from Bavaria) to take up his throne, and it was decided that the capital of newly independent Greece should be established here, there was a scramble to find a house in a fit condition for him to live, while his palace (now the Greek Parliament) was being built.

Right from the earliest plans of the 1830s, a principle of respectful divorce was established between the ancient ruins and the modern city. You don't often in Athens find yourself looking down from a busy modern square into an excavated area where you can easily imagine people just like you going about their business five hundred, a thousand, or two thousand years ago. You get nothing of that "layer-on-layer" sense of continuous habitation that you do, for instance, looking up from the ancient Forum in Rome, to see the foundations of Renaissance churches all but suspended above you, or that you do in descending into the vast underground cisterns in the centre of Istanbul. The only place where you might have done so would have been on the Acropolis; but the accumulated works of Byzantines, Catalan mercenaries, Florentine dukes, and a whole Turkish village, were demolished down to the bedrock in the nineteenth century.

So in Athens, either it is very old (more than 1,500 years minimum) or it is really pretty new (less than 180 years maximum). The only exceptions are the city's handful of surviving Byzantine churches, all of them tiny (because it was a small place in those days), and these truly are gems. Scandalously, several others went the same way as the later buildings on the Acropolis, during the 1830s and 1840s.

But of course it would be impossible to imagine Athens without the Acropolis at its centre. For a long time, while the modern city was growing, visitors to it, and many of those who lived there too, used to cast their eyes upwards past the trolley-bus wires, television aerials, above the stationary honking traffic and through the yellow-brown blur of smog, to gaze in despair at the columns of the Parthenon high above, and curse the modern city as an abomination. The worst times were probably the 1970s and 1980s. Since then, successive mayors have had some success in controlling pollution, in preserving older (as opposed to ancient) buildings, in landscaping public spaces and introducing traffic-free zones.

The main streets closest to the Acropolis have been progressively closed to traffic since 2000; beautifully paved and landscaped thoroughfares now lead you beneath the "Sacred Rock" with its temples in peace and quiet (though the occasional rogue motorbike remains a hazard). Many of the houses lining these roads, which for years were so shabby and filthy from the dust and fumes of traffic that you never even glanced at them, suddenly turn out to be rather beautiful neoclassical villas, and after years of neglect are being renovated, with tasteful modern ideas about colour and uplighting. It has become possible to imagine, as it was not a few years ago, what a dignified, leisurely, hopeful, even spacious place Athens must have been during the nineteenth century.

Among the recent transformations in central Athens, perhaps the greatest has been the opening of the Metro in 2000. This, too, has done its bit to bring the modern city into a new kind of contact with the old. The Athens Metro, although not yet very extensive, and with trains which do not run very fast, is worth making a detour just to travel on. Not only are the stations beautifully designed, immaculately maintained and fairly orderly places, however crowded, but many of them contain small museums showing archaeological finds discovered during the building. Commuting to work past the clay pipes of the ancient water-supply, the marks of cart-wheels on the roadway, and even an open sarcophagus, its occupant caught there, in cross-section above your head, must make you feel that bit closer to the daily life of those ancient Greeks, in a way that you never did before.

It is this modern, and still rapidly evolving, Athens that Michael Llewellyn Smith brings evocatively to life in this book. I can think of no one better qualified to do so. As a historian, Michael Llewellyn Smith has lived in Greece, travelled the country, and written several previous books about it; he has a fluent understanding of the Greek language and knows modern Greek literature well. But to all of these he adds the special "inside knowledge" that comes from having served as British Ambassador for three years at the end of the 1990s. This is at once an authoritative travel book, that brings alive the colours, sounds, even the tastes of the modern city, and a thoroughly reliable, non-specialist guide to its modern history, written by someone who as a diplomat has been close to that history in the making.

As Michael Llewellyn Smith knows well, and reveals in these pages, Athens is a city where daily life is hard to separate from politics; where every Friday the neighbourhood street-market bursts into life in the middle of the staid streets near the British Embassy; where the most unpromising street-corner may suddenly open out into a glimpse of the ancient temples of the Acropolis, almost as though floating on air. And yes, despite the smog, you do still sometimes catch one of those famous violet-coloured sunsets that have inspired poets, both ancient and modern.

—Professor Roderick Beaton
Kings College London, 2004

Preface

"Were it... an acknowledged maxim, that the hospitality of a country could only be repaid by a general panegyric on its inhabitants, few travellers would escape the censure either of partiality or ingratitude."
The Hon Frederick North Douglas, *An Essay on Certain Points of Resemblance between the Ancient and Modern Greeks,* 1813

I did much of the work on this book while staying at the British School at Athens, a venerable and friendly institution which has served as home to generations of scholars. I am grateful to the Director, James Whitley, the Librarian, Penny Wilson-Garganas, and the staff of the school; also to the Directors and staff of the Gennadius Library, Athens, the Greek Literary and Historical Archive (ELIA), the National Historical Museum, and the Benaki Museum.

I am grateful also for advice and help to Robert McDonald, Roderick Beaton, Kalliope Kontozoglou and Eleana Yalouri. Debts to other writers and historians of Athens will be clear from the text. The greatest of them are to Robin Barber, until recently editor of the *Blue Guide* to Athens (from whom I learned about Giorgio and Andrea de Chirico in Athens), Eleni Bastea, Kostas Biris, and Alexander Papageorgiou-Venetas. I have found the *Epta Imeres* (*Seven Days*), the weekly supplement of *Kathimerini,* which often covers the history, culture and neighbourhoods of Athens, particularly useful, and would like to thank Aristides Alafouzos and Marta Dertili.

This is not a guidebook, so anyone who visits Athens will need one in addition to this book. I recommend the *Blue Guide* and the *Rough Guide.* Walkers will find David Rupp's book *Athenian Walks* useful. So is Diane Shugart's *Athens by Neighborhood.* These and other guides are listed in the Further Reading.

Anyone who writes about Athens treads in the footsteps of past writers and travellers, the famous such as Thucydides, Pausanias, Byron, Chateaubriand, Henry Miller, and the less famous: Edmond About, George Finlay, Dimitrios Kambouroglou, Ellen Bosanquet, William Miller, George Horton, Rex Warner, Lisa Micheli, Kevin Andrews, Edmund Keeley and others. Each of these writers has his own

Athens, as every Greek writer and artist presents his own Athens, in poetry or prose, paintings or photographs. Their work often tells us as much about themselves as about the city. There are too many aspects to the city and its people to be caught in a single vision.

There is a vast literature about Athens, especially ancient Athens. My reading list is selective and concentrates mainly on books in English, omitting therefore some of the classic Greek histories, by Kambouroglou, Kydoniates, Benizelos etc. Interesting works of local history, on neighbourhoods, squares and streets, and on periods of the history of "Old Athens", have proliferated recently, many of them under the imprint of the Athens Municipality. Of journals which have recently devoted special issues to Athens, I have read with interest *I Lexi* (*The Word*), no.166, Nov-Dec 2001 (in Greek); and *Highlights*, no 6, Sept 2003 (bilingual edition).

This is a book about the modern city, which was born in the early 1830s after the Greek War of Independence. The ancient city exists within the modern city, and is a very important part of it, both physically, and in the effects it has had on the society, politics and economy of Athens. For example, it was the main factor which led to the institution of Athens as the capital of the Greek state. Insofar as the ancient city is still present and influential, it is part of this book. The same is the case for Byzantine, Frankish and Turkish Athens, though partly because of the ravages of time, and partly because of the deliberate project of the nineteenth-century governors to model the city in a Hellenic fashion, purging alien elements, I have less to say about these periods.

I have chosen for a starting or vantage point the arrival of the young Bavarian King Otho in Athens in 1834, which coincided with the designation of Athens as the capital of Greece. This enables me to trace the development of the capital city, its culture and society, from that important turning point, and to look at the remains of classical Athens rather as Otho and his advisers did, when they considered how to integrate them in the city, and contemplated what was their meaning and potential contribution to the formation of a new Hellenic identity.

Transliterations from Greek are my own and are a mixture of what is familiar in English (Aeschylus not Aishylos, Socrates not Sokrates) and what looks or sounds better in a form more closely approximating to modern Greek (Eleftherios not Eleutherios). Inevitably, there are inconsistencies.

I thank our friends in Athens, and in particular Paul and Ariane Condellis, Tim and Tina Cullen, George and Kaity David, Costas Petropoulos and Anthy Doxiades, Peter and Aline Haritatos, Costas and Kalliope Mitropoulos, Christos Psaltis, Dori Skoura, and Mr A. Theofanis. John Leatham died just as I was finishing this book, and it is dedicated to his memory. I hope he would have enjoyed it. It would certainly have benefited from his comments.

—Michael Llewellyn Smith
Childrey, November 2003

The publisher would like to thank the following for permission to reproduce extracts from:

Petsalis-Diomedis, Thanasis, *Deka Tria Chronia (Thirteen Years)*, 1964 (courtesy Hestia, Athens)

Mazower, Mark: *Inside Hitler's Greece: the Experience of Occupation, 1941-44*. New Haven/London: Yale University Press, 1993 (courtesy Mark Mazower and Yale University Press)

Hirschon, Renée: *Heirs of the Greek Catastrophe: the Social Life of Asia Minor Refugees in Piraeus*. New York/Oxford: Berghahn Books, 1998 (courtesy Renée Hirschon)

Translations are generally by the author, but translations of Thucydides are by Rex Warner and of Plutarch by Ian Scott-Kilvert. The passage from Elytis on p.92 is from John Chioles's translation in Artemis Leontis, *Greece: A Traveler's Literary Companion*. The quotations from Ludwig Ross on p.60 and Ralph E Griswold on pp.83-4 are from Alexander Papageorgiou-Venetas, "The Ancient Heritage in Modern Metropolitan Life: Landscaping the Archaeological Sites of Athens". The quotations from Anna Akerhjelm on p.68 and Bishop Michael Choniates on p.180 are from Kevin Andrews's compilation *Athens Alive*. Fuller references can be found in the Further Reading section.

Chronology
Some Key Dates in the History of Athens

c. 4000 BC	Neolithic settlements on Acropolis
14th-13th century BC	
	Substantial Mycenean settlement with palace and fortifications on the Acropolis
c. 620	Aristocratic legal code of Dracon
c. 594	Solon's economic and political reforms
mid-6th century BC	
	Period of the tyrants: Peisistratus and Hippias: beginnings of Athenian drama; Panathenaic Festival re-founded; temple of Olympian Zeus started
c. 510	End of period of tyrants. Democratic reforms of Kleisthenes
490	Persian invasion of Greece. Athenian victory at Marathon. Period of Aeschylus
480	Athens evacuated. Persians sack the Acropolis. Athenian victory over Persian fleet at Salamis. End of Persian threat Growth of Athenian empire (Delian League) financed by tribute from "allies"
454	Treasury of Delian League moved to the Acropolis. Pericles uses money to finance immense series of public works: Parthenon (447); Erectheum; Propylaea; temple of Athina Nike built. Period of Pericles, Phidias, Herodotus, Sophocles
431-404	Peloponnesian War: Athens and her allies against Sparta and her allies. Period of Thucydides, Euripides, Aristophanes
430	Plague in Athens. Pericles dies in 429
399	Death of Socrates
c. 385	Plato founds the Academy
338	Athens defeated by Philip of Macedon at Chaironea
c. 335	Aristotle founds the Lyceum
c. 315	Zeno founds Stoic school of philosophy; teaches in Painted Stoa
c. 300	Epicurus teaches Epicurean philosophy in Athens
86 BC	Sulla sacks Athens Cicero, Horace, Brutus and other cultivated Romans attend Athens philosophical schools and university
117-138 AD	Emperor Hadrian, benefactor of Athens; benefactions of Herod Atticus

267	Heruli (Goth tribe) sack Athens Agora
312	Christianity the official state religion of Roman empire
330	Emperor Constantine establishes Constantinople as capital of the Eastern Roman, later Byzantine, empire
361-3	Julian the "Apostate", formerly student at Athens, tries as Emperor to restore paganism.
396	Alaric the Goth takes Athens
Late 4th century AD	
	Theodosian anti-pagan legal codes
	Parthenon becomes Christian church of the Virgin Mary
529	Emperor Justinian closes the philosophical schools
580	Slavs sack Athens
1018	Emperor Basil, the "Bulgar-slayer", visits Athens
1040	Harold Haardrada and Norwegian Varangians in Athens
1204	Fourth crusade: Frankish crusaders sack Constantinople
	Frankish rule in Greece: Otho de la Roche becomes ruler of Athens: period of the Duchy of Athens
1260	Guy de la Roche becomes Duke of Athens
1308	Walter de Brienne becomes Duke of Athens
1311	Walter killed by Catalan mercenaries at battle of the Cephissos; period of rule by the Catalan Grand Company
1394	Acciajuoli family, Florentine bankers, become Dukes of Athens
1453	Ottoman Turks capture Constantinople
1456	Ottoman Turks under Omar take Athens
1456-1832	Period of Turkish rule
1687	Venetian forces under Morosini besiege and briefly take Athens. Parthenon blown up when Venetian shell explodes in Turkish powder magazine
1751-3	James Stuart and Nicholas Revett (*The Antiquities of Athens*) visit Athens
1801-	Lord Elgin, British Ambassador to Turkey, removes Parthenon sculptures from the Parthenon
1806	Chateaubriand in Athens
1810-11	Byron in Athens
1821	March: Greek revolt in the Peloponnese leads to Greek war of independence from Turkey
	April: Patriarch Gregory V executed in Constantinople: his remains will be taken to Athens in 1871

1833	Otho, son of King Ludwig of Bavaria, becomes hereditary sovereign of Greece, placed under guarantee of Britain, France and Russia; disembarks at Nauplion, provisional capital
1834	Athens declared capital of the Greek Kingdom; Otho and court move to Athens First city plan by Kleanthes and Schaubert Modified plan by Leo von Klenze Athens University founded
1843	Revolt of armed forces: Otho forced to concede a constitution and parliament
1856	French School established
1862	King Otho forced to abdicate and leave Greece
1863	Prince William of Sonderberg-Glücksberg, Prince of Denmark, ascends Greek throne as King George I of the Hellenes
1874	German Archaeological Institute established
1881	American School of Classical Studies established
1886	British School at Athens established
1896	First Olympic Games of the modern era held at Athens
1897	Greco-Turkish war in Thessaly: Greece defeated
1909	Military coup d'état at Goudi outside Athens
1910	Eleftherios Venizelos becomes prime minister
1912-13	Balkan Wars: Greece and Balkan allies drive Turks out of Ottoman European provinces. Greek population and territory doubled
1913	George I assassinated in newly liberated Salonica: Constantine becomes king
1916	Greece divided between Royalists and Venizelists over issue of war or neutrality. Anglo-French forces occupy part of Athens. Venizelist Greece joins Entente
1919	May: Greek forces land at Smyrna (Izmir) with allied mandate to occupy Asia Minor zone
1922	August-September: Greek army defeated in Asia Minor. Greek refugees expelled from Asia Minor arrive in Athens and Salonica
1923	Lausanne Convention provides for compulsory exchange of populations between Greece and Turkey: more refugees
1924	Greece declared Republic

1935	Monarchy restored
1936	Ioannis Metaxas dictator: regime of 4th August
1941	German forces invade Greece, occupy Athens. Winter famine
1944	October: liberation of Athens. December: military confrontation between ELAS and British forces. Churchill visits Athens. Archbishop Damaskinos becomes Regent
1946	King George II returns to Greece after plebiscite
1946-9	Greek civil war
1947	Death of King George. Paul becomes king
1964	Death of King Paul. Constantine II succeeds
1967	April 21 military coup d'état leads to regime of the Colonels' junta. King Constantine's attempt in December to restore legitimacy fails, and he leaves the country
1973	November 17: student uprising at Athens Polytechnic put down by force: terrorist group N17 later name themselves after this event
1974	President Makarios of Cyprus deposed in coup engineered by Greek regime. Turkish forces occupy northern Cyprus. Collapse of Greek junta. Constantine Karamanlis returns from Paris in July to take up reins of government as prime minister. Greek monarchy abolished after December plebiscite
1980	Karamanlis becomes president
1981	Andreas Papandreou (PASOK) becomes prime minister
2000	Athens metro opens
	Murder of British defence attaché Stephen Saunders by N17
2001	New Athens airport opens at Spata
2002	Members of N17 arrested, brought to trial
2003	December: Members of N17 convicted and sentenced
2004	August 13: Olympic Games in Athens

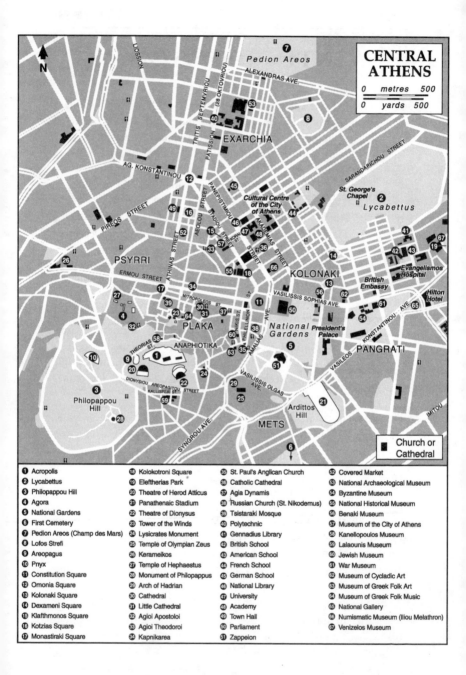

CENTRAL ATHENS

| 0 | metres | 500 |
| 0 | yards | 500 |

■ Church or Cathedral

❶ Acropolis
❷ Lycabettus
❸ Philopappou Hill
❹ Agora
❺ National Gardens
❻ First Cemetery
❼ Pedion Areos (Champ des Mars)
❽ Lofos Strefi
❾ Areopagus
❿ Pnyx
⓫ Constitution Square
⓬ Omonia Square
⓭ Kolonaki Square
⓮ Dexameni Square
⓯ Klafthmonos Square
⓰ Kotzias Square
⓱ Monastiraki Square
⓲ Koiokotroni Square
⓳ Eleftherias Park
⓴ Theatre of Herod Atticus
㉑ Panathenaic Stadium
㉒ Theatre of Dionysus
㉓ Tower of the Winds
㉔ Lysicrates Monument
㉕ Temple of Olympian Zeus
㉖ Kerameikos
㉗ Temple of Hephaestus
㉘ Monument of Philopappus
㉙ Arch of Hadrian
㉚ Cathedral
㉛ Little Cathedral
㉜ Agioi Apostoloi
㉝ Agioi Theodoroi
㉞ Kapnikarea
㉟ St. Paul's Anglican Church
㊱ Catholic Cathedral
㊲ Agia Dynamis
㊳ Russian Church (St. Nikodemus)
㊴ Tsistaraki Mosque
㊵ Polytechnic
㊶ Gennadius Library
㊷ British School
㊸ American School
㊹ French School
㊺ German School
㊻ National Library
㊼ University
㊽ Academy
㊾ Town Hall
㊿ Parliament
51 Zappeion
52 Covered Market
53 National Archaeological Museum
54 Byzantine Museum
55 National Historical Museum
56 Benaki Museum
57 Museum of the City of Athens
58 Kanellopoulos Museum
59 Lalaounis Museum
60 Jewish Museum
61 War Museum
62 Museum of Cycladic Art
63 Museum of Greek Folk Art
64 Museum of Greek Folk Music
65 National Gallery
66 Numismatic Museum (Iliou Melathron)
67 Venizelos Museum

INTRODUCTION

Athens (Greek AθῆνΑΙ) *is situated in 37 58' 20" N. lat. and 23 43' 9" E. long., in the great plain of Attica, which is watered by the* Kephisos *(Cephissus), the only Attic river that is not dry in summer, and by the* Ilissos. *On the N. and N.W. the plain is bounded by* Parnes *and its spur Aegaleos; on the E. and S.E. by* Brilessos *or* Pentilikon *and* Hymettos; *on the S. and S.W. by the* Saronic Gulf. *In the centre of the plain rises a range of hills, now called* Tourko Vouni, *running from N.E. to S. and separating the valleys of the Kephisos and Ilissos; its southern spur, the* Lycabettos *(Mt. St. George), rises abruptly immediately to the E. of Athens. The latter is separated by a broad depression from the precipitous rock of the* Acropolis, *with the* Areopagus, *and from a range of hills farther to the W., which includes the* Philopappos *or* Museion, *the* Pnyx, *and the* Hill of the Nymphs, *and descends to the sea in gentle wooded slopes.*

Baedeker's *Greece: Handbook for Travellers,* 1909

In the middle of the plain of Attica, framed by a ring of mountains and bounded by the sea to the southwest, a crystalline limestone outcrop rises sharply to some 500 feet in height above sea level.

This is the Acropolis. It is ringed now by the modern city of Athens, so that from most viewpoints it stands against a background of whitish urban sprawl, in what is often a hazy atmosphere. In former times—at any time in fact between the late fifth century BC and the end of the nineteenth century—it stood out sharply, against a setting of grey mountainside, green and ochre fields and olive groves, a formidable citadel settled solidly on the plain, with its temples and straw-coloured columns.

The Acropolis is the reason Athens is here, the thread of continuity between ancient and modern Athens. For the varied histories of Athens fall into two main parts or movements. The ancient movement described a wave shape. It started in remote antiquity. It grew to maturity in the times of the legislator Solon, the tyrants Peisistratus and Hippias, the democratic reformer Kleisthenes in the sixth century. It blossomed in the fifth century, the time of successful resistance to the Persian empire, the creation of the Athenian empire, the building of the Parthenon and the other great monuments of the Acropolis, the literary, philosophical and artistic flowering of Periclean Athens. The city's cultural pre-eminence lived on in the fourth century but its independence was lost at the end of a long struggle against the supremacy of Macedon. Eventually Athens fell under the sway of expansive Rome, enduring siege and bloody sack by the army of the Roman leader Sulla in 86 BC. It continued to be the nursery and finishing school of educated Romans such as Cicero, living off the prestige and great names of past philosophers. It enjoyed a renaissance under the philhellenic emperor Hadrian, who adorned the city with public works.

The ancient movement came to an end at some point after the pagan philosophy of the Olympian gods gave way to the new religion, Christianity, and Athens became an outlying, not particularly distinguished, city of the Eastern Roman, Byzantine empire. Two milestones commonly quoted are the decrees of the emperor Theodosius ordering the closing and destruction of pagan temples, and the order of the emperor Justinian closing the Athens philosophical schools in 529 AD.

This, ancient Athens, and especially fifth-century Athens, was what interested people in western Europe, to such an extent that when they visited Athens they hardly saw anything else. The reason was that their education, their culture, and—as they were told—their laws, their philosophy, their art and literature were largely derived from the achievements of fifth- and fourth-century BC Athens. However, there was and is another Athens, the capital city of the modern Greek state, the city that you see today. Athens became capital of Greece in 1834. Much of this book is about the period since then. The modern city can repel with its great stretches of concrete and cement, its mass, its fumes and noises of motor cars and klaxons. But it can also fascinate. It has its culture, its charm, its literary figures, its distinguished Athenians and visitors, above all its dramatic, sometimes tragic, pages of history. The history of the modern city is not so much a wave as an upward

curve of growth and expansion to a size and complexity which places great burdens on its planners and inhabitants. The future cannot be predicted.

Between Ancient and Modern

There is also the Athens which lies between the ancient and the modern. After the centuries of Byzantine empire, during which Athens acquired some of its attractive surviving churches and monasteries, the city passed into the hands of westerners. Following the sack of Constantinople in 1204 by the crusaders, Athens was assigned to Frankish *Grands Seigneurs*, later Dukes of Athens, the de la Roches and Briennes, who were followed by Catalans and Florentine rulers. None of them left much physical or cultural mark, except for the tower on the Acropolis built by the Florentines, which features prominently in early photographs but was knocked down in 1874 as part of the process of purging the sacred rock of non-Hellenic elements. I do not write much about this period, because where possible I have started in this book from what survives in today's city, and little that is Frankish survives. More survives from the Ottoman period of rule, which started in 1456, including some public and religious buildings and also remains of the old Turkish town.

Throughout the period of Byzantine and Ottoman rule, Athens remained a relatively small and politically unimportant town, by comparison with either the ancient or the modern city. That and the lack of impressive physical remains were partly why it was possible for western visitors to pay so little attention to the intervening centuries. But more important was the selective vision which concentrated on the ancient city, aided by the impressive physical continuity of the Acropolis and a few surviving ancient monuments around it.

John Addington Symonds, a British author and aesthete who visited Athens in the early 1870s, is a good example of this vision. Here is what he wrote about Athens:

Unlike Rome, Athens leaves upon the memory one simple and ineffaceable impression. There is no conflict here between Paganism and Christianity, no statues of Hellas baptised by popes into the company of saints, no blending of the classical and mediaeval and Renaissance influences in a bewilderment of vast antiquity. Rome true to her historical vocation, embraces in her ruins all ages, all creeds, all nations. Her life has never stood still, but has submitted to many transformations, of which the traces are still visible. Athens, like the Greeks of history, is isolated in a sort of self-completion: she is a thing of the past, which still exists, because the spirit never dies, because beauty is a joy for ever. What is truly remarkable about the city is just this, that while the modern town is an insignificant mushroom of the present century, the monuments of Greek art in the best period... survive in comparative perfection, and are so far unencumbered with subsequent edifices that the actual Athens of Pericles absorbs our attention. There is nothing of any consequence intermediate between us and the fourth century B.C. Seen from a distance the Acropolis presents nearly the same appearance as it offered to Spartan guardsmen when they paced the ramparts of Deceleia. Nature around is all unaltered... All through the centuries which divide us from the age of Hadrian—centuries unfilled, as far as Athens is concerned, with memorable deeds or national activity—the Acropolis has stood uncovered in the sun... Thus there is no obtrusive element in Athens to distract the mind from memories of its most glorious past.

In this way the entire history of Byzantine, Frankish and Ottoman Athens is obliterated, as is the Greek revival, War of Independence and the modern city.

We (and "we" includes the Greeks) are still, to some extent, in the grip of Symonds' vision. Athens was chosen as capital of the Greek state, although some thought that it should not have been, because of this glorious past, symbolized by the Acropolis and its monuments. And the first thing the new rulers of the new Greek state set about doing was to obliterate all traces of Ottoman presence from the Acropolis, creating a Hellenic site recalling fifth-century BC Athens.

However, things have moved on since Symonds' time. The Greeks have reclaimed their Byzantine past and integrated it within their continuous history. The modern city is seen not as an insignificant mushroom but as a complex modern creation, of mixed beauty and ugliness, worthy of attention in its own right.

The ancient city, the Acropolis, the precinct and temple of Olympian Zeus, the Panathenaic Stadium, the monuments of Hadrian, the Agora, and the other monuments which remain, have been a challenge to the Athenians since 1834. How to treat them, how to restore and present them, how to combine them with the modern city, have been main questions for planners and citizens, and still are. The current debate over the planned new Acropolis Museum, designed to hold and display the Parthenon sculptures (otherwise known as the Elgin Marbles, a term which the Greeks dislike) is only one recent example.

In this book I present the modern city and its history, concentrating mainly on the period since 1834. But the ancient city is always present, and I have incorporated it, just as the Athenians have had to incorporate it in their vision and construction of the modern city.

CHAPTER ONE

Markets, Kiosks, Holes in the Ground, Sound and Light

"Here sky is everywhere, on all sides the sun's ray,
And something all around like the honey of Hymettus;
The lilies emerge unwithering from the marble;
Divine Penteli flashes, begetter of an Olympus.

The excavating axe stumbles on beauty;
In her entrails Cybele holds gods instead of mortals,
Athens gushes violet blood
Each time the shafts of twilight strike her."

From Kostis Palamas, *Athens*

Every Friday morning, early, vans and trucks laden with produce converge on Xenokratous Street in the Kolonaki area on the southern side of Mount Lycabettus, and the market traders set up their stalls. This is the *laiki*—the people's street market, from *laos*, the people. It takes place every week, on a predetermined day, in each of the quarters of Athens. It is one of the most vivid displays of everyday life in the city, with its regularity, the personal encounters with neighbours, the cheerful noise of the vendors crying their wares, the quiet purpose of the shoppers stocking their trolleys and baskets. The seeming spontaneity of the market conceals a well-regulated structure. Each Athenian has his own local market. The Kolonaki market has been mine, because this is the area in which I have lived at different periods from the 1960s to the new millennium.

The lay-out of the market stalls does not vary. At the western end towards the Acropolis, near Philippou's taverna and the stone tablet in memory of former Prime Minister Panagiotis Kanellopoulos, is a stall of inexpensive clothes hanging on racks: jeans and blouses, underwear in dun and beige shades and of ample proportions. Cheap plastic objects are also for sale here, near the kiosk on the pavement, just above the steps leading down towards the British Embassy and up towards the Mount Lycabettus funicular railway.

Then there are stalls of dried herbs and spices: several varieties of the wild teas in which the Greek mountains are rich, sage, *phaskomilo*, ditanny and mint. They come both in generous bunches and in clear plastic bags with labels. There are sacks of different dry beans and pulses. There are the egg stalls, the eggs arranged in racks and baskets by category, with descriptions, superior eggs being labelled "for babies", *yia mora*, the Greek for a baby being a *moro*, or moron, unable as yet to reason.

These stalls are austere by comparison with the profusion of colour and scent of the fruits and vegetables that follow. Depending on the season, there will be red, hard apples from Edessa in the north, russets, golden apples, green apples, pears, plums, plump rozaki grapes from Crete, clustering sultana grapes from the northern Peloponnese. The oranges in the winter and spring are fat and juicy, most of them of the Merlin variety, navel oranges from Crete and Laconia, some with dark green leaves attached. There are grapefruit too, and various mandarins, tangerines and clementines. The stall keepers call their wares and chalk their prices on miniature blackboards, with brief descriptions: "nice apples", "tender", "incredibly sweet". When business is slack they can be seen polishing up the apples. On the vegetable stalls there are beans, garlic, rocket, cauliflower, cabbage, broccoli, beetroot, kiwi fruit (a relatively recent appearance), tomatoes of the fat and the long plum varieties, lettuce, glossy aubergines and peppers, green, yellow and red, in season; and many varieties of parsley, mint and other fresh herbs. The olive stall has more than twenty big bowls, each full of a different variety, sweetish, bitter, hard, soft and squashy, green, black, dark brown, the cracked variety, from Kalamata, Agrinion, Pelion, Crete and Amphissa.

The fish stall is at the eastern end of the market. Most of the fishes are fresh, and not frozen, marked with Greek names and difficult to identify with an English name unless you have Alan Davidson's *Mediterranean Fish* in hand. There are sea bass, sea bream, red mullet, salmon, sole, mackerel, and whitebait. Nearby are stalls with bedding plants and plastic household goods.

The market starts slowly, with a sprinkling of early birds. By eleven o'clock it is in full swing. The shoppers are of all local backgrounds, housewives, retired generals and ambassadors, office workers, professors and their wives, Filipino cooks and daily or live-in helps. The women push big wire trolleys, filling them up with beans, potatoes, oranges and tomatoes for the coming week. By one o'clock the crowd is thinning out and the sellers are reducing their prices. By the early afternoon it is all over for another week.

These stall keepers, who move on the next day to another market site, form an organized guild with social security benefits, managed by an elected committee. The market operates under license from the Municipality, and is supervised by the market police. There are several such guilds in the Athens area. The market has its "elders", members of the committee, who organize it, allocating places for the stall keepers (for some positions are preferred to others). The vendors are subject to price controls so as not to undercut the local shops by too much. None of this is visible, but these traditional rules create an efficient and competitive institution. So far organic produce has hardly featured in the big traditional popular markets, though a baby organic market has sprung up, also on Fridays, in Dexameni (Cistern) Square not far from the Kolonaki *laiki*.

These local markets are more intimate and sociable than the big central meat and fish market and vegetable and fruit market which are down town, off Athinas Street, or the cheap and cheerful Chinese market below Omonia Square. Then there are the kiosks, or *periptera*, another integral feature of Athens life. You are never far away from a kiosk, purveying the essentials and the little luxuries of everyday life: cigarettes, chocolate, bottles of water, phone cards, newspapers and magazines, packets of biscuits, lighters and lighter fuel, matches, services such as telephone calls, and so on. In the days when most people smoked cigarettes (many Greeks still do) you would hand your basic lighter to the kiosk keeper and he would top it up with lighter fuel. Kiosks vary from the simple box-like kiosk to the grand pavilion kiosk, encrusted and hung with every kind of product. In downtown Athinas Street the kiosks carry a hanging assortment of leather belts and straps (2,000 drachmas, now 6 or 7 euros, for a belt labelled Armani or Calvin Klein), electronic goods, cheap watches, pirated false perfumes with exotic brand names. There is a fluffy doll that speaks a four-letter obscenity when its tail is pulled. Licenses to run well-placed kiosks, which used to be a prerogative of the war wounded, are eagerly sought and defended. They can bring riches.

These are some of the surface aspects of life in Athens. If you have time to stroll, this life provides a street theatre. But strolling is not easy on pavements that are often cramped, uneven and cracked. Since the nineteenth century they have provoked complaints from residents and visitors. Athens is a city of hills and narrow streets, and of recent years most of the pavements have been occupied by parked cars. Nevertheless they support mulberry, false pepper, and orange trees, which fill the streets with the scent of blossom in April. Walking in the city becomes a mixture of sweet sensation and discomfort.

Or you can watch the drama from a ringside seat of a pavement café. Here or in a taverna some of the action will come to you: the gypsy child selling a carnation, or the lottery seller, usually an old man, carrying his tickets festooned on a tall pole, like some celebrant carrying a banner in a religious procession.

Street Life

For the Athenians, daily life revolves around the neighbourhoods where they live, each with its café, its bakery, its taverna and shops, its square with kiosks, its cinema (preferably an open-air cinema for the summer months), and its communications with the centre of town. Athens is a city of neighbourhoods, not necessarily distinguished by different architecture or planning, but each with its own character owing something to the origins of the migrants who settled there—for Athens is a city of immigrants.

The journalist Antonis Karkayiannis, who lives not far from the centre, between the Acropolis and Constitution Square, catches the flavour in one of his Sunday columns for the newspaper *Kathimerini.* The day starts at 5.30 a.m. exactly, with the grinding noise and fumes of the municipal rubbish lorry. In order to get through the narrow street to the big bins, the rubbish collectors are often forced to shift illegally parked cars, heaving them up and sideways onto the pavements with rhythmic shouts of encouragement. This is symbolic of contemporary concerns, for the collection and disposal of rubbish are hot issues in Athens. There are articles every week in the press about the need for new waste disposal sites in addition to the appalling landfill site in the suburb of Ano Liosia. Greece is regularly fined by the European Commission for infringing European regulations on rubbish.

The journalist's neighbourhood consists of the area from the traditional Anaphiotika, little houses huddled on the northeast slopes of the Acropolis, through the old Plaka quarter, to the centre of town. Walking down to Constitution Square, he passes through Hyperidou Street, which has been dug up five times in the last year and shows the signs in its deep ruts, and then down Voulis or Nikis Street, stopping on the corner of Voulis to pick up neighbourhood gossip from his friend who runs the open-air parking lot: the comings and goings, which house is being sold or rented, all the trivial but interesting bits of news. He passes the point where Voulis crosses Admiral Nikodimos Street, where at peak hours two streams of traffic clash, Voulis being the only way in to the Plaka, and Nikodimou the only way out. Just at the point where the two streams meet is his favourite *ouzeri,* Evgenia's, serving ouzo and *mezedes,* little bites. Both Voulis and Nikis are narrow streets, crammed with parked cars, which occupy the pavements as well as the street. He knows some unfortunate car owners who get up at 4.30 a.m. in order to secure a parking place here. Apollo Street, a shopping street, which crosses Voulis and Nikis, is said to be going to be pedestrian-only. A bit further on is Constitution Square, which is going to be remodelled for the Olympic Games: the third time in fifteen years. Leading down from Constitution Square to Monastiraki, Ermou Street ought to be the pride of the district, with its recent traffic-free status, and its lighting at night, but it is not. Its upper section has been turned into a luxury open-air parking lot and an al fresco market for imitation western products and for colourful goods from the Far East and Africa. It is a place of wandering musicians and barrel organs. And then the whole area is the home of homeless dogs, for which the Greek word is *adespota,* meaning dogs "without masters". The journalist fears that they will pay the price of the decent appearance that the city will wish to put on for the Olympic Games.

This is an unusual neighbourhood. Most people live outside the city centre, though there are recent signs that people are beginning to move back. But whether in the centre or the suburb, their lives revolve around the local shops, cafés, taverns and street markets. The masterless dogs are indeed a striking feature of central Athens, and of suburbs including smart areas such as Kiphissia. Apparently harmless mongrels, they lie on the pavements or on little triangles of grass, sometimes stirring themselves to cross a busy street when the traffic light halts the flow. Their fate arouses impassioned debate between those who would clean up the streets and have them removed and those who see them as part owners of the city. The compromise solution is sterilization. Motor cars, dogs, street traders, rubbish bins, cracked pavements, these are some of the daily ingredients of life in Athens.

The best time to visit is in the winter and spring and autumn, avoiding the heat of the summer from June to August, though Athens in August has the big advantage of being half empty, since so many residents go away on holiday to the seaside or the mountains. The time to stroll is on a Sunday, or better still a public holiday. The city then is relatively empty, especially at the great holidays when people leave for their home villages and three quarters of a million cars drive out of Athens. When they drive back after the holiday, there are blockages miles long on the national road from Corinth to Athens.

Business and Pleasure
Athens is the capital, the political heart, the hub of the Hellenic world, the centre of Hellenic arts and culture. It is a melting pot of Greeks

who arrived as successive waves of immigrants, and now it is the home of immigrants from outside the world of Hellenism too. It has a fizz about it which other Greek cities lack. As Edmund Keeley writes, "almost all Greeks south of Salonika believe that Athens is where the action is, whether your pleasure is business, entertainment, culture, politics, or simply an escape from boredom."

Those whose pleasure is business are legion. The Athenians are and always were traders. The city breathes deal-making. It is structured to make this easy. You know that you will find spare parts for a car, truck or other engine-driven thing in the downtown area around the Sacred Way, the broad, noisy modern road that takes its name from the ancient and holy route from Athens to Eleusis. You know that you will find textiles, haberdashery, buttons, brass knobs and knockers between Stadiou Street and Monastiraki and Athinas Street; lighting and furniture and cars on the broad streets leading out of Athens to the north or to the sea; and so on. Every object has its place.

Small businesses still predominate, because Athenians still prefer to have their own hands on the levers of control. They prefer family and close associates to impersonal managers. You catch the flavour of Athenian business in the downtown Omonia Square area, where if you stand on a pavement in working hours thousands of shirt-sleeved men bear down on you, all apparently moving towards some assignation in the myriad shops and offices in these streets and stoas (porticoes). The stock exchange in Sophocles Street is not far away, a form of business which suddenly became a talking point, almost a national obsession, in the mid-1990s. Athens acquired young men in red braces constantly communicating by mobile phone. Fortunes were won in the boom years and lost again in the crash.

If your pleasure is entertainment, Athens ranks with other European capitals in providing it. The musical scene has been transformed by the creation in the late 1980s of the Megaron Mousikis, a state-of-the-art concert hall near the US Embassy. This is the brain child and love child of Christos Lambrakis, a cultivated millionaire who wrote the libretto for an opera about Helen of Troy as well as running a media empire. It is now being extended below ground, with a new stage and auditorium. Not to be outdone, the Onassis Foundation is to create a cultural complex on Syngrou Avenue, with a chamber opera. For summer visitors, the Athens Festival provides orchestral concerts, opera, ballet and ancient Greek drama in the theatre of Herod Atticus beneath the Acropolis. Those with long memories say that the Festival has fallen away since the glory days of Callas, Mitropoulos, Karajan and Margot Fonteyn in the 1950s and 1960s.

For Greek music, the choice ranges from updated versions of the *rebetika* songs which developed in the hashish dens of Piraeus to the polished variants of Mikis Theodorakis (*Zorba the Greek*) and Manos Hadjidakis (*Never on Sunday*) and their successors, composers with classical training who drew on folk and popular songs and dances. Greek popular song uses simple, rhymed lyrics strongly imbued with the pain of separation, nostalgia (a Greek word) and sentiments of love and loss. At its best, in for example Theodorakis' settings of George Seferis (*Epiphaneia*) and Yiannis Ritsos (*Epitaphios*), or Hadjidakis' music for Pirandello's *Tonight We Improvise*, it is unforgettable. In what other country, one may ask, have settings of Nobel Prize-winning poets such as Seferis gone to the top of the hit parade?

You may still be able to find popular dives where *rebetika* music can be heard accompanied by the *bouzouki* in the tradition of the great singers such as Vamvakaris and Tsitsanis, and the singers seen through a fog of cigarette smoke, but it has moved a long way from the earlier music of the waterfronts of Piraeus, Thessaloniki and Asia Minor. A more sophisticated modern generation goes to places around the Sacred Way and on Syngrou and Poseidonos Streets to hear newer stars such as Eleni Arvanitaki. The Athenian satirical *chansonnier* has always been popular too. The albums of Dionysis Savopoulos, the singer as social commentator, are in Diane Shugart's words "the history of post-war Greece". In all the haunts of popular music the standard drink is whisky, the level of decibels ranges from uncomfortable to unendurable, and the hours (not uncommonly from around midnight to 5 a.m.) are cruel punishment for the older clients.

For these older clients, and the young, an old western or thriller or romance seen at the open-air cinema screen on a summer evening is a particular delight of Athens.

Café Culture

The most popular sports are football and basketball. Business tycoons like to own the popular clubs. In football Panathinaikos and Olympiakos dominate the Greek league and cup and have established a European presence. The former is the fief of the Vardinoyiannis family from Crete, big in ships, oil and media; the latter is owned by Socrates Kokkalis, the controversial multimillionaire owner of Intrakom telecommunications. Panathinaikos, the senior club, was established in 1908. It is Athenian, its home stadium on Alexandras Avenue. Olympiakos, founded in 1925, is from Piraeus. A third club poignantly reflects in its name the twentieth-century history of Greece. This is AEK, the Athletic Union of Constantinopolitans, founded in 1924 by immigrants from Constantinople. Its stadium is in the refugee quarter Nea Philadelphia. Its emblem is the Byzantine double headed eagle and its colours the Byzantine yellow and black.

Apart from sports, the Athenians' favourite leisure pursuits are the café, the taverna, and the *ekdromi* or expedition by car at the weekend. (As economic prosperity increases, the latter is often to a second home near the seaside.) There are cafés on every square. Kolonaki Square is a good place to try them. You eat out well, without having to pay too much. The range is wide, from the traditional taverna which can be found in every quarter to the sophisticated Italian-style restaurant in the little park below the Evangelismos hospital, or the seafood restaurants on what used to be called Tourkolimano or Passalimani on the peninsula of Piraeus. It is now Mikrolimano, the small harbour, out of political correctness. The essence of eating is the company, *parea*, and the talk, and not to stint but to enjoy the good feeling of plentiful choice. Fast food arrived in the 1970s in the form of pizza parlours and McDonalds, and the new immigrants are bringing their own contribution to Greek cuisine. The wines of Attica have improved (try Semeli for example) though you are just as likely to find excellent wines from the north or the Peloponnese on the wine list. You can still buy resinated Attic wine by the bottle, or half-litre flask, but it is not so easy now to find the wooden barrels which used to line the sides of tavernas, and from which the waiter would draw *retsina* in a tin cannikin.

If your pleasure is politics then Athens is the right place. It is also the centre of the standardized modern Greek language. The language is all around you, in the press, in graffiti, on advertising hoardings and neon signs, and above all in talk and song. Because the Greek language is so ancient, carries so many layers of association, and has infiltrated English at so many points, its words, roots and phrases offer endless material for exploration and analysis. It is also quick to adopt and adapt English words, in the Greek equivalent of Franglais, just as in the past it has adopted Arabic, Slavic, Turkish and French words. A striking recent coinage is *fastfoodadika* (φαστφουδαδικα) for fast food outlets. There is no straightforward equivalence between Greek and English sounds, since Greek lacks noises such as "sh" as in sheep and ship and "ch" as in cheap and chip, and cannot distinguish between sheep and ship or cheap and chip anyway, since they have the same vowel sound. Because of these discontinuities, and because we are indoctrinated with ideas as to how Greek names should look in English or French or German, any logical system of transliteration of Greek words into English gives results that look wrong, which is why my transliterations are inconsistent. It is a remarkable fact that the Greek transliterations of George, as in Lloyd George or George Bush, and Church, as in General Richard Church, are the same: *Tzwrtz* (Τζωρτζ), which would be transliterated back as Tzortz.

The Story of a Hole

Athens is full of gaps, voids and holes: holes in pavements, gaps between office blocks, filled "temporarily" with parking lots which look improvised but are often lasting parts of the city's structure. In the early 1980s, just behind the bulk of the War Museum on Vasilissis Sophias Avenue, on one of the best sites in central Athens, a massive hole was excavated in the ground, about the size of the War Museum itself. The hole was still there in the 1990s. It had acquired its own ecosystem of flora and fauna. There were even trees growing deep below ground level.

As with any transaction involving property rights and large sums of money, the history of this hole in the ground was complicated. It started in the late 1970s, when a young and radical liberal minister named Stephanos Manos was responsible for environmental policy. To simplify a long and complicated story, the state wished at that time to acquire as much as possible of the land south of Vasilissis Sophias

Avenue near the Rizari religious foundation so as to create a park. The authorities succeeded in doing so through complex negotiations involving the landowners, which included the Rizari foundation and the army. The transactions included the acquisition and demolition of a horrific green utility building that had served as transit accommodation, or a useful perk for senior army officers, in central Athens. The prime minister, Constantine Karamanlis, soon to be president, wished to see a museum built on this site, which most people thought a rotten idea. At this point Manos was shuffled into another job. His successor dug the large hole in the ground, to contain the museum.

In October 1981 Karamanlis' New Democracy party was comprehensively defeated in general elections, and Andreas Papandreou's Panhellenic Socialist Party, PASOK, assumed office. The new Minister of the Environment, an engaging politician named Antonis Tritsis, ruled against the museum project, leaving the hole in the ground with no purpose. Manos says that at this stage he predicted that the hole would still be there in five years time.

In 1989 PASOK fell and New Democracy took power again, with the veteran Cretan, Costas Mitsotakis, as prime minister. As minister again, Manos held a tender for the construction of a garage in the hole in the ground. By now Tritsis was mayor of Athens. He convinced the prime minister that building garages was the proper function of the Municipality, not the government. This intervention was enough to hold up any action, but not to lead to a solution. The hole in the ground remained. In the early 1990s I would sometimes walk by on Rizari Street and be reminded of it. I assumed that it had become permanent.

However, this story has an ending. One day in the spring of 2003 the hole began to fill up. It filled with scaffolding. A crane hovered overhead. Men in hard hats walked around the site looking busy. The garage project, with places for 660 cars, was coming to fruition. Like many other projects, it is to be completed in 2004, before the Olympics.

By then the hole in the ground will have been there for 23 years, a good innings for a mere hole. The story shows the difficulty of carrying out long-term projects (the metro, the airport, the new Acropolis

Museum) when ministers and mayors are transient figures. It shows the sheer intractability of Athens, its resistance to easy solutions. Even when this problem is solved, there will always be other real or symbolic holes in the ground.

Growth of the Modern City

The modern city grew in waves. The town where Byron stayed in 1811 had about 10,000 inhabitants. By 1840 there were 26,000, reflecting the arrival of a court and governing class, the growth of a bureaucracy and army, and the migration to Athens of those from Greek lands and abroad attracted by the prospects of jobs in the new capital city. Fifty years later, at the time of the 1896 Olympic Games, the population had increased to between 120,000 and 130,000, with a further 50,000 in Piraeus. Rapid growth continued until the next great burst between the wars, signalled by the arrival in Greece of one and a half million refugees from Asia Minor and Thrace following the Asia Minor catastrophe of 1922. The city grew outwards to accommodate the refugees in the 1920s and 1930s, spawning new suburbs. By the Second World War the population of Athens and Piraeus had reached 800,000.

A further burst of growth followed in the late 1950s and 1960s, when a combination of factors led to the wholesale destruction of neoclassical Athens and the construction of the present "cement-city" of apartment blocks. There were strong pressures of immigration from the countryside, ravaged by the Greek Civil War. The Public Works Minister, Constantine Karamanlis, later prime minister and president, let things rip. He and probably most Athenians at the time saw the solution of immediate social and economic problems as having a higher priority than environmental considerations and conservation policies (which hardly existed). Athenian society developed its own methods of solving the housing shortage, under the Greek terms *antiparochi* and *afthaireta*, meaning roughly "part exchange" and "illegal buildings". These decades saw an orgy of construction, with virtually no control of density and height. In the short term such methods worked, but at the cost of problems stored up for later in the form of crowding and congestion, unplanned development and lack of green spaces. The result was an irrecoverable loss of houses and amenities, a tragedy which the Athenians took years to appreciate, but at the same time an effective rough and ready answer to the housing shortage.

Migration and Crime

Nineteenth-century Athens was a city of internal migration, as Greeks and Albanians were sucked in from the countryside and the islands by the prospect of work in the construction of the new city and in the burgeoning bureaucracy. Most of the immigrants from outside Greece came from Ottoman lands. Today, for the first time, the city is host to large numbers of immigrants from further afield, whose arrival has caused less social tension than might have been expected: Kurds, Bangladeshis, Pakistanis, Indians, Arabs, Poles, Chinese, Africans, Filipinos. They cluster around Koumoundourou Square and downtown Omonia. Lines of Bangladeshis could be seen in recent years queuing outside their consulate for papers. By far the greatest numbers are Albanians, who are found not only in Athens but in every Greek town and village, in domestic work, construction, and seasonal agricultural labour. With a strong tradition of expertise in stone masonry, they have made themselves indispensable in the building trade. Immigrants identifiable by the colour of their skin have more need for green cards than those who, like the Albanians, can merge into the Greek urban landscape. The 2004 Olympic Games have offered good opportunities for employment in construction projects, and people now fear a slump after the games are over.

Even before this new opening of Athens to immigration, the agreeable suburbs to the north of the city were becoming more genteel, as the wealthy built private houses, with swimming pools, in well protected plots secure behind high fences. Suburbs such as Maroussi and Kiphissia have developed American-style shopping malls and fast food outlets. The Athenians' concern about security has sharply increased. It is difficult to disentangle facts from urban and rural legends in this area. But everyone seems agreed that security of property, and even persons, has deteriorated. From the eighteenth century onwards, observers have commented on the personal honesty of the Greeks. In the 1960s, personal experience and anecdotal evidence suggest, you could leave your car or even your house unlocked, with little fear of burglary. The morality of the village survived in the town. (But the villagers brought their own vendettas with them, and homicide rates rose rapidly in late nineteenth-century Athens.) Now Mafia-type gangs from Russia and Eastern Europe have brought drugs and prostitution with the other forms of crime which come in their wake. The press reports shoot-outs between Albanian gang leaders and police in downtown Kypseli. People lock up their belongings. Old ladies who used to walk freely are now beginning to stay at home after dark. Security firms providing guards and alarm systems do good business. Accurate statistics are unavailable, but at the popular level there is widespread belief that Albanians are responsible for much of the increase in crime.

Security has become more of a concern also at the political level. The only Greek prime minister to be assassinated in Athens was Theodore Deliyiannis, an elderly figure who was struck down in 1905 by a frustrated gambler's knife after closing the gambling saloons. There were several unsuccessful attempts on the life of Venizelos, the great prime minister of the first half of the twentieth century. But assassinations and beatings-up were not uncommon in periods of tension, such as the First World War, when the country was divided between Venizelists and Royalists. The poet and political philosopher Ion Dragoumis, whose poem about Athens is at the back of this book (see p.237), was murdered by political thugs in 1920. The Nazi occupation raised the level of violence to a new level.

It was Andreas Papandreou, a mixture of the modern American and the traditional Greek politician, who introduced the blaring motorcade to bring him down from Kastri in the northern suburbs to his office in parliament when he became prime minister in 1981. His predecessor in that post, George Rallis, still an upright and familiar figure on the Athenian scene, could be seen modestly walking from home to office. Costas Simitis, the present prime minister, who combines competence and decency with boredom of political utterance raised to the nth degree, makes the quarter-mile journey from his apartment just north of Kolonaki Square to the prime minister's residence at the Megaron Maximou in Herod Atticus Street by car, in a modest convoy.

A high degree of protection is not just ostentation. Greek politicians and businessmen have had real cause for concern in the terrorist group N17 (November 17, named after the date of the Athens Polytechnic students' uprising against the Colonels' regime in 1973), which perpetrated 25 murders over a period of nearly twenty years, including that of the British Defence Attaché Stephen Saunders. The leading members were convicted and sentenced to life imprisonment in December 2003.

Attica had about three and a half million inhabitants in the 1991 census, more than 34 per cent of the population of Greece. Taking account of population growth and illegal immigration, the number today is probably nearer to four million. Athens is still one of the more secure urban environments in Europe. But given the increasingly multi-ethnic composition of Athenian society and the developments in global terrorism, drugs and crime to which Athens is not immune, it seems depressingly clear that the honest Athens that some inhabitants still remember will not come back.

Heat and Light

The Scottish historian and philhellene George Finlay, who lived in Athens for many years, noted in his journal for 6 October 1869 that two hours after his return to Athens from a summer absence there was a hail storm of unusual violence, which appeared to be most damaging about the university and the palace, where it broke much glass. "In the garden opposite the Mint and the British Legation (which in those days was in Klafthmonos Square) hundreds of sparrows roosting in the trees were killed and the people went out with lanterns to collect them. One collected nearly 200. In the small garden of the Legation about 150 were found dead."

Finlay is one of those people whose journals and letters bring old Athens to life. He first came to Greece in 1823, inspired by Byron's example, to take part in the War of Independence from the Turks. He settled in Athens in 1829 and stayed until his death in 1875. He is buried in the Protestant cemetery of Athens, where his impressive monument, topped by a bust of the man himself, was at the time of writing sadly decaying, the marble of the plinth chipped and crumbling, the iron railings bent. His fine library was left to the British School at Athens, which also has his archive of journals and correspondence.

The epiphany reported by Finlay may be unique. Yet the weather of Athens is not so uniformly fine as it seems to summer visitors. The air can be hot and heavy and sometimes a yellowish cloud of pollution hangs over the city until a sharp wind blows away the cloud: then the light changes, the outlines of the distant hills and islands are etched clearly, the columns of the Parthenon stand out sharply on the ancient rock. On rare occasions the cloud which covers the bowl of the Attic plain has a brownish tinge, the day darkens, and the rain which then falls in torrents is loaded with sand from the Egyptian desert, leaving brown blotches on the bonnets of the cars which fill the streets of the city and crowd onto the pavements.

Rain may be infrequent but when it comes it can be dramatic, turning the steep roads on the sides of Mount Lycabettus to torrents, flooding the basements of apartment blocks in the low-lying areas. In recent times, weather patterns have been changeable. The summer of 2001 was rainless from April to October, whereas in summer 2002 it rained almost every day in Attica throughout August and September. Usually dust ("mud's sister") is more familiar than mud; clear light and sharp outlines more familiar than lowering skies. But the dust is nothing now as compared with the nineteenth century, when almost every visitor commented on the tribulation of the journey by carriage from Piraeus to Athens.

Clear light, sharp outlines. It is the light that now characterizes Athens and Attica for so many Athenians and visitors, not least artists. There has grown up a literature of light. Thus Edmund Wilson on post-war Athens ("You still have to learn in Athens to appreciate everything in terms of light"), and Henry Miller in 1941 on the Sacred Way from Athens to Eleusis:

Everything here speaks now, as it did centuries ago, of illumination, of blinding, joyous illumination. Light acquires a transcendental quality: it is not the light of the Mediterranean alone, it is something more, something unfathomable, something holy. Here the light penetrates directly to the soul, opens the doors and windows of the heart, makes one naked, exposed, isolated in a metaphysical bliss which makes everything clear without being known. No analysis can go on in this light: here the neurotic is either instantly healed or goes mad.

That says more about Miller than about the Attic light. But the old boy was onto something. The poet George Seferis, Miller's friend, commented on "the monotony of provincial English towns. I think sometimes that the only thing that makes the English different from us (thought, expression, architecture, language) is the light."

Attica and Athens have always been renowned for their climate and the quality of their light. But I believe that Miller's emphasis on the sharpness and penetration of the light is a comparatively new phenomenon. It seems to be an aesthetic fashion of the twentieth century. Ancient writers would be more likely to write about the coolness and verdure of the Athenian groves than about the dry, hot atmosphere and the sharp noonday contrast of sun and shadow. Eighteenth- and nineteenth-century watercolourists such as Francis Penrose, the first Director of the British School at Athens, would soften rather than sharpen the contrasts. Chateaubriand on the Acropolis referred to the "lumière éclatante" but left it at that. Byron was more interested in the generalities of the climate, the bracing air, and the sea in which he swam every day. John Addington Symonds noted in the 1870s that the specific quality of the Athenian landscape was light—"not richness or sublimity or romantic loveliness or grandeur of mountain outline, but luminous beauty, serene exposure to the airs of heaven." The light was seen as an aspect of harmony and balance of the landscape. By the time of Henry Miller and the painter Nikos Hadjikyriakos-Ghikas (Ghika), the light had assumed a more hard-edged quality, in keeping with a twentieth-century aesthetic.

A romantic author called Pericles Yannopoulos, one of those intellectuals who tried to found a new aesthetic on authentically Greek values and history around the turn of the nineteenth and twentieth centuries, helped to start the trend with his book, *The Greek Line* (1904). In this he searched for the essence of Greek landscape, thought and light. He became an object of veneration to modernist writers and artists, and was included in the pantheon of artists of the influential periodical *The Third Eye,* which was founded in the 1930s by a small group of artists and writers including Ghika and the architect Dimitrios Pikionis. But poor Yannopoulos went mad, and committed suicide by riding his horse out into the sea near Eleusis.

The most extraordinary epiphany of Athenian light is the way the flank of Mount Hymettus turns from bluish grey, as the sun sets, to a violet-rose which seems to flood the atmosphere. The first to note this, in the fifth century BC, was the poet Pindar, not himself Athenian, who discovered the word ιοστέφανος (*iostephanos,* violet-crowned), to describe the phenomenon. "O glorious Athens", he wrote, "shining, violet-crowned, worthy of song, stronghold of Greece, city of the gods." This is no poetic fiction. It really happens. It is the "violet blood" spoken of by the poet Kostis Palamas.

The climate and vegetation have probably not changed much since ancient times, for all the talk about erosion and deforestation. But the city is always in a process of transformation. Even in my short span of acquaintance there have been big changes in its physical stuff, not to speak of the lives and habits of the Athenians: the building of a metro system, still new and gleaming; the construction of a brand new airport in the heart of the Attic plain (which entailed slicing off the top of a hill, and moving a Byzantine church to a new site); the creation of pedestrian streets in the heart of the city, and the gradual improvement and linking up of the classical sites in preparation for the Olympic Games. In 2003 it seemed that much of the city had turned into a building site, as buildings were spruced up for the Games, and state-run museums and sites closed for reordering or refurbishment.

Athenians Observed

It is the Athenians who give life to the city, and it is to them that the city belongs, though you might not think so to read the proprietary observations of some western travellers. Most visitors came to see the glory that was Greece, not the Athenians. But the Athenians impose themselves. They are as differentiated a body of several millions as any other. Yet for reasons related to ancient Greece foreigners have always felt obliged to comment on their morals and habits, and those of the Greeks generally, whether to praise or blame. St Paul was an early example ("Ye men of Athens, I see that ye are too superstitious..."). You only have to read the British periodical *The Spectator,* or daily papers at the time of some incident involving Greece, such as the arrest of British plane spotters, or the row over the Macedonian name and flag, to see that national stereotypes of Greeks are alive and well.

The intrepid composer Dame Ethel Smyth, student of Brahms, demanding lesbian friend of Virginia Woolf, and composer of the rarely performed opera *The Wreckers,* made what she called a "three-legged tour of Greece" in 1925 with her great-niece Elizabeth Williamson. It was three-legged because the exuberance of the younger and more active partner had to be toned down to the scale of the older, who thereupon became equal to feats of pace and endurance that could never have been accomplished in single harness. Dame Ethel referred to the "perpetual electric shocks of beauty, and an air so intoxicating that, once your lungs and eyes have sampled it, you feel certain it must have been a factor in the evolution of the Greek miracle."

Yet even the broad-minded but bossy Dame Ethel felt obliged to scold as well as praise. Contrary to expectations that she would find a clever but unsympathetic race, she and her niece found the Greeks of town and country kind, courteous and "superlatively well bred". On the other hand, compared with the southern Italians they seemed slow on the uptake. She criticized the launching of roads that were never finished, the profusion of electric bulbs and switches and bathrooms in places where, as far as could be seen, the authorities had no intention of installing either electric current or water supply. She ticked off the Greeks for spending their time playing with worry beads, for which the "true explanation is idleness and love of fidgeting."

For Frederick North Douglas a hundred years earlier, the modern Athenian showed in exaggerated form the characteristics of the ancient Greeks: "lively, ardent, and ingenious, he is still famous for the smartness of his repartees; his inconstancy and his eagerness for news, are proverbial; τι κινουριο (What news?) is still heard in the streets of Athens as was formerly the τι καινον which so often struck the ears of St Paul and Demosthenes." Edmund Keeley's account of today's Athenians is not so different: he writes of the "split character of the contemporary Athenian: intensely individualistic, charming with both men and women, arrogant (anybody is clever enough to be a tycoon or a prime minister), as much on the make as the citizen of any other city, but at the same time as filled with domestic pride as any villager and almost as traditional." He goes on to write that "the Athenian has little concern for public enterprise or communal responsibility and much cynicism about politics," at which point one begins to ask "which

Athenian?" There are counter-examples to such generalizations, in citizens' groups such as the *Elliniki Etairia*, which works for the preservation and restoration of the built and natural heritage.

Generalization is the writer's stock in trade. But the line between fair comment and prejudice is a narrow one. Thackeray crossed it when he wrote of "yonder dirty, swindling, ragged blackguards, lolling over greasy cards three hours before noon, quarrelling and shrieking, armed to the teeth and afraid to fight." Mark Twain claimed that "the modern inhabitants are confiscators and falsifiers of high repute, if gossip speaks truly concerning them, and I freely believe it does."

Thackeray, who hated his ten years of classical education and his time at Charterhouse, set out to deflate romanticism, and to squash Byron, a more sharp-eyed observer than himself: "What are the blue hills of Attica, the silver calm basin of Piraeus, the heathery heights of Pentelicus, and yonder rocks crowned by the Doric columns of the Parthenon, and the thin Ionic shafts of the Erectheum, to a man who has had little rest, and is bitten all over by bugs?" Witty.

Mark Twain and the Acropolis

Mark Twain was more sympathetic. He visited Athens during a novel pleasure excursion of the paddle steamer *Quaker City* to Europe and the Holy Land in 1867. The journey was the beginning of American cultural tourism to Europe. It cost the travellers $1,250 per adult, and they were advised to allow $5 a day in gold for overheads on shore. (These sums should be multiplied by between 5 and 10 to give today's prices.) The promised celebrities dropped out and most of Twain's companions were professors, ministers of religion, widowed ladies, and doctors—a Swan Hellenic cruise without the guest lecturers. Twain paid for the journey through a series of letters at $20 a time to the *Daily Alta* in California. He was as intrigued by his fellow tourists and the local inhabitants as by the ruins. But he had no opportunity to do for Athens what he did for Constantinople, sketching the richness, variety and grotesqueness of life in the streets. In any case, Athens was then as now a tamer, more manageable, more "European" place than Constantinople, which was the paradigm "oriental" city.

When the *Quaker City* made landfall at Piraeus, while the American tourists examined distant Athens through telescopes, disputing which monument was which, the port authorities forbade them to disembark. An eleven-day quarantine was in force. Nineteenth-century quarantine was no joke, though much more bearable on board a comfortable ship than in primitive quarters on land. Twain and three companions decided to jump ship. They slipped ashore at night and struck out through Piraeus, waking the dogs as they made for Athens, under a moonlit sky obscured by cloud. They pushed on over dry, loose, newly ploughed ground, past vineyards, stealing the juicy grapes until a dark shape rose mysteriously up out of the shadows beside them. They continued along a broad white road past a stone aqueduct, up over rocky ridges, until suddenly they came to the Acropolis. They failed to break through the gate or to climb round it and woke the four Greek guards with their noise. "We clamored at the gate," Twain wrote, "and they admitted us. [Bribery and corruption.]"

There followed the confrontation with the Acropolis. Twain and his friends

stood upon a pavement of purest white marble, deeply worn by footprints. Before us, in the flooding moonlight, rose the noblest ruins we had ever looked upon - the propylae (the grand gateway to the Acropolis); *a small Temple of Minerva* (the temple of Athina Nike); *the Temple of Hercules* (the Erectheum), *and the grand Parthenon. [We got these names from the Greek guide, who didn't seem to know more than seven men ought to know.] These edifices were all built of the whitest Pentelic marble* (from the quarries on Mount Penteli, a few miles north of Athens), *but have a pinkish stain upon them now. Where any part is broken, however, the fracture looks like fine loaf sugar. Six caryatides, or marble women, clad in flowing robes, support the portico of the Temple of Hercules, but the porticos and colonnades of the other structures are formed of massive Doric and Ionic pillars, whose flutings and capitals are still measurably perfect, notwithstanding the centuries that have gone over them and the sieges they have suffered... Most of the Parthenon's imposing columns are still standing, but the roof is gone. It was a perfect building two hundred and fifty years ago, when a shell dropped into the Venetian magazine stored here, and the explosion which followed wrecked and unroofed it. I remember but little*

*about the Parthenon, and I have put in one or two facts and figures for
the use of other people with short memories. Got them from the guidebook.*

Twain's cursory treatment of the Parthenon is reflected in his
carelessness of fact—the shell which dropped into the powder
magazine was Venetian, and the magazine Turkish. And how could he
see a pinkish stain under moonlight? But his cultural conditioning
stirred Twain to be moved even by what he could not see:

*Here and there, in lavish profusion, were gleaming white statues of men
and women, propped against blocks of marble, some of them armless,
some without legs, others headless—but all looking mournful in the
moonlight, and startlingly human! They rose up and confronted the
midnight intruder on every side—they stared at him with stony eyes
from unlooked-for nooks and recesses; they peered at him over fragmentary heaps far down the desolate corridors; they barred his way in the
midst of the broad forum, and solemnly pointed with handless arms the
way from the sacred fane; and through the roofless temple the moon
looked down, and banded the floor and darkened the scattered fragments and broken statues with the slanting shadows of the columns...*

*We walked out into the grass-grown, fragment-strewn court beyond
the Parthenon. It startled us, every now and then, to see a stony white
face stare suddenly up at us out of the grass with its dead eyes. The place
seemed alive with ghosts. I half expected to see the Athenian heroes of
twenty centuries ago glide out of the shadows and steal into the old temple
they knew so well and regarded with such boundless pride.*

*The full moon was riding high in the cloudless heavens, now. We
sauntered carelessly and unthinkingly to the edge of the lofty battlements of the citadel, and looked down—a vision! And such a vision!
Athens by moonlight!... It lay in the level plain right under our feet—
all spread abroad like a picture—and we looked down upon it as we
might have looked from a balloon. We saw no semblance of a street,
but every house, every window, every clinging vine, every projection, was
as distinct and sharply marked as if the time were noon day; and yet
there was no glare, no glitter, nothing harsh or repulsive—the noiseless*

city was flooded with the mellowest light that ever streamed from the moon, and seemed like some living creature wrapped in peaceful slumber. On its further side was a little temple, whose delicate pillars and ornate front glowed with a rich lustre that chained the eye like a spell; and nearer by, the palace of the king reared its creamy walls out of the midst of a great garden of shrubbery that was flecked all over with a random shower of amber lights—a spray of golden sparks that lost their brightness in the glory of the moon, and glinted softly upon the sea of dark foliage like the pallid stars of the milky-way. Overhead the stately columns, majestic still in their ruin—under foot the dreaming city— in the distance the silver sea—not on this broad earth is there another picture half so beautiful!

True or false? Some of Mark Twain's facts were wrong, but his romantic description preserves for us an Acropolis still rich in unexpected fragmentary visions, not yet purged by the archaeologists and cultural managers and turned into a bare, controlled museum.

The Acropolis remains the core of visitors' experience of Athens. We shall meet a number of visitors in these pages, and encounter their sense of recognition, combined with ownership, often excluding the Greek people. It was this sense which led them to moralize about Greece and the Greeks. The first Earl of Lytton was a minor poet and diplomatist of the nineteenth century who rose to eminence as Viceroy of India and died at his desk at the British Embassy, Paris, in 1891. Like others of his generation, Lytton had been exposed, through his upbringing, to the power of the Greek spirit, and as a young diplomat in Athens he confronted the irritating reality that Greece regularly threatened to frustrate the plans conceived by the Great Powers in their wisdom. This is how Lytton put it in his poem "Athens" (1865):

The burnt-out heart of Hellas here behold!
    Quench'd fire-pit of the quick explosive past
Thought's highest crater—all its fervours cold,
    Ashes and dust at last!

And what Hellenic light is living now
    To gild, not Greece, but other lands, is given:

Not where the splendour sank, the after-glow
  Of sunset stays in heaven.

But loud o'er Grecian ruins still the lark
  Doth, as of old, Hyperion's glory hail.
And from Hymettus, in the moonlight, hark
  The exuberant nightingale!

Matters could not be clearer. The Hellenic light had moved, with the Parthenon sculptures and more intangible products of the Greek spirit, to the British Museum, the Louvre, and the classrooms and country houses where the enlightened could absorb the message. The nightingale and the lark could not be moved from their ancestral groves and ruins. As to the people of Greece, they did not feature in the picture at all. They hardly featured for many travellers either, unless they were dead. As Chateaubriand said to the Bey of Mistra in the Peloponnese, who asked why he travelled, since he was neither a merchant nor a doctor, "I answered that I travelled so as to see the people and especially the Greeks who were dead." This made the Bey laugh. He replied that since he was in Turkish lands, Chateaubriand should have learned Turkish.

Byron was an exception. He too moralized about the Greeks. But he learned what he could about them, their customs, language and literature, and he saw them as individuals not as types. Of all foreign visitors to Athens, he is the one whom the Greeks have taken closest to their hearts, which is why his portrait features on the cover of this book.

CHAPTER TWO

Nostalgia and Retrospect: Impressions of Forty-five Years

"Already the Athens of our fathers belongs definitively to the past."
Giorgos Theotokas, 1957

"A place which I think I prefer on the whole to any I have seen."
Byron, letter to his mother, 20 July 1810

I first visited Athens in 1957 as a sixth former. We were three, travelling around Greece in local buses with rucksacks and sleeping bags. We stayed in a hostel high on Sina Street, from which there was a view of the Acropolis. Our main interest, as classicists, was in the ruins; less so in those who inhabited them. In this we stood in a long tradition.

I returned to Athens in 1962 and spent a year living in a small house at the corner of Ploutarchou (Plutarch) and Aristippou Streets. This is on the southern flank of Mount Lycabettus, as high as it was possible to go before houses gave way to scrub, cactus and pine trees. Lycabettus is the conical hill that thrusts up into the sky above Kolonaki, and is so visible from the Acropolis and central Athens. Aristippou Street was an earth road. Most of its houses were single-storey ochre buildings with tiled roofs and an earth yard. Tall apartment blocks, in Greek *polykatoikies* ("many-homes"), had not yet advanced this far up the hill.

Some of the families up here kept chickens, and a goat or two tethered in the yard. The early morning wake-up call was the crowing of cocks. All this within half a mile, or a fifteen-minute walk, of the centre of Athens. There were cats everywhere. If you stayed at home during the day you would hear the raucous, irregular cries of the junk seller, *paliatzis*, the yoghurt seller and other street traders. (In the late

nineteenth century, according to US Consul George Horton, they cried their wares in Greek, Turkish and Italian; "in no other city of the world are the street-cries so varied, so harrowing, so vocally picturesque.") In the afternoons you would catch a glimpse of middle-aged Greeks at their windows in pyjamas or nightgowns before or after the siesta, or on their balconies watering the potted plants. In the heat of summer some would take to their flat roofs and sleep there.

During the period in which I lived on Aristippou Street, engineers began to tunnel into Mount Lycabettus, some ten or twenty yards away from the house, in a project designed by the National Tourist Organization, to construct a funicular railway which would carry visitors to the top of the hill, where a new café was to be installed. I took a dim view of this incursion of modernity, particularly when an inefficient blasting operation sprinkled the neighbourhood with stones, one of which shattered the glass roof of my flat. On another occasion, a highly-strung American neighbour, distracted by the noise of drilling at eleven p.m., climbed on to his flat roof and loosed off two blank cartridges at the workmen from a pistol, which led to my only appearance in a Greek court of law, as a witness. As Ethel Smyth observed, you cannot escape noise in Athens.

Most people look back to a rosy period in the past before things started to deteriorate. The eccentric Anglo-Irish scholar J. P. Mahaffy wrote in 1884, "When roads and rail have been brought into Greece, hundreds of people will go to see its beauty and its monuments, and will congratulate themselves that the country is at last accessible," but

the real charm will be gone. There will be no more riding at dawn through orchards of oranges and lemons, with the rich fruit lying on the ground... no more watching the glowing east across the silver-grey glitter of dewy meadows; no more wandering along grassy slopes, where the scarlet anemones, all drenched with the draughts of night, are striving to raise their drooping heads, and open their splendid eyes to meet the sun... no more watching the serpent and the tortoise, the eagle and the vulture, and all the living things whose ways and habits animate the sunny solitudes of the south.

No more a-roving.

"Old Athens"

Athenians like to recall "Old Athens". There is a category of songs of nostalgia: *Rendezvous in Athens, Athens and Again Athens, London Paris Athens,* sung by the formidable Sophia Vembo, *Athens by Night, The Athens Tango, Beautiful Athens,* and best-known of all Manos Hatzidakis' song *Athens* to words by the poet Nikos Gatsos. Parties celebrating at tavernas in the Plaka during carnival time can be heard heartily joining in this last.

The novelist Thanasis Petsalis-Diomedis caught the mood in his 1964 description of childhood in the late nineteenth century:

I was born in Athens, when Athens had a hundred and fifty thousand inhabitants. Horses pulled the trams in Stadium Street, cut right through Constitution Square, and toiled uphill up Philellinon Street. In the early afternoon the milkman passed by with his goats and milked them in front of the door of our house. In the early evening, on the corner of the street a man with a long pole stood below the gas lamp standard and with a smart movement or two lit the gas, which shone a pale blue-green in the pallid orange late light of the day...

When I was born, herdsmen from the villages around herded turkeys and guinea fowls with their canes in front of the Palace and Ermou Street. There was no cinema. The first motor car had only just made its appearance...

At that time, Athens drowned in mud in the winter and choked with dust in the summer. The dirt rose in a cloud at the least breath of wind and Athens suddenly wore a crown of dust. At sunset this dust became golden-red and little by little, as evening set in, took on the classic violet colour. This was the apotheosis of the City—the so-called Violet Crown...

I was born in an Athens where everyone knew everyone else 'like himself'—it is not an exaggeration, because after all, who knows himself? Wherever you passed, wherever you went, everybody was known to you, so you greeted them, you raised your hat, you passed a few moments in talk, as in a little provincial town.

I must seem like a prehistoric being, like something palaeolithic, to today's Athenians, for sure.

Those who indulged in such nostalgia tended to be of a comfortable social background. There was a harsher, poorer Athens of the suburbs and "picturesque" downtown quarters, evoked by Emmanuel Roides, the author of the scandalous novel *Pope Joan* (1866), in a series of articles on "Walks in Athens" published in the 1890s. He castigated the open drains, the smells, the health hazards, the butchers' shops spilling onto the pavements with pedestrians forced to take evasive action to avoid the bloody carcasses of sheep, the dust, the contrast between the opulent façades of shops and cafés and the meagre contents, the Potemkin village aspects of Athens's preparation for the 1896 Olympic Games. Both aspects were real, the picturesque charm and the filth and poverty.

Seen in retrospect, the period from the late nineteenth century to the outbreak of the Great War had a seductive charm. Ellen Bosanquet, the wife of an early director of the British School at Athens, described it:

> *A city of orange-trees and violet beds; of new white marble houses behind very old dark pines; of public gardens planted with seedling trees; of private gardens demurely circling round a central palm. That city had streets scored by winter torrents and patiently remade each spring; and up and down those streets raced the rare but noisy tram drawn by four or five stringy little horses; white horses on fine days, red blue and orange in wet weather when the dye streamed from their harness pads. There were plebeian carriages with cotton roofs like tester beds, and there were patrician landaus that moved slowly behind large British horses. There were donkey-hawkers with glass show-cases set upright on their panniers; there were shoe-shine boys dressed in grey cotton jumpers; there were men carrying trays of sesame-covered rolls and yaourti sellers with shining bowls of the cool sour curd made from sheep's milk, there was the train that jolted and screamed and whistled itself down from Cephissia and came to a halt between four religious-looking palm-trees; there was the blue and silver of the royal liveries, the starched fustanellas and red-bobbled shoes of the Household Guard, and there were the young princes cantering to Phalerum in uniforms of bronze and pink. There was the sun-filled central square with family parties grouped around its little*

iron tables; the children with their ludicrous carnival costumes, and the carnival camel that occasionally at a corner wine-shop dissolved itself into two thirsty men. There were the country folk strolling through the town in gay Albanian dress, and the farmers in their highly coloured carts; there was the modern theatre built and patronized by royalty, and the jolly little open-air theatres patronized by anyone who had a drachma to spare; there were lace-sellers from Cyprus spreading geometric webs on sunny hotel steps, and the handsome Rhodian who turned up each spring with his exciting bundle of embroidery and faience. There was the morning-scene of the 'Rally-Fox' when smart Athenians on beautiful horses rode out to Cephissia for the drag-hunt. There were the political crises when every head in the square was buried behind a newspaper, and the crowded election days with emblems instead of colours for the rival parties.

So the surface life ticked on busy with its weddings and funerals and baptism parties, blessings of waters and cherishings of Easter fire; church ceremonies and court balls following each other like the quick chiming of a busy little clock. And then suddenly everything was changed...

"Everything was changed" by the assassination of the Greek king and the outbreak of the European War. The golden age was over.

The early 1960s is my time of nostalgia, though the city was in many ways more attractive in the period described by Mrs. Bosanquet. But people have looked back with regret and nostalgia at every period. As early as 1839, the Earl of Carnarvon was lamenting a vanished orient, writing that emancipation from Turkish rule had had an unpleasing effect on the external appearance of Athens: "The flat roofs, the stately minarets, the cypresses, and tufted palms, —all that invested it with the character and circumstance of the East had gone with its ancient lords; and houses in the modern German style, and absolutely without effect, had replaced the Asiatic and picturesque irregularities of the old town."

In its turn the new became old and lamented. A case in point was the historic house of the nineteenth-century prime minister Harilaos Tricoupis, on the corner of Akadimias and Mavromichali Streets, where with his devoted sister Sophia he received political clients and hangers on, students, and members of the public with their petitions. It was knocked down in 1936. The old British Embassy, known as the Ambrosios Rallis house on Klafthmonos Square, fell to the demolition men in the late 1930s. Churches also disappeared. The little Church of the Prophet Elisha in Monastiraki, where the short story writer Alexandros Papadiamantis chanted in the choir during his years in Athens, was knocked down during the Great War. One of Papadiamantis's students, Father Philotheos, suggested that the Greek literary establishment should petition the Ministry of Education, the Holy Synod and the Archaeological Association for a new chapel to be built on the site of the old one; but curiously enough—"or it would be curious anywhere else but here"—neither the ministry nor the religious or archaeological bodies showed much interest. The comment "it would be curious anywhere else but here", which comes from an essay on Papadiamantis by the essayist Zissimos Lorenzatos, is characteristic of a sort of Athenian fatalism about the way things happen in Greece, usually as a product of sinister "interests".

But the loss of these and many other nineteenth-century houses was as nothing besides the mania for destruction and construction that gripped Athenian landowners in the late 1950s and the 1960s. By 1963, when I left, the work was well advanced on the funicular railway and it was clear that the street would soon by covered in tarmac, the old houses demolished to make way for new apartment blocks.

At about the time at which Athens was first fixed in my imagination, the writer Giorgos Theotokas, a distinguished member of the literary "generation of the thirties", wrote a lament for the old Athens and a warning for the future. Theotokas, and he was not the only one, thought it a historic mistake to have made Athens the capital of the Greek state. He conceded that the planners of the small, neat capital city of Otho and King George I could not have foreseen what would happen. For Theotokas the old Athens lasted until the 1920s. Then the influx of refugees from Turkey after the Asia Minor disaster of 1922, and the pressures of economic development, began to break up the old structures of the capital. "The city quickly took on a new look, unsettled, confused and dynamic." It was at this stage that nostalgia for the "good old days" began, the lament of the summer reviews and popular song-writers for the courtyards with their vines, the windows with pots of basil, and the other idyllic simplicities which fell one after the other.

The second, and larger, wave of change came with the end of the civil war and the beginning of the new period of peace. It came like an explosion, as if the new forces of the state had suddenly ripened, burst out and overflowed in all directions.

Our town planners, pulled in all directions, stitch and cobble, dig roads, make pavements narrower and broader, change the look of the squares, then later repent and change it back again, and maybe will change it yet again, in brief they are in a state of feverish activity. But we have never understood exactly what they are after, what in the end are the general lines they have in their minds. Nor have they taken the trouble to explain to us, perhaps because they don't have time. Rather one has the impression that they are hunting a mad bull and trying to seize him by the horns.

Theotokas wrote in 1957 that the "Athens of our fathers" already belonged definitively to the past. It had been covered by an enormous new city, half built, shapeless but dynamic, a "Great Athens", in which Piraeus and the once self-standing surrounding villages had been incorporated, with oil refineries, shipyards, new industries, broader roads, longer runways for the aeroplanes. All these things, Theotokas saw, were only a beginning and would continue. He foresaw that Athens would develop from his one million eight hundred thousand people to two million within a generation and on towards three, that all of the Attic plain would be given over to public works, industry and aerodromes, so that the city would stretch from the foothills of the mountains to Eleusis in one direction and Varkiza in the other, like a Los Angeles of the Mediterranean.

As a sign of what was happening, Theotokas pointed to the little Church of the Saints Theodore, a gem of Byzantine architecture, at the corner of Euripides and Aristeides Streets on the lower side of Klafthmonos Square. Here the modern city had swallowed the old building, surrounding it with concrete office blocks. The Saints Theodore Church is not the only one to be swallowed up: the tiny Church of the Holy Power in Mitropoleos Street is actually tucked into the corner of an apartment block, and even the church of Kapnikarea, to some extent protected by being situated in the middle of a crossroads of Ermou and Kapnikareas Streets, has to be seen against the background of office blocks.

The unsettling immediate effects of this building craze of the 1950s and 1960s were described by Patrick Leigh Fermor:

The fever of demolition and rebuilding has the Athenians by the throat. Streets gape as though bombed, masonry crashes, the dust of a siege floats in the air and the clatter of pneumatic drills has replaced the little owls' note as the city's leitmotiv. Rusting whiskers of reinforced concrete prong the sky-line: new hotels soar from the rubble like ogres' mouth-organs. Athens is in a state of headlong flux.

By the time I returned in 1967, Theotokas's warnings were coming true. The old one- or two-storey houses were now in a minority, crouching between gleaming new blocks. The building mania of the 1960s was still in full swing, as owners of property sought to solve their families' housing problems and to profit by the system of *antiparochi.*

George Prevelakis, a specialist in urban planning, describes the system well in his book *Athènes: Urbanisme, Culture et Politique* (2000). It was devised by the ingenuity of the Athenians to make up for the lack of finance in the post-war period, and depended on a balance of interests between three parties, the owner of land, the builder/project manager and the buyers. The builder would contract with the landowner to construct an apartment block on his land, in return for which the owner would get to keep some of the apartments, the builder the rest (typically in the proportions of 30 per cent to the owner, 70 per cent to the builder). The building operation would be financed by buyers of new apartments who would pay in instalments (Greek *doseis*, like doses of medicine) while the construction work proceeded. In this way the garden plots of Athens were filled in with tall blocks, and the old neoclassical and inter-war houses were demolished.

This time we lived round the other side of Lycabettus, on the broad ring road, Sarandapichou Street, which circles the hill just below the line of the pine trees. We rented part of an old house from a landlord who much approved of the sense of order temporarily induced by the new regime of the military junta, Colonel Papadopoulos, Brigadier Pattakos and Colonel Makarezos.

In this our landlord was far from unusual among people of his social background. Though most people have forgotten this now, in the early period of their unpleasant regime the Colonels could count on some approval and widespread tolerance, though not from the political world nor from the liberal intelligentsia. It was only gradually that people realized how inefficient and oppressive they were, and began to forget how unpopular politicians had become in early 1967. Two or three doors down the street from us lived the Canadian journalist Robert McDonald, who had recently taken over the BBC portfolio. McDonald did not at that stage know much Greek. He therefore put work my way, translating some of the documents that came to him, which gave us an unusual insight into the undercurrents of feeling about the political regime. Dissidents would push papers under his door recording instances of arrest or torture. He would receive mysterious phone calls. We spent the day of Sunday 13 December together, listening on the ham radio of a friend to crackling messages between military units as the young King Constantine tried to raise support in his counter-coup against the Colonels' regime. He failed and flew out of Greece into exile, first in Rome and later in London.

Though we did not fully appreciate it at the time, under the sometimes grotesque canopy of the Colonels' regime profound changes were taking place in Greek society. In the city of Athens too there was change, not least in the scrapping of the existing height restrictions on buildings, the development of the Papagos region into a privileged area of housing for the military, and closer to home, the erection of the chunky, buff-coloured War Museum on Vasilissis Sophias Street, blocking the view from the British Embassy down towards Phaleron and the sea.

The Colonels' regime fell, in the chaos and shame following their attempted coup d'état in Cyprus in 1974, which led to the Turkish occupation of the north of the island. The day in July when Constantine Karamanlis returned from Paris to assume the reins of government was one of the historic moments of Athenian history, along with the liberation from the Nazis in October 1944 and the arrival of King Otho in 1834, when Athens became the capital of the new Greek state. Extraordinarily, it seems that Karamanlis' return was witnessed by the future British prime minister Tony Blair, who happened to be in Greece on a student holiday. He tells of how riding into Athens he could hear the radios broadcasting the good news minute by minute on every balcony and in every house and apartment. That day inaugurated a period of recovery, reconciliation and political development for which the Greek people have cause to be grateful to Karamanlis.

The early 1980s, when we returned to Athens, were years of radical political change. This was the time when Karamanlis stepped down from his position as prime minister and assumed the presidency of the Hellenic Republic, the king's departure having been confirmed in a constitutional plebiscite in December 1974. In October 1981 Andreas Papandreou and his PASOK won a sweeping victory at the polls, inaugurating a twenty-year period in which the party came to seem the natural governing party of Greece. Under Papandreou's successor Costas Simitis PASOK is still in power today, though by the time this book appears it may have given place to the conservative New Democracy party under another (nephew) Karamanlis.

Between the early 1980s and the turn of the millennium the city of Athens improved. The earlier period was the time of the *nephos*, or cloud of pollution, which in certain conditions of temperature inversion hangs over the city and fills the Attic bowl. At that time we lived in the agreeable wooded northern suburb of Kiphissia. Driving down to work in Athens on a bad day I could see the evil yellowish cloud hanging in the air below me; once you drove into and through it the *nephos* was no longer visible, but could be felt in the throat and nose. There were days when hospitals reported casualties from aggravated respiratory diseases.

Curse of the Car

The causes of pollution were industrial emissions and exhaust fumes from motor vehicles. The number of cars has increased seemingly inexorably since the 1960s. There are now almost two million passenger cars in the Attica area. The number in Athens has increased by more than six per cent each year over the last decade and continues to increase at about the same rate each year, with registrations of new cars running at more than 10,000 a month. The average age of the fleet has deteriorated over the last ten years, reaching 11.2 years compared with a European Union average of about 7 years. More than one-third of cars are without catalytic converters, much the highest figure in the EU. Cars that run on diesel fuel are not allowed to circulate, which made sense in the 1980s, but is beginning to look outdated now that new technology has produced relatively clean diesel engines.

People will tell you now that the motor car is choking Athens. It is the greatest joy of the Athenian family and the greatest threat to the amenities of the city. Enlightened mayors and ministers of the environment from opposing political families, notably Antonis Tritsis and Stephanos Manos, have created some relief by banning vehicles from certain streets. The Plaka has been transformed from a seedy area of noisy nightclubs into a graceful quarter in which house after house has been restored to neoclassical elegance. But the native Greek genius has found a way to invade even car-free precincts with delivery vans, motor cycles and scooters. Athens is a battleground on which the driver struggles to assert his dominance and to evade the attempts of authority to shackle him, by pedestrian precincts or parking meter. An attempt by the City to install parking meters on the pavements of Kolonaki was defeated by a successful appeal to the Council of State, so that the pavements are now sprinkled with useless metal boxes labelled Siemens.

By the 1990s, when we lived in Athens again, the pollution was less bad. Relief came about through a variety of measures. First the authorities introduced a so-called "Odd and Even" system—*Mona-Zyga*—whereby a car is allowed into the central "ring" of Athens only on alternate weekdays, depending on whether its number plate ends in an odd or even number. The rules are announced each day in the press. This measure brought temporary relief, but by the law of unintended consequences caused problems of congestion outside the ring, and was in any case soon bypassed by the Athenians buying second cars. It remains in force, though rendered largely pointless. Manos's effort to get motorists to acquire catalytic converters for their exhausts was more effective. In 1990 he introduced a scheme of tax incentives for those who destroyed their old, pre-catalytic vehicles and bought new ones with converters. This led to an unprecedented renewal of the car fleet, with some 400,000 cars changed for new.

As much as the pollution, it is now the sheer physical presence of motor cars that oppresses. According to one estimate, more than half the paved surface of roads in Athens is occupied permanently by cars. They park on both sides of roads and on pavements, and double park freely, in rows which block in the inner cars and lead to angry confrontations. The roar of engines, the hooting and the scream of tyres on the tarmac are a nuisance. The city continues to build roads, which immediately fill up with vehicles.

The most important experiments in urban management and traffic control of recent years are the new metro system, and the project to link up the main archaeological sites. Both of these have a long history of planning and debate. The metro is a success, in its engineering, its architecture, and the way it displays the layers of history uncovered during its construction. To appreciate this, the visitor should go down into the central metro station at Constitution (Syntagma) Square, and look at the cross section of the ancient city displayed behind glass, not forgetting the skeleton behind the glass. The metro has made life easier for shoppers, commuters and tourists; but it remains to be seen how much it will ease the congestion of Athens's motor traffic in the longer term.

The linking of the archaeological sites by pedestrian ways and parkland, a long-standing dream, has been stimulated by the prospect of the Olympic Games in 2004. It proceeds slowly, and not all that has been promised will be achieved by 2004. Welcome in itself, it brings in its train new problems of traffic management for the vehicles displaced by new pedestrian ways. The visitor who wishes to judge should walk up the broad paved pedestrian street of Dionysius the Areopagite (an early Christian) on the south side of the Acropolis, and thence up to the Acropolis itself, imagining the roar of traffic and the lines of parked coaches which this now quiet street had to sustain until recently. The designers have paved the street in oblong paving stones or cobbles, with bands of stonework to vary the design, and varying levels, width and angles. The inner side, towards the Acropolis, has been planted with olives, rosemary, and other shrubs.

Preserving sites of repose in the teeming modern city is a constant battle. But the city centre is greener now than it was 25 years ago.

The View from Mount Lycabettus

To see the city as a whole the best vantage point is the top of Mount Lycabettus. The path winds upwards, starting from near the end of Aristippou or Deinokratous Street, bordered by tough cacti of the type called "immortal" (*Agave americana*, the century plant, an introduction from Mexico), their leathery milky green leaves carved with initials. This is a place appropriated at night by couples, as the discarded condoms among the bushes show. Half way up there is a café; at the top a good restaurant. The path is steep and the walk a good fifteen-minute hike to the top, with its chapel of St George. Over to the north, carved out of the hill, is an open-air theatre.

From the top of Lycabettus, looking southwest, the eye is drawn out across the sea to the island of Aegina with its pyramidal mountain, some twelve miles out from the port of Piraeus. It is a beautiful island with a lively waterfront at the main town, which faces away from Athens towards Methana and the Argolid. Athens and Aegina were rivals in classical times, and Pericles called the island the eyesore of Piraeus. For a short time in the War of Independence Aegina became the capital of the new Greek state. It is now a holiday place of second homes for Athenians, and an easy three-quarter hour's commuter ride away.

Sweeping the horizon from the left, or southeast, to the right, or northwest, you see the whale back hump of Mount Hymettus stretching out towards the sea, the old airport and the Glyphada golf course; then an agglomeration of housing stretching down to Phaleron and Piraeus, a whitish mass with flashes of green from which the eye gradually picks out individual features and buildings; in the centre the Acropolis and the Plaka at its foot; on the right Mount Aegaleo; and further to the right Mount Parnes.

From here you can appreciate the essential physical facts about Athens and the Attic basin. The great rock of the Acropolis, solidly settled in the heart of the modern city, was the original citadel and defence of the inhabitants, commanding the Attic plain. It is one of a series of hills that stretch in a south-westerly direction across the plain, forming a long, interrupted limestone ridge. The limestone rests on marl, and is pierced by fissures that issued in springs on the northwest side. With additional fortifications in the form of walls on the north, south and west sides, it was made nearly impregnable. As the city grew at the foot of the Acropolis, the further line of defence came into play, the natural protective barriers of the Athenian plain, its ring of mountains, Hymettus to the south, Penteli to the northeast, Parnes to the north, and the sea to the southwest. The citadel was a convenient distance from the sea: far enough to deter casual raiders, near enough to make it possible in the classical era to yoke together Athens and Piraeus in a single political and economic unit. The magnificent natural harbours of Piraeus and its promontory were crucial to the development of the Athenian economy and to the Athenian war machine, reliant in the classical period on naval power.

The bones and knuckles of the ancient city—the Acropolis, the temple of Olympian Zeus, the stadium—poke up through the modern residential and light industrial cityscape. From this height the movement and noise of the streets are remote and muffled. You can see how the modern city has grown around the ancient core, and how planners have had to struggle to defend and conserve the monuments, which risk being swamped in the post-war high rise of apartment blocks.

Lycabettus towers over Athens, yet it is the Acropolis that commands the city. The artist and author Osbert Lancaster, who served as press attaché at the British Legation at the end of the Second World War, described the prospect from the Acropolis at an unusually dramatic period in the bitter winter of 1944:

For more than a week a handful of British paratroops had held the summit against repeated attacks and only the day before had they been able, as the result of the arrival of reinforcements, to advance their perimeter to the edge of the Agora. Above us the skies were those one finds more frequently in the Derbyshire landscapes of Mr Piper than in the posters extolling the beauties of the eastern Mediterranean; below, the whole overgrown city sprawled across the plain of Attica to the foothills of Parnes and Penteli. The usual deafening hubbub of Athenian life—the clanging of trams, the shrieks of the street-vendors, the crowing of backyard fowls—which in normal times is here audible as though detached from its background and existing, as it were, in a void, was stilled and the prevailing quietness was emphasized rather than broken by the continuous machine-gun fire in the streets immediately below, the detonations from the direction of Patissia (where the proletariat were blowing up houses to form street barricades) and that peculiar sound, half-whistle, half-rending calico, which shells make as they pass immediately overhead. Somewhere beyond Omonia Square a group of buildings was on fire, probably a petrol dump, as the tall column of smoke was oily black against the snow of the distant mountains; behind the Theseon mortar shells fell with monotonous regularity on a corner house by the tram-stop, sending up yellowish-white clouds that hung in the air, round and compact, for a full five minutes before dispersing. On the Acropolis itself a group of trigger-happy gendarmerie lounged with an assumed nonchalance by the lower entrance; alongside the Themistoclean wall a pile of cartridge cases indicated where until very recently a machine-gun had been emplaced; in the empty museum a few grubby plaster casts surveyed an accumulation of military debris. Over all towered the Parthenon, its clear unequivocal statement in no way blurred by the barricades hastily erected from fragments of its pillars and caissons, its own internal rhythm uninterrupted by mortar fire or rockets.

For once the eternal underlying significance of the Acropolis was immediately apparent...

That significance was of course defensive. We shall see later how British and Greek troops found themselves in this unhappy confrontation.

CHAPTER THREE

Otho Takes Possession: What to Do About the Acropolis?

"At present the Acropolis is the most complicated archaeological site in Greece; it has been a Mycenean fortress, an archaic complex of sanctuaries, gradually but never quite transformed into an integrated series of great monuments, an elaborate forest of Hellenistic and Roman art, a walled town, a Turkish castle, a battlefield, and an archaeological carcase stripped to the bone. Traces of all these periods can be made out, but no one period can be perfectly recovered. Yet in its present state the Acropolis can still take one's breath away; its classical buildings seem to be the most wonderful of the works of man."

Peter Levi, note to Pausanias *Guide to Greece,* vol. 1

Athens's new life as a modern European capital city began in 1834.

Greece emerged from the turbulence of her War of Independence as a small, poor but nominally independent state with frontiers—fixed by the "Great Powers" of Europe, Britain, France and Russia—which included the Peloponnese, some of the islands, and Attica, but extended north only as far as a line between Arta in the west and the gulf of Volos in the east. The first president of the independent state had been assassinated in the provisional capital, Nauplion. To replace him, the Powers selected Otho, the seventeen-year-old son of the philhellenic King Ludwig of Bavaria.

Nauplion is a pretty little seaside town on the gulf of Argos, dominated by a massive citadel. Otho disembarked there on 6 February 1833. He was a tall, serious young man, rather deaf, devoted to his mission and to Greece, obedient to his dominant father's ideas. It soon transpired that he was also stubborn, obsessed by detail, and suspicious of democratic ideas such as constitutions and parliaments. But that was to come. For the time being, in the anarchic conditions prevailing in free Greece, he was welcomed as a symbol of statehood, sovereignty, and the protective interest of the Great Powers. Until his majority, power was exercised by a three-man Bavarian Regency.

Nauplion had strong nationalist credentials earned during the war. It was a good place for the king and fledgling court to test their wings, but hardly the capital city of a serious European state. The debate on the site for a new capital began even before Otho's arrival.

Some argued for Athens, with its glorious past; some for Corinth, well placed on the isthmus; others for Argos, Tripolis bang in the middle of the Peloponnese, Syra, Megara, or Piraeus. Some even took the view that there should be no fixed capital, but rotation between a number of Greek cities, ending hopefully with Constantinople when that city, the capital of the Byzantine empire, became Greek once more. The latter conceit was later reflected in the dream of the Great Idea (*Megali Idea*), that the unredeemed Greeks in Ottoman lands should be recovered for Greece. All of these candidates had some claim based on classical renown or distinction in the recent war. But the claims of Athens were unrivalled both in ancient prestige and natural advantages of climate and location.

The choice fell on Athens, although in the early 1830s the town was in a pitiable state. Before it became the capital, young Otho had already made several visits to scout it out, observe its antiquities, and look for a suitable house to live in. In August 1834, with the regents, ministers and other notables in his entourage, he officially visited the Acropolis, ascending on horseback. Seated on a throne in the Parthenon, near the mosque which the Turks had built inside the temple, surrounded with the debris of war and occupation, the king heard a speech by the German architect Leo von Klenze, who had come to Athens to draw up a plan for the new city. Speaking in German, Klenze welcomed the king to "the symbol of your glorious reign", and inaugurated the excavation of the Acropolis. He promised that all the remains of barbarity would be removed, and that the remains of the glorious past would be newly revealed, as the "solid foundation of a glorious present and future".

Klenze invited the king to initiate the restoration of the Parthenon by sanctifying the first restored marble drum. This solemn moment

marked the formal enlistment of scientific archaeology in the service of the Greek nation. Another German, Ludwig Ross, had already been appointed the first director of the newly established Archaeological Service. The Acropolis and the Parthenon were rightly seen then as the symbolic capital of the new nation. They represented in stone the direct link between ancient and modern Greece, integral to the identity and "presence" of the new nation state. One hundred and seventy years later, the temple is still being restored today.

What Otho saw as he entered through the Propylaea, the gateway to the Acropolis, was not what we see in 2004. The Acropolis today is a bare rock surface with a number of semi-ruined monuments on its surface, most of them recalling the fifth century BC, the period of Pericles and the "Athenian miracle". As you pass through the Propylaea, you see the Parthenon looming ahead and to the right and the Erectheum slightly left against the northern wall. The little temple of Athina Nike overlooks from the right the stairway up to the Propylaea. The Acropolis Museum, containing the finds from the nineteenth-century excavations, is hidden behind the Parthenon, lying discreetly low so as not to spoil the line of the ancient ruins.

Short of a massive historical reconstruction or pastiche, based largely on guesswork, we could never see the Acropolis as it existed in the fifth century BC or at any other stage of its development. And no one has suggested such a reconstruction—though a complete project for the development of the Acropolis as a neoclassical theme park, palace and gardens was proposed, as we shall see, by one of the Bavarian architects of the early Othonian period. The problem for the planners and archaeologists in the early period of Greek independence was therefore to decide what sort of Acropolis they wanted. Their answer was an Acropolis closely related to the time of Pericles, cleared of later accretions. It could be restored where possible using original materials, as with the temple of Athena Nike. Modern stone and metal could be used where this was deemed necessary, but without fanciful large-scale reconstructions using modern materials.

The Acropolis: A Brief History
In the days of the earliest human settlements, the Acropolis-citadel was the city itself, a place of huddled houses and primitive wooden shrines. It became an impressive Mycenean fortress-palace, of which traces remain of the walls and fortifications of the late thirteenth century BC. As time passed, the people began to live on the surrounding slopes and the Acropolis was left as a sacred place for temples and a defensive fortress in emergency. At some early point in time, possibly in the late Bronze Age, the hamlets, farms and settlements of Attica were brought together into one state, the process which the Athenians themselves attributed to their legendary King Theseus. From that point on Athens and Attica were one, the plural origins of the city state recalled by the plural form of the name Athens, *Athinai* in Greek.

The city developed by stages from kingship through aristocracy and tyranny to democracy, the stages being associated with great legislators, especially Solon, whose political and economic reforms in the 590s widened access to the political system, and Kleisthenes, whose reforms late in the sixth century created a cohesive democratic state, capable of confronting the might of Persia. It was a very large city state—nearly 1,000 square miles—and it had the advantages of size, good natural defences in the ring of mountains and the sea, and mineral wealth in the silver mines of Laurion.

In 490 BC Darius, the Great King of Persia, sent his forces to subdue the Athenians, who had made trouble for him in his own backyard, Asia Minor. The Athenian infantry marched out to Marathon on the eastern coast of Attica, where the Persian forces had landed, and inflicted a severe defeat on them, although much outnumbered. This was the battle which John Stuart Mill called a more important event even in English history than the battle of Hastings. The Persians took to their ships and sailed round the tip of Attica at Sunium, gliding in towards Phaleron, looking to capture the city of Athens while it was still undefended. But the Athenian hoplites by a rapid forced march had returned in time to face the enemy down. The Persians gave up their plans and sailed away.

Ten years later, in 480 BC, they were back, with much greater land and naval forces, under Darius' successor King Xerxes. Turning the flank of the small and gallant Spartan and allied force holding the pass at Thermopylae, on the east coast of Greece, the Persian forces moved on Athens. Following the advice of the leader Themistocles, the Athenians decided to abandon the city, taking refuge in Troezen and Salamis, and to trust in their ships, the "wooden walls" that, perhaps, the oracle of Delphi had referred to when consulted. Only the very old and the sick remained on the Acropolis. Xerxes' army took the Acropolis by storm, looting and burning the limestone temples and the proto-Parthenon that was then being built. This was the low point in the city's history. But Themistocles' tactic was justified. He drew the Persian navy into combat in the bay of Salamis and routed it. Athens was saved.

There followed the period of Athens's cultural flowering and imperial dominance, in which the Athenian leader Pericles launched the building programme which gave to the city the Parthenon (the temple of the virgin goddess Athena, built in 447-32), the Propylaea (gatehouse temple, 437-32), the temple of Athina Nike (also known as Nike Apteros, Wingless Victory), and finally the Erectheum (temple of Erectheus). These buildings still exist, though the little temple of Athina Nike had to be rescued from the fortifications and reconstructed; and this is the period which lay in the mind's eye of the nineteenth-century restorers and landscapers.

Plutarch, the Greek biographer and historian from Chaironea in Boeotia who wrote in the early second century AD, left a fascinating description of this Periclean programme of public works. He knew what he was writing about because he had studied in Athens. He wrote that the programme had given the greatest pleasure to the Athenians, and caused amazement among the rest of mankind, but at the same time was the cause of slander and misrepresentation. Pericles' enemies accused him of using the contributions of Athens's allies, which had been extracted for use in the war against Persia and to protect them from future wars, to gild and beautify the city "as if it were some vain woman decking herself out with costly stones and statues and temples worth millions of money."

Pericles rebutted these accusations firmly. He argued that if Athens provided the services paid for by the allies, it was not their business how she used the surplus, which should go towards beautifying the city and at the same time providing employment to the people. Plutarch wrote:

So he boldly laid before the people proposals for immense public works and plans for buildings, which would involve many different arts and industries... The materials to be used were stone, bronze, ivory, gold, ebony, and cypress-wood, while the arts or trades which wrought or fashioned them were those of carpenter, modeller, coppersmith, stone-mason, dyer, worker in gold and ivory, painter, embroiderer, and engraver, and besides these the carriers and suppliers of the materials, such as merchants, sailors, and pilots for the sea-borne traffic, and waggon-makers, trainers of draught animals, and drivers for everything that came by land. There were also rope-makers, weavers, leatherworkers, road builders and miners. Each individual craft, like a general with an army under his separate command, had its own corps of unskilled labourers at its disposal... So the buildings arose, as imposing in their sheer size as they were inimitable in the grace of their outlines, since the artists strove to excel themselves in the beauty of their workmanship. And yet the most wonderful thing about them was the speed with which they were completed. Each of them, men supposed, would take many generations to build, but in fact the entire project was carried through in the high summer of one man's administration... It is this, above all, which makes Pericles' works an object of wonder to us - the fact that they were created in so short a span, and yet for all time. Each one possessed a beauty which seemed venerable the moment it was born, and at the same time a youthful vigour which makes them appear to this day as if they were newly built. A bloom of eternal freshness hovers over these works of his and preserves them from the touch of time, as if some unfading spirit of youth, some ageless vitality had been breathed into them. The director and supervisor of the whole enterprise was Phidias, although there were various great architects and artists employed on the individual buildings...

Plutarch was writing at a period when these great works could still be seen, in good condition. Nowadays much is missing even from this golden period: not least Phidias' gold and ivory statue of Athena from inside the Parthenon, and the tall bronze statue of Athina the Champion (Promachos), also by Phidias, which stood in the open air, facing anyone who entered the Acropolis. We know that seafarers approaching Piraeus from Cape Sunium could see the sun's rays glinting on the spear tip and helmet crest of this statue, because the slightly obsessive recorder Pausanias says so in his second-century AD guidebook to Greece. Altars, shrines, sculptures and statues vanished or were recycled in the course of the centuries.

The description of the Acropolis by Pausanias conveys what a luxuriant, colourful open-air museum of Greek religion and history it had become by the time of the emperor Hadrian. The modern visitor used to a stripped, bare aesthetic might be disconcerted to see it, yet the forest of ghostly statues described by Mark Twain conveys some (romanticized) flavour of those times. Statues, both of historical figures and of gods, above all Athina, proliferated. The only imperial figure represented was Hadrian himself. As well as temples, shrines and statues there was a picture gallery.

The changes did not come to an end with the decline of the ancient world. Statues were carried away (including the bronze Athina, to Byzantium). Buildings and statuary were plundered for their valuables: ivory and gold were filched, even the marble itself was taken as building material. Pagan temples became Christian churches. The Parthenon was converted to the Church of the Virgin, probably in the sixth century. Though alternating between Greek Orthodox and Latin rites according to who held power, it remained a Christian church, and a noble and impressive shrine as contemporary descriptions show, until the Ottoman Turks took Athens in 1456 and occupied the Acropolis two years later. Then it became a mosque, which from the description of the Turkish traveller Evliya Chelebi in the late seventeenth century was as splendid as the cathedral church had been. The Erectheum became a harem.

The Acropolis of which Otho and his followers took possession had served both Franks and Turks in its traditional role as a garrison fortress. This caused it to be exposed to attack by Venice in the seventeenth century, when a Venetian shell exploded the Turkish powder magazine in the Parthenon, causing irremediable harm. The Acropolis was again the object of fierce fighting, between the Greeks and Turks, during the War of Independence. In 1834 the evidence of recent warfare and of Turkish occupation was everywhere to be seen, in the rubble and detritus of war, and the low Turkish houses clustered on the surface of the Acropolis around the monuments. These, and the mosque inside the Parthenon itself, can be seen in drawings and prints from the eighteenth and early nineteenth century. Apart from these Ottoman relics, there was the Frankish Tower at the western end of the Acropolis, which had been erected by the Florentine rulers of Athens in the fifteenth century. It is a prominent feature in early photographs. The ruins of the pretty little temple of Athina Nike, which the Turks had demolished in 1686 to make way for gun emplacements, were still there, buried in the bastion at the west end of the Acropolis.

Restoration and Excavation

If there was any choice as to how to treat this complex architectural site, the early archaeologists of the new state showed little sign of it. Following Klenze's lead, the Bavarian garrison that had replaced the

Turks was also removed from the Acropolis, and the archaeologists set about a vigorous programme of cleansing, restoring and excavating, which extended over decades because of the richness of the material and their lack of resources for the task.

Ross, the German architect Schaubert and his Danish colleague Christian Hansen carefully reconstructed the little temple of Athina in the late 1830s. Progressively the archaeologists turned their attention to the ruins on the surface of the earth, and those beneath, excavating down to the bedrock that forms today's surface. The richest haul was the series of wonderful early male and female sculptures—the *kouroi* and *korai*—which were unearthed from the spoil near the Parthenon in the 1880s and can now be seen in the Acropolis Museum. They owe their survival to the fact that the Persian invaders broke them up and threw them into wells during their spoliation of the Acropolis in 480 BC. The removal of the Frankish Tower in 1875 by Heinrich Schliemann, the excavator of Troy, caused some fluttering in academic dove-cots (the liberal historian E. A. Freeman saw it as vandalism, the classicist Mahaffy favoured it). It had become a familiar part of the landscape, and some people were beginning to admit the claims of other architectural and historical traditions than the classical Greek.

This programme of cleansing, restoration and excavation, though controversial in some of its details, reflected a Greek and foreign consensus that the recovery of Greece's classical heritage lay at the heart of the construction of the new nation. The process in archaeology paralleled that in the Greek language, where the enlightened creators of the nation created also an archaizing language, the *katharevousa*, drawing on ancient forms. Classical Greece was the nation's unique asset for the first thirty to forty years. It was only towards the end of the century that Greek scholars discovered a more subtle national identity, based on a continuity traced from the ancient world through Byzantium, and kept alive in the folk songs and customs of the Greek people.

By the end of the nineteenth century, the Acropolis was much as it is today: an "archaeological carcass stripped to the bone", cleaned down to the bare rock, the marble sculptures and fragments displayed in the Acropolis Museum, the whole site fenced off and guarded as both a sacred place and a tourist attraction. But nineteenth- and early twentieth-century photographs still show the surroundings as scrubby and bare, and until the 1880s the southern side was slashed with a prominent landslide of spoil which had been thrown over the southern wall during the excavations. One of the most important features of the integration of the Acropolis into the modern city was still to come: landscaping.

Chapter Four

Landscaping the Acropolis

*"When the last marble tile was laid
The winds died down on all the seas;
   Hushed were the birds, and swooned the glade;
   Ictinus sat; Aspasia said
'Hist!—Art's meridian, Pericles!'"*
        Herman Melville, from "The Parthenon" (Ictinus was the archi-
               tect; Aspasia was Pericles' well-educated partner)

*"And now on the Acropolis we have, if not the real thing, the pure thing,
which some people like better: a monument that never existed in history."*
                    Kevin Andrews, *Athens*

The story of the Acropolis winds through all of Athens's history from earliest times to the present day.

The best vantage point for the visitor is the hill of Philopappus, southwest of the Acropolis. From high on this hill, near the monument of Philopappus, you see the Parthenon looming over the little temple of Wingless Victory, with the Propylaea on the left. Below the Parthenon and the south wall of the Acropolis is the distinctive façade of the theatre of Herod Atticus with its arches. This is much the same as the view enjoyed by the *Son et Lumière* audience at night, but for them, instead of the austere daylight colours of marble, the Parthenon and other buildings emerge from the darkness floodlit, not only with white light but in lurid red to illustrate the Persian invasion and sacking of the citadel in 480 BC. Lighting the Acropolis, to the dismay of purists, is not new. Nineteenth-century witnesses describe the striking effects of fireworks and Bengal lights on festive occasions.

The walk to the Philopappus belvedere takes you up a broad path following the line of the hill, undulating between pine trees and low bushes, with stone-paved way-stations and benches. There is a timeless, natural feel about this peaceful landscaped environment. It is the masterpiece of the architect and teacher Dimitris Pikionis.

Pikionis is one of the little-known masters of twentieth-century Greek art. He was born in Piraeus in 1887, of a family which came from Chios as part of the great dispersion caused by the Turkish massacre of the Chiots in 1822. As a child he explored the landscapes of Piraeus, Athens and Attica, still largely rural. He was a fellow-student of Giorgio de Chirico at the Athens Polytechnic, and impressed him. After further studies in Munich and Paris, Pikionis returned to Greece in 1912. Starting from modernism, he proceeded, first in painting and then in architecture, to develop an aesthetic that came to reflect the Greek vernacular traditions which he found in island architecture and crafts. He left few buildings, but was one of those teachers and practitioners who exert a strong moral and aesthetic influence on their pupils. He was one of the artists who helped to found the progressive journal *The Third Eye* in the 1930s.

Pikionis was an ascetic visionary, searching always for the form and essence underlying the surface of things, the relationship between building and earthscape. In the Acropolis landscaping, which he was commissioned to carry out in the 1950s by Constantine Karamanlis, he drew on his lifetime's experience of the Greek vernacular and of Japanese architecture. The paving of the paths and way-stations avoids the four-square and uses subtle patterns that break the lines of the site, recalling the stone causeways of Zen temples and gardens. Most of those who stroll on these paths are probably hardly aware that the whole area has been carefully landscaped, let alone of the name Pikionis.

Pikionis followed, and developed, the approach of the nineteenth-century pioneers in opening up and excavating Athens's archaeological sites. The problem is that excavation leaves an unsightly mess of stunted walls and ditches. Attractive objects are removed to museums. If the site is left bare, it is ragged and hot under the summer sun. If it is planted with trees, the topography of the archaeological landscape is concealed. The pioneers decided on an approach based on selective planting of shrubs and trees, which would enhance and not conceal the lines of the ancient city. As early as 1832, in their comment on the new city plan, its two authors Stamatios Kleanthes and Edouard Schaubert argued for planting the slopes of the Acropolis with trees which would survive without needing too much water, leaving alleys for walkers. Two years later Ludwig Ross prescribed that each autumn, after the excavation season, the site should be planted with trees appropriately grouped "so as to present the area of the ancient city neither as a barren land nor as a compact wood." Ross concluded that in this way Athens would have a park that was instructive and venerable because of the unique ruins of the past, and rich in natural beauty.

The idea of selective planting was therefore present from the beginning. Pikionis's version of it, sharply contested by the painter Tsarouchis, who condemned it as a manic love of greenery, was informed by respect for indigenous plants and for the contours of the Athenian hills. He thought it unrealistic and misguided to try to recapture the actual look of the ancient city; no one knew what it had looked like. He respected the ancient ruins in their setting, and set out to improve and develop the setting with plantings of native Greek shrubs and flowers which would help to bring out the topography of the ruins, enhancing their readability. The surroundings of the Acropolis are his monument.

Revelation and Rapture

The Acropolis is the citadel, but is also the "sacred rock"—*ieros vrachos*—of the Greeks today. It combines the practical, the religious and the aesthetic. There is an impressive continuity about the sacredness, though it has meant something different to Greeks of the archaic and classical periods, for whom the Olympian gods were real, to Greeks of the modern period, and to foreigners.

This rock has been an object of interest for travellers since antiquity, and since the eighteenth century the focus of a self-conscious enthusiasm. Everyone has been here and most of them, it seems, have left their impressions: Chateaubriand, Lamartine, Flaubert, Thackeray, Twain, Melville, Freud, Virginia Woolf, Arnold Bennett, Robert Byron, Le Corbusier, Evelyn Waugh, and hundreds more. Some of them seem to feel the reader leaning over their shoulders comparing the intensity of the experience with that of all those predecessors. Some are moved to poetry, others, like Cyril Connolly, to tears. It is not a bad thing for the first time visitor to try to gain his impressions unmediated by previous raptures.

At one extreme there is a sense of religious revelation. Ernest Renan, the eminent French author of the *Life of Jesus*, visited Athens in 1865 and was struck down, but not rendered wordless, by the strongest impression he had ever experienced; drawn to the past as by a cool, penetrating breeze coming from far away. "There is one place where perfection exists; and only one. It is there. I had never imagined the like of it. What I beheld was the Ideal, crystallized in Pentelic marble—that and nothing less." Renan saw in the Acropolis a type of eternal beauty transcending every frontier of nation or of race, "a glimpse of the divine". The hours he spent upon the "sacred hill" were hours of prayer. Later, disingenuously, Renan claimed to have unearthed an old paper among his travel notes, containing what he called the Prayer on the Acropolis:

A PRAYER
COMPOSED BY ME ON THE ACROPOLIS
AFTER I HAD COME TO REALISE
ITS PERFECT BEAUTY

The prayer seems in fact to have been composed some time after the event. It does not suit today's fashion for the un-heroic, but there is no doubting the force of the revelation.

Some visitors have tried to grasp the essence of the experience on the wing. Herman Melville wrote in his journal for Saturday 7 February 1857, "Tomorrow prepare for the Acropolis," as if visiting it was a spiritual exercise that required appropriate discipline. The following day he reported, "Acropolis—blocks of marble like blocks of Wenham ice—or like huge cakes of wax. Parthenon elevated like cross of Constantine. Strange contrast of rugged rock with polished temple. - At Stirling—art and nature correspond. Not so at Acropolis. Imperceptible seams—frozen together. - Break like cakes of snow. -"

Melville tried to capture his impressions later in poetry, reworking the image of the Parthenon as a Cross, and worrying away at the spiritual dimension of his experience:

Estranged in site,
Aerial gleaming, warmly white,
You look a suncloud motionless
In noon of day divine;
Your beauty charmed enhancement takes
In Art's long after-shine.

This is the same poem on the Parthenon which ends with the striking image of the winds dying down, the birds hushed, when the last tile was laid.

Some visitors deliberately go against the grain, as if determined not to be impressed. Writing to his friend Francis Hodgson on 20 January 1811, Byron concealed his delight in a facetious comparison:

I am living in the Capuchin Convent: Hymettus before me, the Acrop-
olis behind, the temple of Jove to my right, the Stadium in front, the town
to the left: eh! sir, there's a situation! There's your picturesque! nothing like
that in London, sir, not even the Mansion House!

Asked by a Greek lady how the Acropolis impressed him, Bernard Shaw replied, "Like a folded umbrella". The poet George Seferis, who tells this story, speculates whether GBS simply could not see anything outside the United Kingdom, or whether the Greek lady had got on his nerves.

Writers have struggled to capture the colours of the rock and of the Parthenon. Mark Twain saw it, by moonlight, as pink loaf sugar. Virginia Woolf scraped her palette to find the right colours: creamy white, tawny, ashy pale. Evelyn Waugh compared the colour of the Parthenon to Stilton cheese. More acutely, for me at any rate, H. V. Morton likened it to the colour of crust on Devonshire cream. It is clear that, with cleaning, the colour of the stone has changed over the last hundred years, for nineteenth-century observers regularly speak of a reddish tinge to the stone, and early photographs show discoloration. Charles Tuckerman, for example, who in the 1870s expected to see it glistening in whiteness, found "a dull reddish brown; stained, streaked and mottled by the action of the elements", with many of the columns blackened with smoke. The colours these writers have tried to capture are of course quite unlike the colours of the Acropolis of ancient times. "Its beauty as it is is the beauty of nature—of lovely material in radiant light; it is not, except in detail, the beauty of art—since the works of art have long since been dispersed and shattered. But most people prefer nature to art," wrote Roger Hinks provocatively.

The writer who best caught the intimate relationship of rocks, temples and landscape, by standing back, as it were, from the close-up imperfections of the stones, was Melville, who in his poem "The Attic Landscape" deliberately renounced colour:

No flushful tint the sense to warm -
Pure outline pale, a linear charm.
The clear-cut hills carved temples face,
Respond, and share their sculptural grace.

On top of the hundreds of thousands of words poured out by visitors and Greeks in attempting to describe the Acropolis and their experiences in viewing it, many further thousands have been written by scholars analyzing these reactions. They have scrutinized the foreigners' approach for signs of colonialist attitudes, and the Greeks' approach for what it says about national identity.

Freud's Memory

The account to have most excited post-modernist theorists is that of Sigmund Freud. It is contained in an essay called "A Disturbance of Memory on the Acropolis", written in 1936 and published as an Open Letter to Romain Rolland on the occasion of his seventieth birthday. Freud claimed in this letter to have been troubled during the last few years by an experience he had had in 1904, which he had never understood and which kept on recurring in his mind. Eventually he decided to analyze the incident. The events were as follows. Freud and his younger brother used to take a holiday together each year in late August or early September, usually in Rome or some other part of Italy or on the Mediterranean coast. This year they decided to travel via Trieste to Corfu for a few days. In Trieste they called on a business acquaintance who advised strongly against Corfu at that time of year and recommended that they visit Athens instead. The Lloyd boat was to sail that very afternoon.

Freud claimed that "as we walked away from this visit, we were both in remarkably depressed spirits. We discussed the plan that had been proposed, agreed that it was quite impracticable and saw nothing but difficulties in the way of carrying it out." They wandered about the town in a discontented and irresolute frame of mind, but when the Lloyd booking offices opened they went there, and despite all the supposed difficulties booked passages for Athens as though it were a matter of course, without discussing the reasons for this decision.

All this might be thought irrelevant to Freud's impressions of the Acropolis, but not so. The crucial passage follows:

> *When, finally, on the afternoon after our arrival, I stood upon the Acropolis and cast my eyes around upon the landscape, a remarkable thought suddenly entered my mind: 'So all this really does exist, just as we learnt at school!' To describe the situation more accurately, the person who gave expression to the remark was divided, far more sharply than was usually observable, from another person who took cognizance of the remark; and both were astonished, though not by the same thing. The first behaved as though he were obliged, under the impact of an unequivocal observation to believe in something the reality of which had hitherto seemed doubtful... as if someone, walking beside Loch Ness, suddenly caught sight of the form of the famous Monster stranded upon the shore and found himself driven to the admission: 'So it really does exist—the sea-serpent we always disbelieved in!' The second person was justifiably astonished, because he had been unaware that the real existence of Athens, the Acropolis, and the landscape around it had ever been objects of doubt. What he had been expecting was rather some expression of delight or admiration.*

Note that Freud is not interested in the Acropolis as such, at any rate for the purposes of this letter, only in his own reactions to it. He goes on at rather impressive length to analyze his own response (Can this really be true? Am I really seeing the Acropolis? So this is the reality we learned about at school), and to conclude that the underlying reason was piety, a feeling of guilt that the sons had been able to travel so much further, in reality and metaphor, than their father. That was why they had felt dissatisfied in Trieste at the thought of going to Athens.

Freud is not the only one to have found the Acropolis mysteriously familiar. Robert Byron felt a sensation of unreality, as if he were the victim of a delusion. The painter Charles Ricketts found it "almost familiar, and as if I had been here in some pre-existence. It has the familiarity and dimness that things have when one dreams about them." Freud's account will hardly bear the weight of analysis that has been loaded on it; it was written more than thirty years after the incident for which it attempts to pin down his motives and thoughts. But the episode does show that when Freud wanted an image of the numinous, of what is so entwined in our childhood experiences and education that we can be tempted to think "Can it be true? Am I really here?" he turned to the Acropolis, as the fountainhead of European culture.

"A Prodigious Bomb"

Looking at the Parthenon from a distance, you can see clearly that the line of the roof has been broken, and some of the columns truncated. The building is badly damaged. Looking from closer, you see that the sculptures that should feature on the pediment, and in what are called the metopes, are missing. The building is incomplete.

The main cause of the damage lies in the rivalry between Venice and Ottoman Turkey, in which Athens was caught up. The year 1683 marked the high watermark of Turkish penetration of Europe. It was then that a Turkish army which had laid siege to Vienna was defeated by a mixed Austrian-Polish army commanded by Jan Sobieski, King of Poland. This epoch-making battle was followed by a counterattack by the West, which ushered in the long decline of Ottoman power. The spearhead of this counterattack was Venice, with its strong commercial and political interests in the eastern Mediterranean.

The commander of the Venetian and allied forces ranged against Turkey was Francesco Morosini. By 1687 he had encompassed the entire Peloponnese, conquering Mistras and Monemvasia, and turned his attention to Negropont, or Euboea. But the season was far advanced and the Negropont garrison was strong, numbering more than 5,000. Meeting in council with his senior commanders, Morosini therefore decided to march on Athens, postponing the Negropont campaign until the next year. His forces reached Piraeus on 21 September 1687.

Faced with the threat of large Venetian forces, the Turks vacated the town of Athens, which clustered around the foot of the Acropolis, and took refuge on the Acropolis itself. The Venetian forces set up camp in the broad olive grove west of the city. They were then harassed by Turkish snipers who approached the camp on horseback. Morosini and his deputy, the German Count Koenigsmarck, wished to avoid the hardship and horror of a prolonged siege, and called on the Turkish garrison to surrender. The Turks refused.

There are conflicting accounts of what happened next. One eyewitness, a Major Sobiewolsky, who served as lieutenant in the Venetian auxiliary troops, reported that on 22 September his men began to bring batteries into position, while at the same time trying to undermine the Acropolis by sapping, which seemed likely to fail owing to the hardness of the rock. At that point a deserter came from the fortress, bringing the news that the Turkish commander had stored all his powder and valuables in the building called the temple of Minerva (i.e. the Parthenon) and that people were taking refuge there in the expectation that the Christian forces would not harm the temple:

Upon this report, several mortars were directed against the temple, but none of the bombs was able to do damage, particularly because the upper roof of the temple was somewhat sloping and covered with marble, and thus well protected. A lieutenant from Lüneburg, however, offered to throw bombs into the temple, and this was done. For one of the bombs fell through (the roof of) the temple and right into the Turkish store of powder, whereupon the middle of the temple blew up and everything inside was covered with stone, to the great consternation of the Turks.

A lieutenant from Lüneburg—*ein lüneburgischer Lieutenant*. The path of the destructive shell can be traced in one of a series of prints drawn by an engineer in the Venetian army.

Sobiewolsky's account suggests that the Parthenon was deliberately targeted because of the information that it contained the powder magazine. At the very least, the bombardment of the Acropolis proceeded without particular regard for the buildings upon it. The Venetian objective was to beat the Turkish garrison into submission as quickly as possible. All the buildings on the Acropolis were therefore held to be military objectives.

Reporting on the events to Venice, Morosini himself attributed the main direction of the attack to his deputy Koenigsmarck. He wrote that the bombardment of the Acropolis was difficult because of the nature of the terrain, but that on the evening of 26 September a lucky hit (*fortunato colpo*) blew up the powder magazine. In a second despatch a week later Morosini reported that the "prodigious bomb" had wrecked the Parthenon itself and killed more than three hundred people, whose corpses were beginning to putrefy.

Koenigsmarck himself left no record. But a Swedish lady named Anna Akerhjelm, companion to Countess Koenigsmarck, wrote to her brother in Sweden on 18 October:

> *The citadel is situated on a mountain excessively difficult (from what they say) of capture, since there is no means of mining it. How it dismayed His Excellency to destroy the beautiful temple that has existed three thousand years and is called the Temple of Minerva! In vain however: the bombs did their work so effectively that never in this world can the temple be replaced. After eight days the Turks hoisted the white flag, seeing that the Saraskier was not likely to come to their relief.*

Anna was right. The damage to the Parthenon was irremediable. The Venetians allowed the Turkish garrison to depart to the ships six miles away in Piraeus, carrying as many of their belongings as they could. Many dropped their burdens on the way. Others were murdered by scavengers.

Anna noted that as soon as the Venetian armada made its appearance before the city the Greek inhabitants of Athens submitted themselves to the Republic, having prudently buried all their valuables under ground. Throughout the hostilities they no doubt waited with interest to see who would come out on top. They hospitably offered the countess orangeade, lemonade, fresh almonds, pomegranates, jams and other sweetmeats.

The Venetian occupation of Athens led to the usual turnover of religious buildings. The Swedes took over a pretty mosque to turn it into a Lutheran church, while two others were made over to the Catholics. But the destruction of the Parthenon served no purpose, for the Venetians occupied the Acropolis for only six months before deciding for strategic reasons to abandon the city. Turkish rule was resumed. But the Parthenon was never to recover.

Classical Symbol

The Acropolis no longer commands the city quite as it did until the nineteenth century. Set in a sea of modern buildings, it does not stand out in the way it once did against a landscape of mountains and olive groves. Pollution sometimes blurs the lines of the columns so that from a distance the rock seems to swim in a haze. Nevertheless, after Lycabettus, the Acropolis is still the dominant feature of the Athenian landscape. The city planners of the nineteenth century took it as their point of reference. It seems to follow you around. As you cross a downtown street such as Athinas or Aeolou and look along its line, your eye comes to rest on a segment of the Acropolis.

A good view of the Acropolis, preferably from a high window with a westward view, is a status symbol for corporate or establishment Athens. The Greek Ministry of Foreign Affairs is a case in point. Private individuals prize their view of the Acropolis from the balconies or roofs of Kolonaki, Mets or Pangrati.

Foreigners, even if they have never gone there, take the Acropolis as their symbol of Greece. They see it as representing ancient Greece and its values, democracy, the proportions of classical art, and by extension the spirit of freedom in time of trouble and war. It is the columns of the Parthenon that spring to the mind of cartoonists when they want to make a point about Greece, whether to admire the country's resistance to Nazi occupation or to evoke the prison house created by the military junta.

For Greeks, the range of references evoked by the Acropolis and the Parthenon is even wider. They represent ancient Greece and its values, but they represent also the continuity of Greek culture and history and all that is good in the Greek spirit. (Inevitably, the Parthenon as the supreme visual symbol also provides the tackier visual aspects of tourist souvenirs and consumer products.) The rock has stood since the earliest Greek times. It has absorbed and survived occupation, siege, spoliation, changes of use of its temples, destruction of the monuments, and still it is there, presiding over the city. If the contemporary Greekness and purity of the Acropolis has required a little help from the state—the destruction of the Frankish Tower and other monuments recalling foreign occupation—this is something of which most Greeks are probably unaware. The priority for nineteenth-century Greece was to assert Greek identity as a member of the European family with roots firmly planted in ancient classical soil.

The sacred status of the Acropolis demands appropriate behaviour from visitors. Western hooliganism is severely condemned. The lager lout who drops his trousers in the face of an ancient Greek monument lands up in court. Inappropriate dress is frowned on. Nelly's delightful photographs of a nude woman dancing ecstatically in front of the columns of the Parthenon are on the borderline of acceptability. Proposals to use the theatre of Herod Atticus, which is built into the south side of the Acropolis, for fashion shows or events regarded as vulgar provoke intense controversy over what should be permissible on this site.

The idea that the stones are sacred is a comparatively recent one. It was not only the Turks who despoiled the ruins. Greeks as well as foreigners in earlier times regarded them as useful resources of building materials and lime. Until the state took a grip on the site, visitors, especially foreigners, made free with it. A party of British midshipmen broke off parts of a recently excavated statue in the 1830s. As late as 1875, Mahaffy was enraged to see a young Greek down below in the theatre of Dionysos at pistol practice, using as a target a fine piece of carved marble. When appeals to a custodian proved useless, Mahaffy and his companion hurled stones at the "wretched barbarian" below and drove him out of the theatre.

The Elgin Marbles

In the light of the modern sense of the sacred and the proper, it is not surprising that the sculptures from the Parthenon which Lord Elgin had shipped to Britain give rise to sharp and continuing debate. For these are the parts of the Parthenon which are recognized as the finest examples of Greek classical art. To the Greeks it seems that a foreigner, using his power as ambassador to extort permission from the then occupying power Turkey, vandalized and violated the monument, stealing the holiest parts of Greece's national heritage.

Thomas Bruce, the seventh Earl of Elgin, was appointed British ambassador to the Ottoman government in Constantinople in 1799. This was the high summer of the period of acquisition of antiquities. As protector of the Ottoman regime against the French, Britain carried

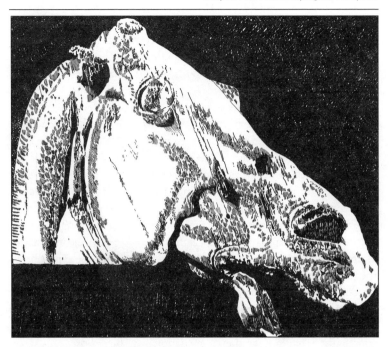

enormous weight in Ottoman councils, and Elgin succeeded in obtaining from the regime a *firman*, or official letter of permission, authorizing him to remove "some pieces of stone with inscriptions or figures" from the Parthenon, as well as to draw and make casts, and excavate fragments on the ground. This document was very fully exploited by Elgin's team of agents in Athens.

The authority of the *firman*, like everything else in the issue of the Parthenon sculptures, is controversial. It is far from clear that it permitted Elgin to remove integral parts of the frieze and metopes by force, as opposed to collecting stones which had already fallen, through the effects of time or the Venetian bombardment. Whatever the legal position, Elgin's team, led by the Italian painter Lusieri, did use force, sawing where necessary through the frieze slabs to detach the parts he wanted. They removed the greater part of the Parthenon frieze, which ran round the inside of the building, sculptures from the triangular pediments, and fifteen of the so-called metopes, the individual scenes that face outwards. The "marbles" were packed up and despatched to

England, where eventually they were bought by the British government and presented to the British Museum. They remain there, and can be seen in the Duveen gallery. Any Londoner or visitor to London contemplating a visit to the Acropolis should go and see them there, either before or after.

The Parthenon sculptures, whose story is told in detail by William St Clair in his book *Lord Elgin and the Marbles*, (1998) have generated immense debate and seem likely to go on doing so. What other issue could bring together Byron, the Greek poet Cavafy, and Melina Mercouri on the same side? Controversy dates from the time of their removal. Contemporaries, including the traveller Edward Daniel Clarke who witnessed them being torn down from the Parthenon, already realized that something momentous was happening. And yet these very contemporaries, and Chateaubriand later, were not above taking home parts of Greece's fragmentary ruins. Since the explosion in the Parthenon in 1687, depredation had become commonplace in Greece and especially in Athens. It was justified in the eyes of visiting scholars, ambassadors and dilettantes by the rapid deterioration of the ancient sites. There was little idea of protection and inviolability. The constraints were not aesthetic or nationalist, but those caused by Ottoman bureaucratic obstruction. However, the wholesale approach of Elgin was something new, and therefore widely deplored. Clarke, Edward Dodwell and others judged that sawing the monument in pieces was going a step too far. A few years later Byron used the strongest of language in denouncing Elgin's vandalism.

Elgin did, as it happens, save the sculptures from the erosion suffered through atmospheric pollution by those sculptures remaining on the Parthenon in Athens. The effects can be clearly seen by contrasting those pieces in the British Museum with those in the Acropolis Museum. In this respect Elgin did the Parthenon a favour. But the favour is irrelevant to the question as to where the sculptures should now be displayed, since no one argues that they should be put back up onto the temple.

The legal arguments are not decisive. The British Museum claims good legal title, though some dispute this. The Greek government, whatever it thinks privately, does not claim the sculptures back on legal grounds. Rather, it argues that in the present world the British Museum could even retain title to them while returning them on permanent loan. Arguments about stewardship are neither decisive nor any longer relevant. At one time it was claimed that the British Museum's stewardship of the sculptures was better than that which could be expected of the Greeks. No longer, once it was known that in the 1930s, on Duveen's instructions, the marbles were scraped with abrasive substances in an attempt to whiten them, with the result that some parts of the surface have lost the patina of the years (one should bear in mind, though, that originally the surfaces would have been covered in paint!). In any case, the Parthenon restoration programme is at the state of the art, and is supervised by Greek archaeologists who know their building and its sculptures better than anyone. If the marbles ever return to Greece, they will be well looked after.

We are left with a confrontation between two irreconcilable views. On the Greek side, it is argued that the sculptures, which are part of Greece's national heritage, belong to the Parthenon, and should therefore be displayed in the context of the building and near to it, in the new Acropolis Museum, where building and sculpture can be appreciated as part of a single aesthetic experience.

On the British Museum's side, it is argued that the museum holds legal title to the sculptures, and that they should remain part of one of the world's great universal collections, where visitors and scholars can study and appreciate them in the context of the whole collection. The British Museum also fears that the return of the sculptures would set a dangerous precedent, which could lead to the progressive erosion of its permanent collection.

For all these elevated arguments, the issue is really a question of finders keepers. The British Museum possesses the sculptures and will not return them unless forced to do so by government; indeed, it cannot under its charter. The government will not force the Museum by legislation unless it comes to the conclusion that it has a serious political interest in doing so. There is no sign of this at present. Although the Committee for the Restitution of the Parthenon Sculptures has mounted a shrewd and persistent campaign, and won the support of some influential voices from the academic world, Greek governments have never taken the issue seriously enough to risk a prolonged row with Britain. The issue has been left to ministers of culture, from the passionate Melina Mercouri to the present minister, Evangelos Venizelos, while prime ministers and foreign ministers argue about more important questions such as the price of olive oil or the Cyprus question. Although one should never say never, the return of the Parthenon sculptures to Athens looks as far away as ever.

CHAPTER FIVE

The Agora and the Classical City

"Behold
Where on the Aegean shore a City stands
Built nobly, pure the air, and light the soil,
Athens, the eye of Greece, Mother of Arts
And Eloquence, native to famous wits
Or hospitable, in her sweet recess,
City or Suburban, studious walks and shades..."

Milton, *Paradise Regain'd*, iv, 237-43

"A place cannot be called a City, nor its inhabitants citizens, if it is with-
out archives, gymnasium, theatre, agora, and a supply of water in foun-
tains."

Pausanias, *Guide to Greece*, x, 4, 1
(paraphrase found in Amphipolis museum)

On the lower slopes of the Areopagus hill, not far from the well preserved Doric temple of Hephaestus (formerly thought to be the Theseion or temple of Theseus), is a standing stone on which is inscribed in fifth-century BC lettering, "I AM THE BOUNDARY OF THE AGORA" (*ΟΡΟΣ ΕΙΜΙ ΤΕΣ ΑΓΟΡΑΣ*). Greek objects like to label themselves in this charming way. Pots do the same: when you see "I AM THE POT OF SO AND SO" written on a pot, the name denotes the potter rather than the owner.

The standing stone, as its name suggests, marks the limit of the ancient Agora, or gathering place or market place, the area bounded by the Acropolis and the Areopagus to the south, the Plaka quarter to the east, the Piraeus-Athens railway and the flea market area to the north, and the Theseion area to the west (for though the name of the temple has changed, the nearby underground railway station has kept the name Theseion). This was the heart of the ancient city. You can get a comprehensive view of the whole Agora from the approach path to the Acropolis high above the Plaka. The views across the Agora from near the temple of Hephaestus towards the Acropolis are spectacular, especially when the trees and shrubs are in blossom.

The Agora presents in dramatic form the tensions of coexistence of the old and new in Athens. It was part of the nineteenth-century city, much of it built on. Yet it was also the civic and commercial heart of the ancient city. What to do? Destroy the houses and excavate? Let the modern city prevail and leave the ancient buried (as has happened with much of the Plaka)? Or dig it up, find what was to be found, remove the treasures to museums, and then replace the buildings? Despite some dissident voices, the priority of ancient Greece in the national imagination meant that eventually the area had to be excavated.

The Agora, the Acropolis looming above it, and their surroundings including the Kerameikos area were the parts of the city which embodied the "miracle" of fifth- and fourth-century Athens. How the miracle took place will be forever debated. Sometime in the late Bronze Age, before or after the turn of the millennium, the villages of Attica came together as parts of a unitary city state of Athens, in a process associated by the Athenians themselves with the legendary King Theseus (hence the inscription on the arch of Hadrian, "THIS IS THE CITY OF THESEUS..."). By the early fifth century BC the city had developed democratic institutions and an informed, patriotic citizen body. Then, for about 100 years after the Persian Wars, by some alchemy, there occurred in Athens, with its population of about 50,000 adult male citizens, and perhaps 300,000 residents in total, an explosion of human achievement in the fields of literature, drama, historiography, philosophy, art, sculpture and architecture. Notoriously, it went along with an imperialist ideology, represented by Pericles, an inferior status of women, the institution of slavery, and a certain brutality in dealing with enemies and renegade allies.

One way of looking at this is to trace the influence of Athens's creative artists in the modern world. Aeschylus, Sophocles and Euripides, the creators of tragic drama, are still performed in innumerable variations. To watch *Agamemnon* or *Oedipus Rex* in the theatre of Herod Atticus, or at Epidaurus, whether performed by a Greek company in modern Greek translation, or by the British National Theatre directed by Peter Hall, is to feel close to the origins of tragedy. Socrates, or rather his medium Plato, still lies at the heart of modern philosophy. Thucydides, much quoted in this book, remains the father of scientific history, and Herodotus the father of history as enquiry. In the arts, Phidias as sculptor and director of the Parthenon project, Ictinus as its architect, inform the neoclassical architecture of the Renaissance and after. Even the best of the Athenian decorative potters, unrecorded in Athenian literature, exert a grip over the western imagination which shows no sign of diminishing.

Not all these people were Athenians. Herodotus came from Halicarnassus in Asia Minor. But they did their best work in Athens. Perhaps that helps to explain the miracle. Athens was a melting pot, a trading centre, and a place where men of talent could make their mark.

The public life and religious observances, the social interactions, the artistic performances of these men all took place within half a mile or so of the Acropolis, though the domain of Athens was enormous— some 1,000 square miles—compared with most Greek city states, including the whole of Attica. This was a crucial point, for the defence of Athens associated with Themistocles and the new fleet was funded by silver mined by slaves at Lavrion, near the tip of the Attic peninsula. If you walk around the old city centre you will see the traces of all these public activities: the religious observances in the monuments of the Acropolis, the plays of Euripides at the theatre of Dionysus beneath the south wall of the Acropolis (this theatre was built only in the fourth century, so that the familiar plays of Aeschylus and Sophocles were actually performed in an earlier and more primitive theatre); the funeral speech of Pericles from a platform in the public burial ground near the Kerameikos cemetery; the great wartime speeches familiar from Thucydides on the Pnyx hill west of the Acropolis, before the full citizen Assembly. The essential Athenian activities of talk and trade, and even dining in dining clubs, took place mainly in the Agora.

Heart of the City

From meaning a place where people meet and talk, the word *agora* came to mean market place as organized markets developed in the early classical period. The area of open ground at the northern foot of the Acropolis took shape as the Agora in the sixth century BC. It was a good area, accessible from the Attic countryside and from Piraeus harbour. It straddled the Panathenaic way, the paved road along which passed the annual procession of men and animals to the Panathenaic festival, pictured (or not, according to some art historians) in the Parthenon frieze in the British Museum. The market area, which was sacred, was marked off from the rest of the city by marker stones such as the one surviving today. Later as the area developed, it came to be bounded by long buildings, colonnades and porticos, including the Stoa of Attalos of Pergamum, built in the second century BC, restored to its former glory by the Americans in the 1950s.

Shopkeepers, moneychangers and peasant farmers came to the Agora to conduct their business and sell their produce, from tables and stalls and later from shops. The Agora came to be the centre of civic life of the ancient city. It was a place for political meetings, for religious festivals, theatre, music and athletic competitions. It contains the traces of civic and religious buildings from successive epochs.

Here, in the open air, Athenian citizens—that is, the adult males—met to talk, walk, shop and even vote. Here they could meet foreigners and see their wares. Access to the market was essential to Greeks of other cities who wished to have good political and commercial relations with Athens, and exclusion from it was a painful sanction. Shortly before the great war with Sparta broke out, Athens passed a decree excluding all citizens of Megara from the harbours and markets of the Athenian empire. The Megarians had cultivated some sacred land that did not belong to them, and given shelter to fugitive slaves from Athens. This was one of the immediate causes of the war.

The life of the Agora is well described in a series of illustrated booklets published by the American School of Classical Studies at Athens. One of them, *Socrates in the Agora*, is about the great philosopher, who used to come to the Agora to find his audience in the second half of the fifth century BC. According to his pupil Xenophon, he would rise early in order to get to wherever he would meet the people with whom he could discuss philosophical questions. He would argue and talk with anyone, using the crafts exercised by cobblers, leather workers, metal workers and other craftsmen in the Agora to develop his analogies. He could commonly be seen in the middle of a group of people. Here Socrates lived and died, condemned to death for impiety and corrupting the youth of the city, and famously refusing to escape. He provoked the jury by proposing outrageously that his penalty should be free meals for life at the expense of the state, rather than death as demanded by the prosecution. Reading Plato's description of the trial, his last days, and his death by hemlock poison, is a moving experience, especially in the Agora itself, where with the eye of faith you can actually see the remains of the prison where Socrates spent his last days.

Thousands of fragments of pottery were found in the Agora excavations. Pots are easily broken, but their fragments, of virtually indestructible baked clay, survive. The universal urge to scratch ones name or some pithy message on pots, walls and bits of paper means that these fragments are often of historical value. Some of the most interesting are the so called *ostraka*, the sherds on which Athenian citizens scratched the names of politicians in the mysterious exercise of democracy known as ostracism, an institution which allowed the citizens to get rid of individuals regarded as politically dangerous. More than 10,000 of these have been found in the Agora and Kerameikos areas, while 190 of them were discovered in a well on the north side of the Acropolis, all inscribed with the name of Themistocles, the saviour of Athens from the Persian threat in 480 BC. These are inscribed in only a few different hands, suggesting that the vote was rigged.

By this provision, the citizens would vote once a year at a meeting of the Athenian Assembly on the question whether there should be an ostracism, that is whether one of the citizen body should be banished. If a majority voted in favour, then some time later the citizens formally voted, in the Agora, by inscribing the name of a citizen on a potsherd or *ostrakon*. Provided a sufficient number—not fewer than 6,000— voted, the man whose name was scratched on the largest number of *ostraka* was obliged to leave the territory of Athens within ten days and retire into exile for a period of ten years. By a civilized provision, however, he retained and could resume his property rights and citizenship, and could draw income from his estate while in exile.

Some of Athens's most prominent political actors were ostracized, including Pericles' father Xanthippus in 484, and the great Themistocles. The process also gave rise to a well-known anecdote told by Plutarch: in the course of voting on an ostracism, an illiterate peasant asked his neighbour in the Agora to write the name Aristides on his fragment of pottery. The neighbour happened to be Aristides, nicknamed the "Just". Surprised, he asked the man what harm Aristides had done him. "None whatever," said the man, "I do not even know the fellow, but I am sick of hearing him called 'The Just' everywhere!" Aristides made no comment, but wrote his name on the sherd and handed it back. When the results of the voting were declared, he was ostracized.

Another who engaged the Athenians in talk in the Agora was St Paul. He came to Athens in 54 AD after his adventurous sojourn in northern Greece, where he received a particularly hostile reception from the Jews of the Thessaloniki synagogue. Paul was shocked to find the city of Athens "wholly given to idolatry". He therefore threw himself into argument with the Jews in the synagogue, and daily in the Agora with anyone who met him there. His encounter with the Athenians gives an interesting thumb nail sketch of the contemporary image of the Athenian character and the disputatious feel of the city in the first century AD.

Then certain philosophers of the Epicureans, and of the Stoicks, encoun-tered him. And some said, What will this babbler say? other some, He seemeth to be a setter forth of strange gods: because he preached unto them Jesus, and the resurrection.

And they took him, and brought him unto Areopagus, saying, May we know what this new doctrine, whereof thou speakest, is?

For thou bringest certain strange things to our ears: we would know therefore what these things mean.

(For all the Athenians and strangers which were there spent their time in nothing else, but either to tell, or to hear some new thing.)

Then Paul stood in the midst of Mars' hill, and said, Ye men of Athens, I perceive that in all things ye are too superstitious.

For as I passed by, and beheld your devotions, I found an altar with this inscription, TO THE UNKNOWN GOD. Whom therefore you ignorantly worship, him declare I unto you. God that made the world and all things therein, seeing that he is Lord of heaven and earth, dwelleth not in temples made with hands.

Mars' Hill, the site of Paul's soapbox preaching, seems to have been the Areopagus just opposite the entry to the Acropolis. A bronze plaque commemorates the occasion. The references to the resurrection of the dead, which was at the heart of his message, had a mixed effect: some mocked, and others said they would hear him again. Paul's aim was to convert the Athenians. Socrates set out to convince his listeners that they should examine their lives, on the principle that the unexamined life is not worth living.

Paul's few converts included Dionysius the Areopagite, and a woman named Damaris; so that the broad street of Dionysios the Areopagite south of the Acropolis, now pedestrianized, commemorates St Paul and the earliest steps in Athens's conversion to Christianity.

Excavating the Agora

Prominent monuments such as the Parthenon, the temple of Hephaestus, and the temple of Olympian Zeus could not be missed. But the Agora was pretty much an unknown quantity. Greek scholars knew it was there under the earth, and knew roughly where to look. Greek and foreign archaeologists started to explore the area in the second half of the nineteenth century, following the clues in ancient texts and making trial excavations. The cutting of the line of the new

Piraeus-Athens-Kiphissia railway through the northern part of the area in the 1890s yielded further information, and gave rise to an evocative short story by Alexandros Papadiamantis, in which a player of the Middle Eastern flute takes up residence by night in the half-completed rail tunnel: his haunting music looks back to a lost eastern heritage, while by day the engineers hack through the layers of the city's archaeological record.

But the real assault on the ancient Agora began in 1931 and was carried out in annual campaigns by the American School of Classical Studies, with John D. Rockefeller funding. The excavation campaigns were intensive, the digging massive, and the costs well beyond what any other archaeological team could aspire to. The site became identified with the Americans. It had been subject to what Homer Thompson, the director of the project, called "feverish building" after Athens was designated the capital of Greece in 1834, so that by 1931 it was covered in housing. The land was expropriated and some 400 houses were demolished. The American team then set to work. The result today is a pleasing archaeological park of fragmentary buildings and foundations, marble, stone and greenery, in which the eleventh-century church of the Holy Apostles stands out as the only whole Byzantine survival.

The cost in terms of destruction of a living part of the city was high. Osbert Lancaster was one of those who regretted the loss of a lively area of the nineteenth-century city, calling the result of the excavation a "dreary bomb-site". The historian of nineteenth- and twentieth-century Athens Kostas Biris was another. But Lancaster wrote just after the war, before the landscaping of the site, and Biris changed his mind when he saw the final result.

By the 1950s the excavations were substantially completed, with only a few modern houses and streets still to be removed. Homer Thompson then invited the American landscape artist Ralph E. Griswold to visit the site, making sure that this took place during the dry summer season, when he would see it at its most arid and severe. Griswold was provided with references to planting in the Agora taken from ancient authors. On this basis he planned a planting scheme for the Agora proper which used only the trees mentioned in these classical authors: oaks, planes, laurel, olive, white poplars and myrtle. On the surrounding slopes he planted other indigenous species, avoiding exotics. ("This policy became difficult to follow when prominent individuals offered gifts of exotic plants," Griswold wrote.) He included many semi-tropical varieties: red bud, tamarisk, oleander, vitax, almond, acacia, pine, cedar, cypress, rhamnus, parkinsonia, rosemary, heather, lavender, teacriums, gorse, clematis, honeysuckle, smilax and English ivy. He also planted as many wild flowers as possible from all parts of Greece, to give visitors a glimpse of Greece's unrivalled display of wild flora.

King Paul planted an oak near the altar of Zeus, and Queen Frederika a bay tree (*laurus nobilis*). The Boy Scouts (oleanders) and Girl Guides (a bay hedge), the Greek Landscape Committee and the Society of Old Athenians (olives, bay, fig and pomegranate), the Ministry of Agriculture schools, and private individuals all made their contributions. Pomegranate and myrtle were planted around the temple of Hephaestus, in the very holes which, the excavators concluded, had contained plants in ancient times. To complete the work, an irrigation system was installed.

Griswold wrote later that if he had not come in the summer he could not have devised a successful planting. He had to negotiate each aspect with the archaeological service, and to train his own workmen in methods totally unfamiliar to them, justifying his instructions at every step. He wrote:

> *It was my intention to have the planting supplement and not compete with the archaeological structures. Each plant was located to help the visitors identify and appreciate the antiquities. The same intention governed the location of modern paths and steps which were essential to make the ruins accessible to the hundreds of scholars and laymen who visit the Agora daily.*

Griswold returned ten years later to make corrections where shrubs had grown too exuberantly. The Agora park that he created looks very well today. It is a tribute to the meticulous and sensitive approach of the American excavators and landscapers, in the tradition of Ross and Pikionis.

Roman Athens

Much of what we appreciate in Athens today dates from the centuries when the political centre of gravity of the Hellenic world had moved away from Athens, first to the Macedonia of Philip and Alexander, then to the capital cities of Alexander's successors, and finally to Rome. The Panathenaic Stadium and the monument of Lysicrates were built, and the Theatre of Dionysus substantially rebuilt, in the second half of the fourth century. The Stoa of Attalus, reconstructed by the Americans on the eastern side of the Agora, was built to a commission from King Attalus of Pergamum in Asia Minor in about 150 BC. It was visited by the heads of state and government of the European Union as part of the ceremonies marking the enlargement of the Union in April 2003.

The loss of independence following the subordination of Athens and other Greek cities to Philip and Alexander, and later to Rome, was accompanied by a loss of creativity. But the city continued to grow and to be beautified as part of the Roman empire, and to command the affection of well-educated Romans.

Greece became a Roman protectorate in 146 BC. Athens continued to enjoy various privileges and a limited sovereignty. But her position was precarious. A bloody landmark was the sack of Athens by the future Roman dictator Lucius Cornelius Sulla, the ruthless general with the mulberry birthmark on his face. Athens had became involved, to its cost, in the wars of Rome against her greatest enemy, Mithridates of Pontus, who stood in the way of her eastern expansion and influence. Mithridates was the wily king who, according to A. E. Housman, built up a resistance to poisons by taking them in small quantities, and "died old." Controlling most of Asia Minor, he invaded Greece in 88 BC, gathering support from cities which resented Roman rule and taxes.

A tyrant named Aristion held Athens on behalf of Mithridates against Sulla's army. The siege and sack of the city by Sulla was remembered as a black moment in the city's history. According to Plutarch, Sulla was in the grip of a terrible, overwhelming desire to conquer Athens, driven by some kind of rivalry to challenge the shadow of the city's past glory. He was in a hurry. He cut down the trees in Plato's Academy and Aristotle's Lyceum (both outside the city walls) to replace his siege engines. He seized the sacred treasures of Greece to pay for his troops. The Athenians were reduced to subsisting on weeds from the Acropolis and boiling and chewing their own shoe leather. When finally the tyrant Aristion sent two or three men to sue for peace, instead of getting down to business they infuriated Sulla by going on and on about Theseus and the Persian wars. Sulla told them to go away and take their speeches with them. "I was sent to Athens by the Romans not to take lessons in its history, but to subdue its rebels."

The city wall was breached, and the lower city taken, on 1 March 86 BC. Sulla then let his men loose in a riot of bloodshed and looting. Long afterwards, Plutarch wrote, people still estimated the numbers of dead by how much ground was covered with blood. Even after the fall of the main city, the tyrant held out for some time on the Acropolis, until reduced by drought. Then the heavens opened and the Acropolis ran with water just after he surrendered.

The city set off the decline in its real independence with a determined assertion of its cultural pre-eminence. It became a philosophical theme park. Well-off and well-educated Romans travelled to Athens as cultural tourists. They spoke the language and read the literature. Like Lord Elgin later, they brought back with them marbles and bronzes as souvenirs of Greece. Cicero and Horace studied here. Atticus, Cicero's rich, cultivated correspondent, lived here for some years. After Greece became formally a Roman province in 27 BC, Athens maintained its special relationship.

Roman leaders and emperors had a special affection for Athens. Mark Antony loved it and showered the city with gifts. It appealed to the extravagant side of his character, which was attracted to shows, athletic games, theatricals, and religious mysteries. The greatest Roman lover and benefactor of Athens was the emperor Hadrian (117-138), the Spanish-born traveller, administrator and Hellenist who was said to speak Greek better than Latin. It was in Hadrian's time that the massive temple of Olympian Zeus, which had been started in the time of the tyrant Peisistratus more than seven hundred years before, was completed. Hadrian created a new city beyond the existing city, adorning Athens with baths, a colonnade, statues, and the library and aqueduct which bear his name. The recent excavations for the Athens metro have revealed how extensive were the bath complexes that the Romans built. It was in Hadrian's time too that the benefactions of Herod Atticus, the emperor's friend, took place, giving Athens a superb stadium and theatre. This period was probably the summit of the city's material prosperity and grandeur.

Incursions from the north ushered in a time of instability. In 267 AD the Heruli, an aggressive tribe of Goths, swept down through Greece, assaulted the city and sacked the Agora. It was the beginning of the end for ancient Athens.

CHAPTER SIX

The Athenian Way of Death

> *"The whole earth is the tomb of great men."*
> Pericles, in his funeral oration, Thucydides Book Two

The Kerameikos, or potters' quarter, is also the area of the ancient cemetery. It lies to the west of the Agora. Part of the ancient cemetery is contained within the present archaeological site, which has been excavated and studied by the Germans. The "First Cemetery" is the first and most interesting of post-independence cemeteries. These two cemeteries contain some of the most poignant art of their eras.

Ancient Athenian custom was to bury the dead outside the city walls. Those who fell in war were normally buried where they fell, but some time in the early fifth century the Athenians began to bring home their dead and give them a state funeral in a public state burial ground outside the wall in the Kerameikos.

The historian Thucydides, writing about the winter of 431-30 BC, at the end of the first year of the war with Sparta, described how the Athenians followed their annual custom by giving a public funeral for the first casualties of the war.

> *These funerals are held in the following way: two days before the ceremony the bones of the fallen are brought and put in a tent which has been erected, and people make whatever offerings they wish to their own dead. Then there is a funeral procession in which coffins of cypress wood are carried on wagons. There is one coffin for each tribe, which contains the bones of members of that tribe. One empty bier is decorated and carried in the procession: this is for the missing whose bodies could not be recovered. Everyone who wishes to, both citizens and foreigners, can join in the procession, and the women who are related to the dead are there to make their laments at the tomb. The bones are laid in the public burial-*

place, which is in the most beautiful quarter outside the city walls. Here the Athenians always bury those who have fallen in war. The only exception is those who died at Marathon, who, because their achievement was considered absolutely outstanding, were buried on the battlefield itself.

So the Athenians invented the concept of the unknown soldier. Thucydides' description is a prelude to the famous funeral oration of Pericles, delivered after the procession from a high platform in front of the communal grave.

Burial was not always so ordered. In excavating the new metro station at Kerameikos (which in the end was not built) the bulldozers uncovered a mass grave, containing the remains of some 150 bodies of men, women and children, thrown pell-mell into a large pit. The experts dated the remains to the decade 430-420 BC, the early years of the war between Athens and Sparta. In his history of the war Thucydides described the plague which ravaged Athens in the year 430-29, when the inhabitants of Attica were crowded into the city while a Spartan army devastated the Attic countryside:

They had not been many days in Attica before the plague first broke out among the Athenians. Previously attacks of the plague had been reported from many other places... but there was no record of the disease being so virulent anywhere else or causing so many deaths as it did in Athens. At the beginning the doctors were quite incapable of treating the disease because of their ignorance of the right methods... A factor which made matters much worse than they were already was the removal of people from the country into the city, and this particularly affected the incomers. There were no houses for them, and, living as they did during the hot season in badly ventilated huts, they died like flies. The bodies of the dying were heaped one on top of the other, and half-dead creatures could be seen staggering about in the streets or flocking around the fountains in their desire for water. The temples in which they took up their quarters were full of the dead bodies of people who had died inside them. For the catastrophe was so overwhelming that men, not knowing what would happen next to them, became indifferent to every rule of religion or of law. All the funeral ceremonies which used to be observed were now disor-

ganised, and they buried the dead as best they could. Many people, lacking the necessary means of burial because so many deaths had already occurred in their households, adopted the most shameless methods. They would arrive first at a funeral pyre that had been made by others, put their own dead upon it and set it alight; or, finding another pyre burning, they would throw the corpse that they were carrying on top of the other one and go away.

There can be little doubt that the mass grave uncovered by the bulldozers dates from the time of the plague.

Not only did the plague cause a breakdown in the normal arrangements for funerals and burial. According to Thucydides—who himself suffered from the plague and survived—it affected the morality of the citizens. Seeing that the plague acted as a great leveller, taking no account of riches or family, men decided to live for the moment, spending their money and enjoying what pleasures they could.

The Kerameikos

The Kerameikos is still a tranquil and attractive site, though set amid the noise of downtown Athens, a few hundred yards from the Piraeus-Kifissia railway. The Eridanos brook runs right through the site. It is dry in September, but is marked by a green channel showing bright orange trumpets and pink oleanders against the ugly backdrop of the Holy Trinity Church. The brook runs beneath the Sacred Gate through which passed the Sacred Way. During the festival of the Eleusinian mysteries, Athenians passed in procession through this gate and along the Sacred Way to Eleusis.

The Sacred Way still exists as the modern *Iera Odos*, passing through some of the most unattractive parts of Athens and its suburbs. Henry Miller made the journey to Eleusis and became intoxicated by the light, the shrubs and stones. "One should not race along the Sacred Way in a motor car—it is sacrilege," he wrote. "One should walk, walk as the men of old walked, and allow one's whole being to become flooded with light." I wonder whether Miller walked the whole way. In any case, since his time the encroaching cement and noise has made it much less feasible to walk. The writer Lizzie Calligas, however, intrepidly traversed the whole route on foot on 19 September 1994, and by car in both directions a year later, and recorded her impressions on film and in a quirky, interesting book, *The Sacred Way*, illustrated with her own photos.

The Kerameikos today is a recovered, constructed site. Ludwig Ross described the view from Holy Trinity (*Agia Triada*) hill in 1832 as a heap of rubble, a shapeless, dreary grey-green mass of ash and dust. The area was then well outside the small modern town. Modern houses gradually appeared. The antiquities lay beneath sand that covered them to a depth of several feet. Towards the end of the nineteenth century the gas works had made its appearance, along with small industries including a soap factory, and kilns. There were sand quarries and an open sewage channel.

The Greek Archaeological Society started excavations and the expropriation of the land in the 1860s, to protect the area from development that would flow from the new Piraeus Street. At that time no one knew exactly where the ancient cemetery was to be found. The discovery of grave *stelai* in 1863 was a clue. Gradually the area was recovered from the sand. In 1913 the German Archaeological Society took over the site from the Greeks, and over a period of half a century conducted a systematic investigation. The Attico metro excavation of the site of the Kerameikos station added to the picture built up earlier by the Greek and German archaeologists.

The site today contains the handsome "street of the tombs" and a small museum. On either side of the street of the tombs are the fourth-century monuments, ranging from simple columns or *stelai* with finials to sculpted reliefs and even miniature temples or mausoleums. One of the most prominent, the monument of Dexileos, in memory of a twenty-year-old knight killed in a skirmish at Corinth in 394 BC, shows Dexileos in the act of spearing his opponent from horseback, in what looks like a prototype of the iconography of St. George and the dragon. But this monument and some others in the open air are casts: the originals are in the museum, which is a miniature storehouse of Greek funerary art.

The reliefs in the museum (as in the National Archaeological Museum) show what image the dead and their surviving families wished to present. They are serene, dignified, but ultimately mysterious, unlike their twentieth-century equivalents in the Athens

cemeteries, which seem to hide little. A crudely carved stele of a woman called Ampharete, carrying a baby which holds a bird, is inscribed:

I HOLD HERE THIS DEAD CHILD OF MY DAUGHTER.
WHEN IN LIFE WE BOTH BEHELD THE RAYS OF THE SUN,
I HELD HER THUS ON MY LAP AND NOW, BOTH DEAD, I
HOLD HER STILL.

These grave steles hold a mystery, which comes on you gradually, and which long inspection does nothing to resolve. What are they trying to tell us, the surviving relatives of this Ampharete, this Hegeso, etc.? They are not portraits, they are episodes of daily life presumably designed to be typical, worked to the instructions of the relatives by rough craftsmen, by no means the Phidiases of their generation. The poet Elytis reflected on them:

> *It is never night or morning, since time no longer has any meaning. But it is always the home, the family, the loved ones, the thread we held onto that keeps unwinding directly from our heart. That girl who looks out with resignation; and the other one opening the jewel box; and the one who prepares to offer the mirror but hesitates, as if she sensed the uselessness of it; or the old man who has thought he first would touch the future moment, but—the little boy is there and looks about to fall asleep— what of all that would be altered now?—and the dog that smells the edge of the cloth. You would say, just letters all of them, letters of an artist's alphabet, if nothing else, that give us the opportunity to sketch out a depiction of our thirst for eternity in the most discreet manner.*
>
> *TIMARISTOS AND KRITO, KTESILAOS AND THEANO, HEGESO, AMYNOKLEIA, MNESARETE, MYNNO—how puzzling! These capital letters in stone, nothing else mentioned, no further comment; these trace us back and locate us. They create the calm of a shadow within the blinding light of death... A kore, so young, so beautiful—it's not possible—surely she's still somewhere combing away at her hair...*

The museum shows what the dead took with them into the grave. The children took their toys, such as a pottery horse on wheels carrying four wine jars, and a pecking bird with a geometric pattern. It is the survivability of ceramics that brings us these insights into the mental and physical world of the Greeks. Much of the art is of poor quality, as is much of the art of any epoch. Some is exquisite, for example the red figure jar showing a woman seated at her distaff opposite a robed man with naked chest, carrying a hare by its front legs, its long ears hanging down. On the other side of the jar the two of them embrace.

Today as in ancient times, the Greeks externalize grief and mourning, not only through monuments and images but also through the rituals of death, burial and mourning. Margaret Alexiou's book, *The Ritual Lament in Greek Tradition* (1974) explores authoritatively the continuity and change in these rituals. From time to time Athenian rulers felt obliged to legislate against excessive ostentation and expense in funerary buildings and in ritual lament. Solon forbade ritual lamentation and excessive spending in the sixth century BC. Centuries later, Cicero reported that because of the excessive grandeur of the tombs in the Kerameikos it had been decreed that no one should make a tomb which required the work of more than ten men in three days, and that there should be no plaster decoration. But sometimes the dead and their graves were enlisted again in the struggle of the living, just as in the chain of history the stones of a classical monument are reused in a Byzantine church and then in a nineteenth-century house. When the walls of Athens were reinforced in 338 BC, said the orator Lycurgus, "the land itself offered its trees, whereas the dead offered their own coffins... as for the living, they all worked, some in charge of the fortification, others constructing moats, others digging ditches; in short, no one was idle in the city."

Funeral Rites

The rituals of death in the Orthodox Church are more immediate, more often celebrated and more external than in Anglican or even many Roman Catholic traditions. The dead man or woman, whether statesman or peasant, seems more present to the Greeks. The mental world of death and its rituals in Athens has been set out by a Greek-American anthropologist, Neni Panourgia, in a complicated, interesting book, *Fragments of Death, Fables of Identity*, which opens out the subject from the coffin and the dead person to the undertakers, relatives and friends, their relationship to the death, how it affects them, and how through this relationship they express their identity as Athenians.

Panourgia is writing mainly about private matters. But there is a public aspect too. Sometimes a funeral has become a "national" event, or served the Athenians as a means of expressing a collective mood. The obvious example from the ancient world is Pericles' funeral oration, in which, in Thucydides' account, he took the event as the occasion for a eulogy of the Athenian way of life, speaking of Athens as a model to other states, of her democracy, equality before the law, and openness to all the talents:

We are free and tolerant in our private lives; but in public affairs we keep to the law. This is because it commands our deep respect... Here each individual is interested not only in his own affairs but in the affairs of the state as well: even those who are mostly occupied with their own business are extremely well-informed on general politics—this is a peculiarity of ours: we do not say that a man who takes no interest in politics is a man who minds his own business; we say that he has no business here at all.

This speech continues to resonate with Greeks across the centuries. It is invoked on solemn occasions. The statesman Eleftherios Venizelos translated it as part of his translation of Thucydides.

On at least three occasions in modern times a funeral has brought the Athenians onto the streets, drawn by something that the dead man expressed about Greece's present plight. In February 1943 Greece's greatest poet, Kostis Palamas, died of natural causes. He was the author of the short poem about Athens at the head of this book, and of the *Olympic Hymn*, which is sung at every Olympic Games. The novelist Giorgos Theotokas wrote later that the terrible years of the war had separated Greeks from Greeks, and Athenians from people of the countryside, and that Palamas's funeral electrified the atmosphere and raised the spirit of Athens in a wonderful outbreak of collective passion and faith. Palamas dead seemed like the most powerful emblem of national resistance and the desire for freedom.

Palamas died in the night of 22-23 February 1943. Theotokas and others such as the poet Angelos Sikelianos, the writer Stratis Myrivilis, the critic George Katsimbalis and Ioanna Tsatsos went to his house in Plaka to see the corpse, laid out in black clothes, on a divan, with branches of almond blossom laid on his body. He seemed smaller than in life. Myrivilis said, "Look what sweetness there is in his face." Candles were lit in the room. There was no other light. Those present felt they were looking at half a century of Greek life.

The funeral became the occasion for a public release of national feeling, as Athenians crammed into the church of the First Cemetery for the service, which was conducted by Archbishop Damaskinos. The crowd filled the paths of the Cemetery and gathered round the grave. Sikelianos placed his hand on the coffin and, though himself ill, recited a poem which he had written the night before in memory of Palamas. Sikelianos then led the mourners, seeming to Theotokas like a sleepwalker. The actress Marika Kotopouli said as he passed her, "Sikelianos is burying Palamas!" And indeed if anyone was Palamas's successor as poet of the nation it was Sikelianos.

Katsimbalis threw a handful of earth into the grave. And then a strange thing happened. Led by Katsimbalis, the crowd joined, at first hesitantly, then in full voice, in the Greek national hymn, the invocation of Freedom by the nineteenth-century poet Dionysios Solomos. The funeral had enabled the mourners to express in public what could not be expressed at other times. Ioanna Tsatsos ended her diary entry for the day of the funeral, "We are free."

This happened again during the military dictatorship of 1967-74. One of the grand old men of Greek politics, George Papandreou, died on 1 November 1968. His body was laid out in the Little Cathedral before the burial in the First Cemetery. Papandreou had been prime minister at the time of the liberation of Athens in 1944. He was the grizzled leader of the centrist opposition to Karamanlis's government in the early 1960s, the author of some of the most stirring political speeches Athenians had heard over the years, and a link with the Venizelist past, whose career went back to the early years of the century. He represented things—freedom of speech, the free practice of politics, a certain respect for liberal values—that had been suppressed by the dictatorship. His funeral was the occasion of another outpouring of national feeling. The BBC reporter Robert McDonald, who did a voice report on the eve of the funeral from the steps of the cathedral, remembers someone coming up to him and saying that his report had encouraged people to leave their homes and attend. The crowd was variously estimated at a quarter of a million to a million.

Then on 20 September 1971 the poet George Seferis died. As winner of the Nobel Prize for literature, he had an aura of prestige for patriotic Greeks. He had reluctantly emerged from his silence two years earlier, speaking as the poetic conscience of the nation, to condemn the military regime as totally inimical to the ideals for which "our world" had fought during the last war, and to prophesy inevitable tragedy for the country. His death was a rallying cry from the wilderness for those who believed in the values that, in Seferis's bleak vision, were about to sink into "swampy stagnant waters".

Seferis represented to the Greek people something larger than himself, and his funeral was the occasion to recognize this. The service took place in the crowded Church of the Transfiguration on the edge of the Plaka, near the house on Kydathinaion Street where Seferis himself, his sister Ioanna and her husband Constantine Tsatsos had lived. Afterwards, as the body in the hearse made the long slow journey along Kydathinaion Street and down Amalias Avenue to the cemetery, the crowds spilled out and stopped the traffic. As with Palamas, music took over. In snatches, spontaneously, and then together, the crowd, mainly young people, sang the well-known Theodorakis setting of *Epiphaneia*. It is a very personal love poem, which on this occasion expressed the nostalgia for freedom that the poet represented for the crowd.

The First Cemetery

Athens has many cemeteries. The most venerable and the most interesting is the First Cemetery, a cool, shaded park in the Mets area not far from the Panathenaic Stadium. The great and the good of Greek life, and members of old Athenian families, are buried here.

The mental world of the Athens First Cemetery is not so far from that of the Kerameikos. The First Cemetery was created in the nineteenth century, and for many decades remained outside the modern city. Now it is a haven of greenery within the city, a place where cats, dogs and birds feel at home, where collared doves settle on the cypress trees whose deep green contrasts with the marble of the monuments. Little sparrows dart down to peck at the boiled wheat *Kollyva* which families put out in dishes on the graves on holy days. A stroll in the cemetery is one of the secret, calming pleasures of Athens. Unless a funeral is in progress, there are usually only a few ladies passing down the alleys towards their family graves, perhaps carrying fresh flowers, and a few workers pottering around the graves. Most of these are well kept, but some are unkempt with withered grasses.

The cemetery contains the finest and most complete collection of nineteenth- and twentieth-century sculpture in Greece, including some figures, such as the "Sleeping Girl", which are known to virtually every

Athenian. (Actually there are two "Sleeping Girls", sculptures by G. Halepa and I. Vitsaris on the graves of Sophia Aphentaki (1876) and Maria Deliyianni (1883) respectively.) Here the great families of Athens—the Rallis, Pesmazoglous, Negrepontis and others—have their family tombs. The prevailing nineteenth-century style is of a little temple labelled FAMILY (*ΟΙΚΟΓΕΝΕΙΑ*) OF SUCH AND SUCH, or a relief following the classical model, with grave maidens inclining their heads and leaning on staffs. Some of the dead are commemorated by busts: Generals Kolokotronis and Makriyiannis, heroes of the War of Independence, are imagined in Greek costume. Twentieth-century generals have imitated this, but less successfully, with crude busts in modern uniform and medals. (The marble workshops where you can

order a bust or relief are near the cemetery, by the flower shops.) Some of the nineteenth-century images are startling in their naturalism, such as the forceful mother who domi-nates the tomb of the Georgoulas family.

Much of the history of Athens can be deciphered here, in the tombs of war heroes, politicians, artists, actors, presidents and prime ministers (but not kings and queens, princes and princesses, who are buried on the royal family's estate at Tatoi under Mount Parnes). The Makri-yiannis family tomb, besides the inscription IOANNIS MAKRIYIANNIS 1797-1864, carries a quotation from his memoirs:

WITHOUT VIRTUE AND PAIN
FOR THE FATHERLAND

AND FAITH
IN THEIR RELIGION
NATIONS DO NOT EXIST

Makriyiannis was an unlettered, patriotic fighter from central Greece who led a troop of irregulars and suffered multiple wounds in some of the hardest battles of the War of Independence. He taught himself to write as an adult in order to record his memoirs of these historic events, in which the nation battled, first for freedom from Turkish rule, and then to create its own state and government. Makriyiannis's memoirs are among the seminal works of Greek demotic literature. They were published only many decades after his death, in 1907, and raised to iconic status in the canon of Greek literature by the poet Seferis, who saw them as an "untarnished spring of life", containing the common lot of Greek popular tradition, the spiritual wealth of the race, something of the essence of Hellenism. Seferis sent a copy of the memoirs to Colonel Woodhouse, the commander of the Allied Military Mission to Greece during the war, with the inscription, "For my learned friend Monty, this illiterate my master in Greek", which was, as Woodhouse remarked, a testimony to which no literary gloss could be added.

On the Makriyiannis family temple there is another inscription:

KITSOS MALTEZOS
1922-1944
DIED MURDERED FOR GREECE
1 FEBRUARY 1944

Kitsos Maltezos, Makriyiannis' last surviving relative, was a brilliant young man who joined the leftist resistance but fell foul of the communists. He was shot dead in front of the Byron statue on the corner of Amalias Avenue, nine months before the liberation of Athens.

When the writer Dimitrios Vikelas visited the First Cemetery in 1884, he found something subtly wrong about it, a certain lack of care in the upkeep of the graves and surrounding greenery. This was a time of expansion of the cemetery to cater for the rapid growth of the city and he attributed his unease to this. Vikelas saw that the cemetery could be a Pantheon and a school of history for the Greeks, and looked forward to the day when thousands more Athenians would visit it. But he gently ridiculed the "archaiolatry" or ancestor worship of the supposedly Christian Athenians, who would represent on the tombstone a scene of farewell, in modern dress, imitating the gestures of a stele in the Kerameikos; and still more the inscriptions in illiterate classical Greek; or worse, in ungrammatical French, recalling the Kolonaki ladies at whose salons conversation would take place in Kolonaki-accented French. Besides these absurdities, Vikelas found many simple and affecting inscriptions and monuments. He noted especially some lines that moved him more than all the pseudo-classical epitaphs, not realizing that they were actually written by his friend, the poet George Drosinis, another devotee of the cemetery. They were inscribed in memory of a young girl who had died earlier than her father, who was to join her later in the common family grave:

> *The flower has its stem and the stem has its flower.*
> *Neither the father is alone, nor is the daughter alone.*
> *Each has the other as companion at his, at her side.*
> *Charos has separated them, the grave unites them again.*

Charos is death, descended from Charon, the figure who in ancient Greek myth ferried the dead across the river Styx. In modern folklore he struggles with men for their souls.

Near the entrance to the cemetery, far from the moral climate of this inscription, are the graves of archbishops of Athens, including Damaskinos, and of some of the large-scale political figures of recent history, including Melina Mercouri and Andreas Papandreou. It is somehow characteristic of Andreas that, although his grave looks at first sight modest, it turns out to occupy a larger plot than most others. I attended his funeral in the cathedral on a hot summer's day in 1996, with John Selwyn Gummer representing the British Government and John Prescott, his leg in plaster, the Labour Party. It was a grand state occasion, but somehow it lacked the national resonance of his father's death. The tension provoked by Andreas's late marriage to the air hostess Mimi was palpable. His son George and his half brother, also George, both made emotional addresses to the corpse, the former full of filial pride, the latter full of reproach to Andreas for never having loved him.

In the entrance to the First Cemetery, outside the cemetery office, there is a notice listing grave plots available for purchase or rent. A family buys a lease on a plot from the Athens Municipality, and pays an annual service charge. If the family dies out or fails to keep up its obligations, the plot reverts to the city and is put up for sale again.

These graves are for the well-off. A select few (29 in 1972), such as Makriyiannis, were given their grave plots free as a mark of respect by the city. According to Greek legislation there is no cremation, which the Orthodox Church prohibits (though there are signs that this position is under threat). The pressure on space is therefore considerable. The standard practice is for burial of the dead to be followed in three years by their exhumation, the bones being returned to the families, and then placed in a family grave or a common ossuary. Three years is not a long time, and lime is used to assist the process of decomposition. Sweet-smelling bones are regarded as a sign of sanctity.

The Protestant Cemetery

In a corner of the First Cemetery is the extensive Protestant Cemetery of Athens, which was moved here early in the twentieth century from its original position at the corner of the Zappeion park, across the way from the stadium. It contains some interesting finds for British, American and German visitors. Besides the names of families well known in the history of nineteenth-century Athens, I stumbled on the graves of T. H. White, author of the Arthurian trilogy *The Once and Future King;* of the documentary film maker Humphrey Jennings (1907-1950) who died in Poros ("Death is a veil which those who live call life/ They sleep and it is lifted"); and of the Cambridge historian A. H. M. Jones (1904-1970), who died at sea off Athens. The most prominent of the Protestant graves is that of George Finlay. The iron rails round his grave are broken and twisted, the marble is chipped, and the plinth just below the bust of his head is cracked and repaired. Finlay awaits a new Scottish philhellene to repair his monument.

CHAPTER SEVEN

Byzantines, Franks, Catalans and Florentines

> "*Sheep graze among the meagre relics of the Stoa Poikile.*"
> Michael Choniates, Bishop of Athens, late twelfth century AD

Where in this teeming construction of asphalt and cement is Byzantium? Where the castles of the Frankish dukes of Athens, the villas of the Florentines, the halls of the Catalans, all of whom ruled Athens in the Middle Ages? The classical city dominates Athens and has been incorporated in it. The Byzantine lies low in the remaining churches in the centre and expands in the monasteries on the outskirts. The Franks, the Catalans and the Florentines have disappeared as if they had never been.

The sack of the Athenian Agora by the Heruli in 267 signalled a new threat from the north. Alaric, king of the Goths, captured the city in 396, but spared the Acropolis. The Acropolis resumed its traditional role as defensive fortress, and the city shrank behind protective walls. It was at about this time, following Constantine's conversion and establishment of his capital Constantinople on the Bosphorus, that the empire split into east and west and the conversion of Athens from paganism to Christianity began, against no little resistance from the forces of conservatism.

Cicero, Horace, Brutus, were among those who had studied in Athens. In the autumnal years of Roman rule, the period known as the Second Sophistic, it held its place as a centre of philosophical study, living off its past reputation. These centuries are recaptured in accounts by some scholars who studied here. They included Longinus, Libanius, St Gregory Nazianzen, and two emperors, the Stoic Marcus Aurelius and the strange pagan Julian the so-called Apostate. Libanius, a student from Antioch, gave a bad account of the fourth-century city. Its intellectual life degenerated into rowdyism, with factions forming around particular sophistical teachers, and fierce competition to poach new students, by force if necessary. "May the accursed ship-captain perish who brought me here," wrote one student, comparing the city to the burnt skin of a sacrificial victim from which one had to try to reconstruct what the city had been like before. Philosophy had departed, leaving only the shells of the famous institutions such as the Academy and the Lyceum. "Athens has no longer anything sublime except the country's famous name... Today only the bee-keepers bring it honour." The atmosphere seems to have been like a university rag day.

With the triumph of Christianity as the official religion of the Roman state, the fate of Athens as centre of the old philosophical schools was sealed. The last spark of life for pagan Athens's resistance to the tide of Christianity was the brief and unhappy reign of the emperor Julian the Apostate (361-3) who was brought up a reluctant Christian, but found his true nature at the schools of Athens, and came out as a pagan when he became emperor. "Vicisti, Galilaee," he is said to have uttered on his deathbed: "You have conquered, O Galilean." The story may be untrue, but it accurately reflects what was happening. The old gods and heroes and spirits of nature lived on in the Greek countryside, adapted and absorbed by the new religion, sometimes making themselves felt even today.

A series of decrees of the emperor Theodosius in the late fourth and early fifth centuries ordered that pagan temples should be destroyed. Some time after this the Parthenon, transformed rather than destroyed, became the Church of the Virgin Mary. Some claim that there was a transitional stage in which it was the Church of the Divine Wisdom, a little closer to the attributes of the goddess Athina than was the Virgin Mary. The gold and ivory statue of Athina by Phidias was carted off to Constantinople, where it disappeared. The great church remained dedicated to the Virgin under both Greek and Latin rites until the Ottoman conquest in 1456.

In 529 AD the emperor Justinian completed the work begun by Theodosius, by closing the philosophical schools of Athens. This was the coup de grace for the ancient, pagan world of the Olympian gods and the old-style scholarly institutions of Athens. It condemned the city to the status of a provincial backwater, in an outlying part of the Byzantine empire ruled from Constantinople. With the southward migration of Slav tribes in the sixth and seventh century, Athens became one of a number of remaining Greek towns in a sea of Slav invasion, largely cut off from the heart of the empire in Constantinople. It was just one city in the province or "theme" of Hellas, outweighed and outranked by Thebes. Athens was the seat of a relatively minor bishop, the senior Metropolitan Bishops sitting in Thessaloniki and Corinth. In the eighth century, a young lady from Athens, Irene, was chosen by the emperor Constantine V to marry his son Leo. She travelled from Athens to Constantinople in 769 AD, rising eventually to the position of sole ruler of the empire, and raising Athens to the status of Metropolitan see.

Traces of Byzantium

A good place to start to see what Byzantium has left to Athens is the Cathedral Square. On the western side of the square there is a statue of Damaskinos, Archbishop of Athens during the Second World War and Regent of Greece, by Churchill's agreement, in the crucial period following the liberation. It was he who celebrated in the cathedral the liberation of Athens from the Germans in October 1944, thanking the Virgin Mary for this deliverance. The cathedral itself, a mid-nineteenth-century foundation, is large and grand, but fails to take wing. Next to it, on the south side, stands a much smaller Byzantine church known sometimes as the Little Cathedral, also as the Church of Gorgoepikoos or of Agios Eleftherios. It is dwarfed by its larger neighbour, and it cannot match the symbolic power of the relics of Patriarch Gregory V which repose in the cathedral; but it beats it every time for grace and rhythm of architecture and elegance of decoration. The building is a mongrel. In Byzantine times pre-Christian antiquities were rifled and old stones were reused. On the west front of the Little Cathedral there is a riot of marble animals, birds, signs of the zodiac and other decorative motifs.

The empire has left little physical trace apart from the churches. What remains and is portable is collected in the Byzantine Museum—fragments of sculpture and carved stone, wonderful icons, vestments, metal and decorated ware. The churches of Athens are all, old or new, of Byzantine inspiration and type, except for the Protestant Church on Philellinon Street and the Roman Catholic Cathedral of St Denis on Panepistimiou. Byzantium therefore plays an important part in the looks and architecture of the city.

The rulers of Byzantium were great builders of churches. This was a religious empire bound together by faith. Emperors and their consorts competed in the grandeur of the foundations they established. But Athens after the closure of the philosophical schools declined into a small town concentrated within the *enceinte* around the Acropolis. It lacked the glory and the grand churches of the imperial centre, such as the Cathedral of St Sophia at Constantinople, or even of Thessaloniki, the second city of the empire. Athens accumulated a mass of parish churches and chapels, some of distinction, in the old city—mainly the present Plaka area. The surrounding villages had their churches too. The most impressive foundations were the monasteries outside the city: Daphni on the road to Eleusis, and Kaisariani in the foothills of Hymettus.

In 2003, along with so many other Athenian museums, the monastery at Daphni, behind its high fortified wall, was closed for conservation and restoration work. By the time this book appears it should be open. It was well placed on the main route from Athens to Eleusis and the Peloponnese, in a gap in the hills. This road now carries a constant stream of traffic and can get blocked at weekends. A few hundred yards back towards Athens is a pleasant botanical garden, largely ignored by visitors. The annual Daphni wine festival used to take place near here, a favourite with tourists of the 1950s and 1960s. The Daphni mosaics include the awesome image of Christ Pantokrator in the dome of the main church, which Osbert Lancaster called the most awe-inspiring and convincing of all the Pantocrators in Byzantine lands, and which drew poetry from the Archbishop of Canterbury, Dr Rowan Williams, when he saw it. The foundation is ancient, dating to the fifth or sixth century AD, but the present buildings date mainly from the late eleventh century. During the Frankish domination of Athens, Otho de la Roche gave them to the Cistercians. Otho and Walter de Brienne are actually buried here. It was recovered by the Orthodox Church only in the mid-fifteenth century.

The harmonious ensemble of buildings of the eleventh-century Kaisariani monastery is set in a wooded fold of Hymettus, surrounded by its own arboretum with splashing water, yet only twenty minutes from the centre of Athens. Here in the courtyard with its fountain, set below towering plane trees, I remember a tasting of olive oils from the best olive-producing areas of Greece, Kalamata and the Mani, Mount Pelion, Amphissa and its vast silvery grove of olives, western Crete and Attica itself. Hymettus attracted other monastic foundations besides Kaisariani, all named after different Saints John: the thirteenth-century St John the Theologian beyond Papagos; the twelfth-century St John the Hunter above Agia Paraskevi; and the eleventh-century St John Kareas high up the mountain. Part of the pleasure of such monasteries is the contrast of their settings with the bare, grey rock of whale-backed Hymettus itself, crowned with its radar installations and pierced with limestone caves. Of the three mountains that ring Athens, Hymettus is the closest to the city, the one whose presence is always felt in its different moods and lights.

Down in the city, most of the Byzantine churches are concentrated in the old town, and can be visited easily on foot in the course of a walk around the Plaka and its surroundings. The finest in their settings are the Church of the Holy Apostles, with its innovative architectural form, which is placed most attractively near the eastern side of the Agora, and the Kapnikarea Church set right in the middle of the crossroads on Ermou Street.

Even though most of the Byzantine churches are dwarfed by the neighbouring accumulation of office blocks, they hold their own, and speak of a past of which much of the history is forgotten but the faith is still alive. They are a constant presence in the life of the Athenians, and they are the survivors, for dozens of churches were destroyed or abandoned in the first decades of the independent state, their stones reused in the cathedral and other buildings. There are usually people, more of them women than men, inside the churches, lighting candles that shine against the sombre interior, kissing the icons, offering prayers for sick relatives. There are prayer boxes handy, with sheets of paper to write on.

The Orthodox Church

But with more than four million people, the great majority of them of Orthodox faith, the city needs a lot of churches. In the densely populated suburbs these are often large, newish structures, built with much concrete in a debased Byzantine style. They lack the subtlety of form and materials of the old Byzantine churches, with their uneven tiles and dog's tooth ornaments in their walls, as often as not incorporating in the structure some old Roman or Greek recycled marble.

The churches are used mainly for weddings, baptisms (by total immersion), funerals, and at the great festivals of the year, especially Easter. All through Holy Week they are busy with fasting worshippers. The streets fill on Good Friday with the Epitaphios procession of the garlanded bier of Christ, and again at midnight on Easter Saturday, when at the climax of the service the priest declares that Christ is Risen and the congregation light their candles one from the other and come out of the church into the streets to walk their way home, candle flame cupped in the hand, to make the sign of the cross on their door with the smoke and to eat the special Easter lamb soup, the *mageiritsa*, breaking their long fast before going to bed. The following day the gardens of those who have stayed in Athens rather than returning to their villages are fragrant with the smoke of lambs turning on the spit, cooking with herbs from early morning until they reach their succulent best around noon. The meat market does a brisk trade in whole lambs before Easter. Out of town, at Phyli in the Parnes foothills, you can see the poor penned lambs being taken one by one and slaughtered for the Easter feast.

St Paul called the ancient Athenians too superstitious. Almost all Greeks observe the external aspects of the Orthodox faith. They cross themselves, they get married in church (which was the only way to get legally married until the 1980s), and they go to church at Easter. They have been brought up in this faith and it is an important part of their national identity. The Church was recently embroiled in a fierce row with the government over whether a new form of identity card should or should not specify the citizen's religious affiliation. Church leaders saw nothing strange in specifying in this way that Greeks, in their vast majority, are Orthodox Christians. Even those, and they are many, who would object on grounds of privacy and human rights to being labelled publicly in this way, would not deny their affiliation if asked. They carry the Orthodox Church's rituals and beliefs throughout their lives and to the grave.

"A Great Ruin"

Athens was not an easy city to govern. The Athenians stoned a senior Byzantine official to death on the Acropolis in 915, and took part in a wider Serbian and Greek revolt in 1040-41, sparked off by a hard-nosed financial administrator known as John the Orphanotrophos, the man in charge of charitable foundations. He was a brother of the Emperor Michael. The revolt was put down on behalf of the empire by the same Harold Haardrada who ended his life at the battle of Stamford Bridge.

The best description of Athens in the Byzantine period comes from the pen of its last Metropolitan Bishop, Michael Choniates, who came from Asia Minor and became Bishop of Athens in about 1180 AD. He wrote of his mission as an exile to a barbarian and irreligious place, painting a contrast of present degradation with past glory that was to become a cliché in later centuries:

O city of Athens, thou who wert the nurse of wisdom, to what depths of ignorance art thou sunk.

The bishop rebuked his flock for their irreverent and irrelevant chattering during prayer time, shuffling their feet on the floor of the cathedral, the Parthenon—that "beautiful and heavenly mansion" — and letting their minds wander. Bishop Michael wrote that he had become a barbarian himself since living in Athens. It took him three years to learn the Athenian dialect. The Attic land was the same as before: lovely, temperate, fertile in fruit and honey. The Acropolis was the same. But the people were boorish and uncultivated, the priests were an evil lot, the plain of Marathon was barren of grain, Eleusis and all Attica were ravaged by pirates from Aegina, and worst of all the see of Athens was being turned into a wilderness by the exactions of a horde of agents, tax collectors and customs officials who came down on the city each year like the plague of frogs which the Lord sent upon Egypt. "The tax-collectors survey our barren soil with measures small enough to check the prints of fleas. The very hairs on our heads are counted: how much more the leaves of vines and plants." His strongest criticism was for the Praetor, the empire's chief functionary in the region, worse than Xerxes or the thirty tyrants, whose depredations with his large retinue wasted the city's coffers and dried up stores of grain.

Now everything in Athens is poor and mean, especially the farm-implements. The great city has become a great ruin. The bellows has failed; there is no iron-worker, no bronze-worker among us, no maker of knives.

You cannot look upon Athens without tears. Not that the city has lost her ancient glory, it is too long since that was taken from her. Now she has lost the very form, appearance and character of a city. Everywhere you see walls stripped and demolished, houses razed to the ground, their sites ploughed under. Time and its dread ally, envy have dealt with Athens more barbarously than ever the Persians did... Sheep graze among the meagre relics of the Stoa Poikile.

... The dying pity those who remain alive.

Michael travelled to the capital of the empire to plead for lighter taxes, and for release from his post. His main consolation was the glorious, radiantly bright sanctuary of the Parthenon in its guise as cathedral, presumably a spiritual brightness, though in the interior lamps hung like stars before the screen on which was fixed the icon of the Virgin with Christ.

One would like to see archaeological evidence confirming or refuting this extraordinarily negative picture. Like other texts in a period when written evidence is sparse, Michael's has been made to bear a lot of weight. There is a strong element of convention in the bishop's complaints. He had an interest in painting a dark picture if he was to persuade the governors in Constantinople to reduce the burden of taxation on his flock; and the contrast he developed between past and present may have gained from touching up. The Arab geographer Edrisi in 1154 described Athens as a populous town, surrounded by gardens and cornfields. The city itself was probably not too different in shape and aspect from the late Roman city, but with ancient monuments dilapidated and often rifled for their marble, and with new and not so new Byzantine churches dotting the roof lines with their red-tiled domes.

Enter the Franks

In these times of feuding imperial agents, provincial warlords, and encroaching predators from the west (French, Venetian and others), Michael led the defence of Athens against the Greek chieftain of Argos and Nauplion, Leon Sgouros, who marched into Attica in 1203. He put the lower town to the torch but failed to capture the Acropolis. A year later Constantinople was captured and plundered in the Fourth Crusade by a western Catholic force of Frenchmen and Venetians, a crime never forgiven by the Orthodox, which ushered in a period of Latin domination of most of the Greek peninsula. Greece was carved up among the feudal barons. Athens and Thebes fell to the portion of Otho de la Roche, a knight from Burgundy, in 1205. Bishop Michael left Athens and settled on the island of Kea. The Parthenon became a Latin cathedral. The "Franks" had arrived.

For more than two hundred years the city continued under the sway of these western feudal chieftains, successively the Dukes of

Burgundy, the Catalans, and the Dukes of Florence. This was a progression from noble knights to rough men at arms to bankers.

The Duchy of Athens of Boccaccio and Shakespeare has a romantic ring. It was a time, at first, of chivalrous pursuits, hawking, hunting, feasting, fighting, archery, dancing. In Shakespeare's *Midsummer Night's Dream* it is an unreal thing of gossamer fancy. Viewed by Athenians, it seems more like a diversion from the course of their history. It has left little trace or influence either physically (apart from the "Frankish Tower" built by the Florentines) or on language and custom. The story of the duchy is a complicated subtext to a larger story of power and influence in the Greek peninsula.

For most of the time Thebes remained the capital of the Duchy of Athens. Otho's title was "Grand Seigneur"; his successor Guy was elevated to the rank of duke. The language of court was French. The legal system was based on the usages and customs of the Kingdom of Jerusalem, the code established in the Holy Land by earlier crusaders. Matters pertaining exclusively to the Greeks were handled by their ecclesiastical authorities under Byzantine codes. Though the Greeks were not required to abandon their rites and traditions, their clergy were placed below the Latins, who pushed them out of their episcopal thrones and houses and contested their ownership of monastic lands.

From the de la Roche Burgundian dynasty, under which Athens prospered, the duchy passed to the French knight Walter de Brienne. Brienne's rule was brought to a violent end in one of the great disasters of Frankish chivalry, in which his thousand knights were drawn by their Catalan mercenaries into battle in a marsh near the Cephissos river in Boeotia, and slaughtered. Rule passed to the Catalan Grand Company (1311) whose tough mercenaries grabbed the widows of the French knights as well as the governing prerogatives of their husbands. From the Catalans, some seventy years later, the duchy passed to the Florentine banking family of the Acciajuoli, described by Gibbon as a family "plebeian at Florence, potent at Naples, and sovereign in Greece". Plebeian he may have been, but at least Nerio Acciajuoli had a certain style. Having ripped the silver plates from the Parthenon doors to pay a ransom, he repented on his deathbed and left his broodmares, and the whole city of Athens, to the Parthenon itself, the Church of the Virgin.

The traveller Cyriacus of Ancona left an account of Athens in 1436 which includes an accurate description of the then state of the Parthenon, the temple of Hephaestus (which he calls Mars), the temple of Olympian Zeus, the Tower of the Winds, and the aqueduct of Hadrian. Clearly these were part of an enlightened traveller's itinerary. But by the mid-fifteenth century the impetus of Florentine rule had been lost, and the aggressive, confident new imperial power of Ottoman Turks was on the march. Athens was about to change masters again.

CHAPTER EIGHT

The Turkish Town

"Setting aside the magic of the name, and all those associations which it would be pedantic and superfluous to recapitulate, the very situation of Athens would render it the favourite of all who have eyes for art or nature."

Byron, Note to Canto the Second of *Childe Harold's Pilgrimage*

Three years after the fall of the Byzantine capital Constantinople in 1453, it was the turn of Athens. According to the chronicler Doukas, before the Turks occupied the city the Athenians were reduced to eating grass, roots, wild herbs and acorns.

Sultan Mehmet II the Conqueror toured the Peloponnese inspecting his new domains and returned through the Isthmus of Corinth to Athens in the autumn of 1458. The Greek historian Critobolus not surprisingly gave him a favourable write-up, saying that he loved Athens and its wonders because he had heard much of the wisdom, prudence, valour and virtues of the ancient Greeks. He came in a spirit of exploration, pilgrimage and investigation of the conditions and fortifications of Greek lands. He was especially struck by the Acropolis, attempting to reconstruct in his mind's eye how it must have looked in ancient times. The chronicler calls him a philhellene and a wise man as well as a great king, who noted the Athenians' respect for their ancestors and rewarded them in various ways. Broadly speaking, the account rings true: the first period of Ottoman domination was one of revival, to be followed by decline and neglect.

Standing on the Acropolis today you will see around you no trace of the Ottoman past unless and until you lean over to look down on the northern slopes of the Plaka. Yet the Acropolis itself was the seat of the Turkish garrison, and until the end of the Turkish occupation dozens of garrison houses were dotted around, in and among the ancient ruins. They can be seen in pictures by eighteenth- and nineteenth-century travellers, such as the painter Edward Dodwell, who left a memorable and much-quoted account (1819) of his meeting with the Disdar, or Governor of the Acropolis, who controlled entry by westerners. The story is as interesting for the light it casts on technical aids to drawing as for the alleged Turkish ignorance and superstition, and invincible western superiority.

Dodwell had concluded a deal with the Disdar—"a man of bad faith and insatiable rapacity"—for free access to the Acropolis as often as he wished in return for a small down payment and a much larger payment of 80 piastres on completion of his work. He spent his time drawing and painting, having his lunch sent up to him, and making friends with the inquisitive children of the Turkish soldiers. But the Disdar became impatient for his money.

After experiencing numerous vexations from this mercenary Turk, a ridiculous circumstance at length released us from the continuance of his importunities. I was one day engaged in drawing the Parthenon with the aid of my camera [i.e. a camera obscura], when the Disdar, whose surprise was excited by the novelty of the sight, asked with a sort of fretful inquietude, what new conjuration I was performing with that extraordinary machine? I endeavoured to explain it, by putting in a clean sheet of paper, and making him look into the camera obscura; he no sooner saw the temple instantaneously reflected on the paper in all its lines and colours, than he imagined I had produced the effect by some magical process; his astonishment apparently mingled with alarm, and stroking his long black beard, he repeated the words Allah, Masch-Allah, several times. He again looked into the camera obscura with a kind of cautious diffidence, and at that moment some of his soldiers happening to pass before the reflecting glass, were beheld by the astonished Disdar walking upon the paper: he now became outrageous; and after calling me pig, devil, and Buonaparte, he told me, that if I chose, I might take away the temple and all the stones in the citadel; but that he would never permit me to conjure his soldiers into my box. When I found that it was in vain to reason with his ignorance, I changed my tone, and told him that if he did not leave me unmolested, I would put him into my box; and that he should find it a very difficult matter to get out again.

Dodwell had no further trouble with the Disdar!

During most of the period of Turkish occupation Athens was treated as just another, not particularly important, town. Though Mehmet the Conqueror was hailed as a philhellene, most Turks had no particular interest in or respect for Athens' classical or Christian monuments. They were not unique in that. During the Turkish period, besides the destruction of the Parthenon, directly attributable to its use by the Turks as a powder magazine, the exquisite little temple of Nike was demolished and turned into a bastion, and the temple of Augustus at the east end of the Acropolis was torn down and made into a guard house for the soldiery.

It was, of course, the fact that the Acropolis served the Turks in its natural function as fortress and citadel that caused it to be exposed to Venetian shelling, and later to be the object of fierce fighting between Greeks and Turks, during the War of Independence. But it was also a place for a promenade. Just below the Erectheum and immediately overlooking the town there was a battery with two cannons, used by the Turks to signal the Bairam. Byron's companion John Cam Hobhouse saw the Turkish ladies walking on this side of the ramparts on a fine day, and leaning over the battlements, to enjoy the amusing murmur arising from the city below.

The Acropolis contained Turkish public and religious buildings as well as housing. The Parthenon was converted from church to mosque after the conquest, and described in its lavish splendour by the Turkish traveller Evliya Chelebi in 1667. After the great explosion of 1687, a new mosque was constructed right in the middle of the Parthenon, its dome and minaret plainly visible in pictures by Stuart and Revett, Dodwell, Hansen and others. The urge on the part of the post-independence Greeks to purge this Ottoman past meant that the Ottoman buildings soon disappeared.

As well as these Ottoman features of the Acropolis, much of the old Turkish city to the north, with its commercial, administrative and religious buildings, has also vanished, under the pressure of archaeological excavation and new building. The Agora excavation, for example, removed the remaining traces of the Turkish town in that area, together with the more extensive nineteenth-century Greek buildings on the same site. There remain in the Plaka a few traces of public buildings (the baths, the Tsistaraki Mosque near Monastiraki), but also a certain atmosphere, in the narrow, twisting streets, and the continuing functions of commerce.

The old Turkish city extended north of the Acropolis up to the late Roman walls, and eventually beyond them. A new Turkish wall was built, enclosing the city and a stretch of adjacent country, in 1787, in the time of the tyrannical Turkish Governor Hadji Ali the Bodyguard (Haseki) who had the favour of the Sultana and whose regime of rapacity and oppression lasted twenty-four years. Entry was by seven gates. The purpose of wall and gates appears to have been mainly commercial, to exert control over taxation of products sold in the city markets. Within these walls, the city was divided into administrative sectors and neighbourhoods corresponding to parishes, within which under the *millet* system the Greeks conducted their own affairs, as observed by numerous travellers including Byron.

Writers and Visitors
The life of the city in the nearly 400 years of Turkish occupation is difficult to recapture, apart from occasional dramatic moments. The Greek population left little by way of written records. Ottoman archives until recent years have been largely neglected by Greek historians, and for Turkish historians Athens is probably not high on the list of historical priorities. Outsiders have therefore formed their picture largely from the accounts of travellers from western Europe, whose interests included the antiquarian, topographical, military and diplomatic: less so, with some fortunate exceptions, the sociological. Various themes recur: the idle, luxurious, rapacious Turkish governing class; the oppressed, demoralized Greeks, not to be compared with their ancestors; the unrivalled beauty of the monuments; the discomforts and the rewards of travel.

Information about the early Turkish period is sparse, but as travellers began to visit in increasing numbers in the eighteenth century we get a good picture of the externals that struck such visitors. Richard Chandler's visit in 1765 set the scene well:

Athens is not inconsiderable, either in extent or in the number of inhabitants. Corsairs infesting it, the avenues were secured, and in 1676 the gates were regularly shut after sunset. It is now open again, but several of the gateways remain, and a guard of Turks patroles at midnight. The houses are mean and straggling, many with large areas of court in front of them. In the lanes, the high walls on each side, which are uncommonly white-washed, reflect strongly the heat of the sun. The streets are very irregular; and anciently were neither uniform nor handsome. They have water conveyed in channels from Mount Hymettus, and in the bazar or market-place is a large fountain. The Turks have several mosques and public baths. The Greeks have convents for men and women; with many churches, in which service is regularly performed; and besides these, they have numerous oratories or chapels, some in ruins or consisting of bare walls, frequented only on the anniversaries of the saints to whom they are dedicated. A portrait of the owner on board is placed in them on that occasion, and removed when the solemnity of the day is over.

Besides the more stable antiquities, many detached pieces are found in the town, by the fountains, in the streets, the walls, the houses and churches. Many columns occur; with some maimed statues; and pedestals, several with inscriptions, and almost buried in earth...

The Acropolis is now a fortress... The garrison consists of a few Turks, who reside there with their families. These hollow nightly from their situation above the town, to approve their vigilance. Their houses overlook the city, plain, and gulf, but the situation is as airy as pleasant and attended with so many inconveniences, that those who are able, and have the option, prefer living below when not on duty. The rock is destitute of water fit for drinking, and supplies are daily carried up in earthen jars. The spectator views with concern the marble ruins intermixed with mean flat-roofed cottages, and extant amid the rubbish the sad memorials of a nobler people...

Chandler was tasked by the Society of Dilettanti, a society of well-born collectors and connoisseurs who funded his journey, to report on the state of the antiquities. Preceding the romantic movement, he was not so interested in his own reactions, for example to the Acropolis, as nineteenth-century travellers, though he was very ready to describe the physical inconveniences of eighteenth-century travel, such as the fleas and bugs. He opened up several themes that became commonplaces of description. One was the conversion of the Tower of the Winds in the Plaka (the combined water clock and sundial of Andronikos Kyrristos) to a Tekke, or place of worship belonging to an order of dervishes. Chandler attended a religious function there, an event which ended with the dervishes' wonderful dance. This was followed by entertainment to pipes and coffee. It became a feature of the traveller's round.

Chandler also commented freely on the character of the Turks and the Greeks, the relations between them, the position of women, and the customs and folk beliefs he came across. He found the Turks of Athens to be in general more polite, social, and affable than was common in that "stately race": "living in more equal terms with their fellow-citizens, and partaking, in some degree, of the Greek character." He saw in them a sense of "habitual superiority", strict honour, punctuality, uprightness in their dealings, narrow-mindedness and avarice. The Greeks on the other hand might be regarded as the representatives of the old Athenians: lively, quick in apprehension, cunning, supple. The Archons, or eight or ten ruling families, were now "mere names, except a tall fur cap, and a fuller and better dress than is worn by the inferior classes". They were shopkeepers, merchants or tax farmers. Both the lordly Turk and the lively Greek neglected pasturage and agriculture, leaving these to the tough Albanians, who were "inured early to fatigue and the sun", and "hardy and robust". The wheel turns: every village in Greece now has its group of Albanian immigrants who have arrived since the early 1990s, some working in seasonal agricultural labour, others in construction, all of them inured early to fatigue and the sun.

The picture that emerges from Chandler and later travellers is of a small, sleepy Greek Ottoman town, largely cut off from the great movements of ideas and of commerce. The population was around 12,000 in the later Ottoman period. Greeks (Christians) far outnumbered Turks (Muslims), probably by about four to one. There was a substantial minority of Albanians in the town, as well as in the surrounding countryside. Writing of the oppressive regime of Hadji Ali in the late eighteenth century, the Athenian Panagis Skouzes referred to a sprinkling of Muslim gypsies, blacksmiths, and blacks from Ethiopia who made straw mats and rush brooms.

The town had 36 parishes, called the Lower Neighbourhoods, but many more churches and chapels than 36, because of the prevalence in Greece, to which Chandler drew attention, of chapels dedicated to a particular saint, which would be opened and used only on the saint's day. The churches played an important social security role, harbouring the homeless and the poor in little cells in the surrounding gardens.

The place which most attracted visitors was the Bazaar, or market, not far from the Roman Agora and the Library of Hadrian. The Ottoman courts, the residence of the Voyvoda or Governor and the Medresse, the Islamic school of instruction, were nearby. The actual markets, daily, weekly and seasonal, each took place in front of one of the mosques. There were hamams or baths, cafés, and shops. Muslim mosques and religious buildings were mixed with Christian churches and Turkish and Greek housing in the same area.

Towards the end of the Ottoman period, Athens's monuments were put on the intellectual map of western Europe by a number of distinguished traveller-reporters. The most influential of these were James Stuart and Nicholas Revett, who came to Greece in 1751. Like Chandler, they were acting on behalf of the Society of Dilettanti. Their task was to capture and measure the surviving monuments of antiquity for a British readership of aristocrats, connoisseurs, architects, and artists who were becoming more and more interested in Greece. Stuart and Revett made meticulous drawings of the monuments of Athens, not only showing their structure, but faithfully reproducing the current mixture of classical and Turkish in, for example, the Parthenon with its mosque, and the monument of Lysicrates (known then as the Lantern of Demosthenes), which was built into the Capuchin convent. The influence of Stuart and Revett's publication of *The Antiquities of Athens*, which came out in three parts between 1754 and 1794, was immense. You can see it in Greek revival architecture in Edinburgh and throughout Britain. In opening up the rhythms and models of Greek art to Europe they were matched in their impact only by the Parthenon sculptures removed by Lord Elgin, and they had an even greater influence on our built environment.

Chateaubriand and Byron

Apart from Stuart and Revett, the visitors to Ottoman Athens whose writings had the greatest influence were Chateaubriand and Byron. Their descriptions increased the exposure of the city to a European readership that was beginning to take an interest in the political state of Greece as well as its artistic heritage.

Chateaubriand came in 1806. He approached Athens from the Eleusis road. He left us a fine description of the prospect of the city which unfolds as the traveller comes up to the gap in the hills near Daphni:

> *The first thing that struck my eyes was the citadel lit by the rising sun: it was right in front of me, on the other side of the plain, and seemed to be propped up on Mount Hymettus, which formed the background. It exhibited, in a confused mixture, the capitals of the Propylaea, the columns of the Parthenon and of the Erectheum, the embrasures of a wall loaded with canons, the gothic debris of the Christians, and the hovels of the Muslims...*
>
> *At the foot of the Acropolis, Athens was revealed: its flat roofs, inter-mixed with minarets, cypress trees, ruins, isolated columns: the domes of its mosques, crowned with big storks' nests, made an agreeable effect in the sun's rays. But, if one could recognise Athens in its ruins, one could see also, from the general appearance of its architecture and the character of its monuments, that the town of Minerva was no longer inhabited by its own people.*
>
> *We were walking towards this little town of which the population was not even equal to that of a Paris faubourg, but whose renown equals that of the Roman empire.*

With such sententious thoughts—for he was always conscious of the effect he wanted to produce on his readers—Chateaubriand proceeded across the plain and through the olive grove to Athens. Here he was entertained and instructed by M. Fauvel, the well-known French consul who features in virtually every traveller's account of his period, as guide to and collector of antiquities. As they walked through the Bazaar, "everyone greeted M Fauvel, and each one wanted to know who I was."

Though parts of Chateaubriand's reportage are second-hand or invented, I think we can take it that his account of Athens is not. It is well done. He commented that the first thing to strike the visitor was the lovely colour of the monuments of Athens, a colour of ripe heads of corn, or of autumn leaves, imparted by the clear sky and brilliant sun of Greece to the marble of Paros and Penteli, by contrast with the black or greenish tones of the rain and smoke-begrimed buildings of northern Europe. Justice, harmony and simplicity of proportion came next, and then the appropriate relation of the monuments to the natural sites and to their uses.

In order to describe the view from the Acropolis, Chateaubriand climbed the minaret belonging to the mosque in the Parthenon, and sat on a broken part of the frieze:

> *Now you must imagine this whole space sometimes bare and covered by yellow heather, sometimes interrupted by bunches of olive trees, squares of barley and rows of vines; you must imagine trunks of columns and chunks of ancient and modern ruins sticking out from the middle of these cultivated patches; whitewashed walls and garden fences across the fields; you must imagine Albanian women scattered through this countryside, drawing water or washing the Turks' clothes*

at the wells; peasants coming and going, leading their donkeys, or carrying provisions to town on their backs; you must suppose all these mountains with beautiful names, all these so famous ruins, all these islands, all these no less famous seas, lit by a brilliant light. I saw, from on the Acropolis, the sun rise between the two summits of Mount Hymettus; the ravens which make their nests around the citadel, but which never fly over it, were gliding above us; their shiny black wings were frosted with pink from the first rays of daylight; columns of light blue smoke rose in the shadow all along the flanks of Hymettus, marking the places of beehives; Athens, the Acropolis and the ruins of the Parthenon were taking on the most beautiful colour of peach blossom; the sculptures of Phidias, struck sideways by a beam of gold, were coming to life and seemed to move on the marble through the mobility of the shadows thrown by their reliefs; in the distance the sea and the port of Piraeus were bathed in white light; and the citadel of Corinth, reflecting the brightness of the new day, shone on the western horizon, like a rock made of fire and purple dye.

The reflections prompted by this remarkable view were, characteristically, of the degradation of present servitude compared with ancient splendour. His consolation was the transience of all mortal things; he too, like the great Greeks who had peopled this citadel, would pass on in his turn. These sombre thoughts did not prevent him from taking a fragment of the marble of the Parthenon with him, as was his practice at every ancient monument he visited.

Byron followed Chateaubriand three years later, a young man, not yet famous, in search of adventure and sexual liberation. He came with his friend John Cam Hobhouse, who left a solid account of Athens in the final years of Ottoman occupation. It is typical of Hobhouse's patient approach that he walked all the way round the city wall of Hadji Ali Haseki and recorded that it took him 47 minutes. You can see in Thekla Street in modern Psyrri the site of the house where Byron and Hobhouse first stayed in 1809, with the family of the widow of a British consul, Theodora Makri. The house was easily distinguished by the flagpole from which the consul had flown the British flag. There were half a dozen lemon trees in the courtyard from which they plucked fruit to season their pilaff. Here Byron flirted with the three pre-nubile daughters, the elder of whom, Teresa, was the Maid of Athens of his poem:

Maid of Athens, ere we part,
Give, oh, give me back my heart!

The romance is tarnished, and the story made more true to life, by the information that Teresa's mother tried to sell her to Byron. In later years Teresa became a feature of Athens. More than one western visitor reported how he had been introduced to her, by then a matronly figure with nothing of the Maid of Athens about her.

On this first visit, Byron did not stay long. He went off to explore the Peloponnese, visited Smyrna and the Troad, and swam across the Hellespont in imitation of Leander, a considerable athletic feat. On his return to Athens, Hobhouse having left for home, he settled in the Capuchin Convent in the Plaka. It was a favourite stopping point for British travellers in a city lacking hotels. The Catholic missionaries were glad of the company and no doubt of the extra revenue. Here Byron spent the winter in company with "many English" and in "balls and a variety of fooleries with the females of Athens". He enjoyed it, reporting to Hobhouse that he was most auspiciously settled in the Convent, which was commodious and by no means solitary: "We have nothing but riot from noon to night... Intrigue flourishes: the old woman, Theresa's mother, was mad enough to imagine I was going to marry the girl; but I have better amusement." Byron took his daily ride to Piraeus for an hour's swimming.

Besides the tomfooleries at the Convent, Byron was educating himself and closely observing what was going on in Athenian society. He wrote to his mother on 14 January 1811, "Here I see and have conversed with French, Italians, Germans, Danes, Greeks, Turks, Americans, etc., etc., etc.; and without losing sight of my own, I can judge of the countries and manners of others. Where I see the superiority of England (which, by the by, we are a good deal mistaken about in many things), I am pleased, and where I find her inferior, I am at least enlightened."

Byron summed up his impressions of Athens in the Notes on the present state of Greece that he wrote in early 1811 and appended to

Canto Two of *Childe Harold*, the poem which made him famous overnight. He was not particularly interested in ancient monuments (though Elgin's depredations excited his scorn) but he responded to the combination of climate, people, politics and antique associations:

> *Setting aside the magic of the name, and all those associations which it would be pedantic and superfluous to recapitulate, the very situation of Athens would render it the favourite of all who have eyes for art or nature. The climate, to me at least, appeared a perpetual spring; during eight months I never passed a day without being as many hours on horse-back: rain is extremely rare, snow never lies in the plains, and a cloudy day is an agreeable rarity... 'Athens,' says a celebrated topographer, 'is still the most polished city of Greece.' Perhaps it may be of Greece, but not of the Greeks; for Joannina in Epirus is universally allowed, amongst themselves, to be superior in the wealth, refinement, learning, and dialect of its inhabitants. The Athenians are remarkable for their cunning; and the lower orders are not improperly characterised in that proverb, which classes them with 'the Jews of Salonica, and the Turks of the Negropont.'*

The picture Byron left of the city is of a small, argumentative, self-satisfied foreign community, constantly running down the Greeks. "Among the various foreigners resident in Athens, French, Italians, Germans, Ragusans, &c, there was never a difference of opinion in their estimate of the Greek character, though on all other topics they disputed with great acrimony." The artistic and civilized Fauvel, who had lived in Athens for thirty years, declared that the Greeks did not deserve to be emancipated, reasoning on the grounds of the "national and individual depravity". A French merchant declared they were the same *canaille* (rabble) that existed in the days of Themistocles. Byron resisted this kind of talk, because, like Gladstone later, he recognized that the "faults" of the Greeks were the product of their situation, and that the remedy was independence.

> *'They are ungrateful, notoriously, abominably ungrateful!'—this is the general cry. Now, in the name of Nemesis! for what are they to be grateful? Where is the human being that ever conferred a benefit on Greek or Greeks? They are to be grateful to the Turks for their fetters, and to the*

Franks for their broken promises and lying counsels. They are to be grateful to the artist who engraves their ruins, and to the antiquary who carries them away; to the traveller whose janissary flogs them, and to the scribbler whose journal abuses them! This is the amount of their obligations to foreigners.

A few weeks later, in a note datelined the Franciscan Convent, 23 January 1811, Byron went further:

To talk, as the Greeks do, of their rising again to their pristine superiority, would be ridiculous... but there seems to be no very great obstacle, except in the apathy of the Franks, to their becoming an useful dependency, or even a free state with a proper guarantee;—under correction, however, be it spoken, for many and well-informed men doubt the practicability even of this.

A free state with a proper guarantee was exactly what Greece, with Byron's unstinting help in the War of Independence, was to become. But he was not to see it. He left Athens for good in May 1811. His return to Greece in 1823, by way of Cephalonia, ended with his death in April 1824 in Missolonghi of fever and the butchery of his own doctors, who bled him almost to death. He is commemorated in Athens by a street in the Plaka, a refugee neighbourhood below Mount Hymettus, and a football team. There was formerly also a Byron Professor of English at the University of Athens.

Greek against Turk

While Byron sweated out his life in the feverish climate of Missolonghi, Athens became one of the cockpits of the war between Greeks and Turks. The Greek insurgents had laid siege to the Acropolis soon after the outbreak of the war in March 1821, but the siege was relieved in July by the Turkish commander Omer Vrionis, whose men ferociously picked off Greeks whom they found isolated in the Attic plain in sorties or "Greek hunts". After Omer's departure in November, successive Greek attempts on the Acropolis failed. The fortifications proved their strength. Greek forces' attempts on the citadel concentrated on the southwest end, through assault, mining operations and artillery bombardment. But in the end it was starvation and lack of water that led the Turks to capitulate in June 1822, after the Greeks had taken the well south of the Acropolis and polluted it.

Following the Turkish capitulation, negotiated on honourable terms, about half of the Turkish garrison were massacred. It was not the last time that this was to happen, in a war of great brutality. The rest were evacuated on foreign transport ships. The devious Captain Odysseus Androutsos, commander of Greek forces in Eastern Roumeli, took charge of the Acropolis; but following a complex series of events which included his collaboration with the Turks, he found himself imprisoned in the Frankish Tower, where he spent months in chains before being murdered and thrown down from the tower onto the bastion of Wingless Victory. His story is told by David Brewer in his book about the War of Independence, *Flame of Freedom* (2001). So ended Odysseus.

In 1826 Missolonghi fell to the Turks. By now the Greeks were confined to a few strongholds in the Peloponnese and to Athens. In June 1826 Turkish forces under Reshid Pasha set up quarters in Patissia and invested the Acropolis again. Makriyiannis was one of the Greek garrison and played a gallant part in the defence. He described these events in his memoirs. His account of his quarrel and reconciliation with Gouras, the commander of the garrison, the song he sang one evening which made Gouras groan aloud, and Gouras' subsequent death, is one of the most moving passages in Greek literature.

The attempts of the Greeks to relieve the Acropolis were a catalogue of military errors and confusion, caused by the tactical disagreements of the leading philhellene and Greek commanders, Cochrane and Church, Gordon and Karaiskakis. The climax was the shambles of the Greek attack of 6 May 1827 across the plain from Phaleron, in which Reshid's counterattack killed some 1,500 out of a force of 2,500 men. At that point the Greeks in their turn decided to negotiate an honourable capitulation. The garrison marched down from the Acropolis on 5 June 1827. Thus when independence was secured, the Acropolis of Athens was the last part of the territory of the new Greek state to remain under Turkish occupation.

The events of the war had confirmed both the symbolic importance of Athens and the continuing strategic value of the

Acropolis. Makriyiannis wrote that whoever holds the Frankish Tower and the storehouses has the citadel in his hands. The events in Athens also confirm the pain and brutality of this war. For the wounded there was little hope: "the lice fought for mastery with the worms." The heads of victims were cut off and displayed as proofs of their despatch. It was a life and death struggle in which even Makriyiannis, who well understood the symbolic value of antiquities to the Greek nation, was prepared to blow himself, the Turks and the Parthenon to smithereens if that was the only way to avoid the shame of defeat.

Such considerations were read two ways by the Greeks: as an argument that Athens should become the capital and strategic centre of the state, and as an argument for the reverse, on the grounds that the antiquities of Athens would hardly survive the further assaults that could be expected on the capital city.

CHAPTER NINE

Athens Revived

"The court has removed here, the country is beautiful, climate fine, government fixed, steamboats are running, all the world is coming, and lots must rise."
> J. L. Stevens, *Incidents of Travel in the Russian and Turkish Empires*, 1839

"I have got a map with squares, fountains, theatres, public gardens and Places d'Othon marked out; but they only exist in the paper capital— the wretched tumble-down wooden one boasts of none."
> William Makepeace Thackeray, *Journey from Cornhill to Grand Cairo*, 1845

The temple of Hephaestus at the western limit of the Agora had served as a church, of St George, in Ottoman times. Protestant visitors unfortunate enough to die in Athens were buried here. It was here that the notables of Athens gathered on 13 December 1834 formally to welcome their new King, Otho of Bavaria. He came, with his retinue of advisers, to take possession of Athens and to inaugurate it as the capital of the newly independent Greek kingdom.

The city was hardly a city, more a rough country town, stretched out across the lower slopes to the north of the Acropolis. It was still surrounded by the wall that had been built in the 1780s by the tyrannical Governor Hadji Ali Hasekis. The city had changed hands twice during the war. It had been the site of fierce siege warfare. Houses not pillaged for stone had been destroyed by artillery and fire. Then in 1830 a large tract of the great olive grove lying between Athens and the sea had been destroyed by fire.

When Benjamin Disraeli visited Athens in November 1830, he described every house as roofless. The windows were without glass. The archaeologist Ludwig Ross, arriving in 1832, found Piraeus harbour deserted, with only a dozen wooden huts for Turkish customs and Greek muleteers as signs of activity. There was no housing. (Nine years later Hans Christian Andersen counted about 120 houses.) Transport between Piraeus and Athens was by two-wheeled carts over rutted tracks. The first four-wheeled vehicle was introduced in 1834. The French poet Alphonse Lamartine, like Chateaubriand no mean exponent of sententious rhetoric, painted a grim picture of the "sombre, sad, black, arid, desolate" Attic land, pronouncing unpromisingly that for poet and painter "c'est fini." This was in 1832.

Around the same time the traveller Christopher Wordsworth, nephew of the poet, future Bishop of Lincoln and headmaster of Harrow School, confirmed this picture of desolation in his *Athens and Attica: Journal of a Residence There* (1837):

> *The town of Athens is now lying in ruins. The streets are almost deserted: nearly all the houses are without roofs. The churches are reduced to bare walls and heaps of stones and mortar. There is but one church in which the service is performed. A few new wooden houses, one or two of more solid structure, and the two lines of planked sheds which form the bazar are all the inhabited dwellings that Athens can now boast. So slowly does it recover from the effects of the late war.*
>
> *In this state of modern desolation, the grandeur of the ancient buildings which still survive here is more striking: their preservation is more wonderful. There is now scarcely any building in Athens in as perfect a state as the Temple of Theseus [now known as the temple of Hephaestus]. The least ruined objects here, are some of the ruins themselves.*

For all the dereliction of Athens, canny Greeks had already started to repopulate it. Wordsworth conceded that it was the most secure place in Greece, which was not saying much given the rampant brigandage in Attica, where the notorious Captain Vassos and his men extorted goods and money freely from farmers and travellers. From 1830 on people began returning from Aegina and rebuilding their houses. It was a reasonable bet that Athens, rather than Corinth or any of the other candidates, would become the capital of the new state.

For the time being however, Athens was an island of continuing

Turkish occupation in an expanse of liberated territory stretching south of Thermopylae. The centre of interest of the town was the Bazaar, the old Turkish market. Wordsworth wrote:

The Bazaar or Market at Athens is a long street, which is now the only one there of any importance. It has no foot-pavement; there is a gutter in the middle, down which, in this wintry weather, the water runs in copious torrents. The houses are generally patched together with planks and plaster. Looking up the street, you command a view of the commodities with which this Athenian market is now supplied. Barrels of black caviar, small pocket-looking glasses in red pasteboard cases, onions, tobacco piled up in brown heaps, black olives, figs strung together upon a rush, rices, pipes with amber mouth-pieces and brown clay bowls, rich stuffs, and silver-chased pistols, dirks, belts, and embroidered waistcoats... Here there are no books, no lamps, no windows, no carriages, no news-papers, no post-office. The letters which arrived here a few days since from Napoli [Nauplion], after having been publicly cried in the street, if they were not claimed by the parties to whom they were addressed, were committed to the flames.

Wordsworth's description still conveys something of a provincial market, in say Chania, Arta or Ioannina, whereas the modern Athens vegetable market on Piraeus Street now offers a different, but equally exotic, selection of produce, gorgeous in its abundance and variety.

Wordsworth recognized that his visit to Athens in 1832 coincided with the end of an epoch, and took this as the occasion for an outpouring of nostalgia:

The Muezzin still mounts the scaffold in the bazar here to call the Mussulman to prayer at the stated hours; a few Turks still doze in the archways of the Acropolis, or recline while smoking their pipes, and lean-ing with their backs against the rusty cannon which are planted on the battlements of its walls; the Athenian peasant, as he drives his laden mule from Hymettus through the eastern gate of the town, still flings his small bundle of thyme and brushwood, from the load which he brings on his mule's back, as a tribute to the Mussulman toll-gatherer, who sits at that entrance of the town; and a few days ago the cannon of the Acropolis fired the signal of the conclusion of the Turkish Ramazam—the last which will ever be celebrated in Athens.

A Greek commissioner arrived to take over the city. A company of 300 Bavarian troops entered the city on 1 April 1833, and on 12 April, Good Friday, the Turkish garrison departed from the Acropolis, to be replaced by the Bavarians, who gave a lunch in the Parthenon for the last Turkish governor. The "sacred rock" was liberated.

Among the foreigners who were there from the beginning, the winter of 1832-3, were George Finlay, who had bought a house in 1828, two American missionaries, King and Hill, Wordsworth, Ludwig Ross, the architect Schaubert, and a sprinkling of other artists and travellers. There was only one hotel, the Hotel d'Europe, run by an Italian philhellene and his Austrian wife, both of whom were one-eyed. Life proceeded on its unhurried way, in a curious post-war symbiosis of Greeks, Turks and foreigners. The Greek elders assured local government. The Greek bishop did his best to reconcile quarrelling factions.

Otho's Capital

Otho had paid his first visit in May 1833, to examine the antiquities and scout out a future residence. He came overland and was met by a delegation of Athenians at Daphni, well outside the city. A large crowd welcomed him at the olive grove. He made three more visits later in the year, pursuing his search for the site of a palace. In the early autumn he came by sea, riding up from Piraeus where the welcoming delegation presented him with an owl, the symbol of Athens, and an olive branch (his future wife Amalia was also welcomed with a live owl on her arrival three years later). He entered the city by the Arch of Hadrian, which was adorned with a wreath bearing the words "This is Athens, the city of Theseus and of Hadrian, now of Otho" (the arch itself bears two inscriptions, made at the time it was completed: on the west side "This is Athens, formerly the city of Theseus," and on the east "And this is the city of Hadrian, not of Theseus").

In October 1834 the Greek government in Nauplion published a momentous decree ordaining that as of 13 December the king would

move his residence from Nauplion to Athens and Athens would become the seat of the king and the capital of the state. Otho rode up from Piraeus on the appointed day to the Church of St George in the temple of Hephaestus. A solemn *Te Deum* was sung. One of the assembled notables read out an address. Otho then proceeded to the house of Kontostavlos, on the site where the Old Parliament building now stands, which he had bought to serve as his temporary residence pending the construction of a palace appropriate to his status. He lived there until 1837. The three-man Regency, the court, the diplomatic ministers of the foreign powers, the government ministries, and the Holy Synod followed him to Athens. Immediately there was a run on rentable property. Athens as political and economic capital had arrived.

The housing problem was acute. In anticipation of the move to Athens, a committee of officials had drawn up a list of Athenian buildings to be used as government offices and official buildings. The list contained 73 named houses. Most of them were quite small, with only three or four rooms. A few had more. It was clear that satisfactory accommodation for ministries, law courts, prisons, and all that went with the status of capital, was simply unavailable. Officials had to make use of what they could get, pending the construction of proper buildings, which was much delayed. Ministries moved from place to place. Everything was provisional.

Buildings such as Turkish mosques and the Medresse, which might have been suitable, for example for the courts, were situated in the area north of the Acropolis that the government designated as an archaeological space for excavation, in which there must be no building or alterations of existing buildings. The government therefore eventually decided to adapt four ruined Christian churches to serve as courts, using local Greek architects so as to save time, although they recognized that this would mean that the work would be imperfect.

Planning the New Athens
Othonian Athens in its early days was an exciting place of growth, change, destruction, and creation both material and ideological. The adoption of Athens as capital led to a construction boom and a period of high rentals. Residents, especially recently arrived Greeks from abroad, were unceremoniously pushed out to make room for public bodies. The owners of the few well appointed houses, such as Negrepontis, who let his house to the British minister, did well. It served as the British Legation for only a short time, but it still stands, in downtown Athens, pockmarked with bullet holes from the civil war.

The British minister Dawkins and his colleagues from France, Russia and Austria, carried enormous political weight in this small, gossipy society. Politics revolved around them, with factions composing English, French and Russian political parties. They in their different interests tried to influence the king and his advisers to support their views, while the king, struggling to escape their constricting influence, identified himself with his people's aggressive nationalism. Gradually, in the face of continual criticism from outsiders, especially the British, Otho and his advisers and the intellectual leaders of the Greek people engaged in the formation of the modern nation and the construction of a worthy capital.

Otho, his father Ludwig, and his Bavarians were European modernizers inspired by ancient Greece. They saw antiquity as vital to Greece's prospects, and they set out to put order into the language, education, society and built environment of the new state. Their model for the planning of new towns, as at Sparta, Patras and other sites, was the rectangular grid plan with broad streets and squares, which was modern but also harked back to an ancient Greek model. But Athens, the new capital, was a greater challenge. It had to be a worthy capital city, and the ancient ruins must be satisfactorily incorporated in it. The first planners to tackle this stimulating task were a Greek and a German, Stamatios Kleanthes and Edouard Schaubert.

Kleanthes and Schaubert had met in Berlin at the Architectural Academy, where they studied under the distinguished neoclassicist Karl Friedrich Schinkel, himself to play a part in Athenian planning. Kleanthes was a Greek from Macedonia, educated at Bucharest, Leipzig and Berlin. Schaubert was a Silesian German from Breslau (Wroclaw in modern Poland). The two architectural graduates made their way to Greece by a circuitous route, taking in Rome. They arrived in Aegina in 1830, presenting themselves to President Capodistria. "In this serendipitous fashion," writes Eleni Bastea, historian of the making of modern Athens, "they became the first civil architects of the new state." As such, they started to survey the city and its suburbs, drawing on earlier work by the topographer Colonel Leake.

In May 1832, before the formal decision to make Athens the capital city, the Greek provisional government invited Kleanthes and Schaubert to make a plan for Athens "equal with the fame and brilliance of the city and worthy of the century in which we live". They submitted their proposal to the government in December 1832, and it was approved by Royal Decree. The memorandum of explanation they put to the government survives. They described the existing city: about 6,000 inhabitants, plentiful water, narrow crooked streets not more than thirteen feet in width, the houses mostly in ruins, and 115 small churches of which only 30 were in reasonable condition. They took as a working hypothesis that Athens would become the capital, and therefore planned for a city of 35,000-40,000 people, with room for further expansion.

Everything pointed to the plateau north of the Acropolis, where there was ample space, healthy air, easy access for building, and convenient possibilities for drainage and sewerage. Moving the city north would have the additional advantage of leaving the old cities, of Theseus and Hadrian, unbuilt upon and therefore available for future excavation. Kleanthes and Schaubert envisaged removing the old houses and huts on the north slopes of the Acropolis, in the Plaka and Agora areas, "freeing the antiquities from their surroundings" so as to display them in all their beauty. A picturesque Byzantine church would be left here and there to provide a contrast (a telling indication of the relative undervaluing of Byzantium at this period). The space between the monuments would be landscaped and planted with trees, creating an unmatchable open-air museum. The idea of the archaeological park was therefore present in the very first plan for Athens.

The best place from which to appreciate the early plans of Athens is the Acropolis, looking north over the Plaka area and the old Ottoman town towards the northern plateau where the modern city was to be built, with the appurtenances of a capital: palace, gardens etc. The plan incorporated the main features of the existing town, and respected the topography. The streets were to be broad, the houses provided with courtyards. There was a place for ministries, the Mint, a senate and parliament, a library, botanical garden, and of course a cathedral. The plan provided for commerce and culture. It was rational, progressive and idealistic.

Within a year, reacting to criticisms of the plan, a revision had been commissioned by Otho's father Ludwig, from the well-known architect Leo von Klenze, who arrived in Greece in July 1834. Klenze modified the Kleanthes-Schaubert plan in a number of respects, but kept the basic shape of a triangle perched above the Acropolis (on a map with north at the top), with its apex at the present day Omonia (Concord) Square, known then as Otho Square. Thus the original plan still determined the basic shape of the new city, and with all its modifications over the years it still does.

Planning, however, was one thing. Implementation was another. It depended on a complex balance of forces, involving the government, the Greek and Bavarian engineers charged with putting the plan into action, the landowners whose properties and wealth were affected, and the general public, which made its voice heard by lobbying and through the media. Government weakness and instability militated against consistency and firm decisions. There were frequent new partial plans and modifications. In some ways this process of change was beneficial. It meant, for example, that some Byzantine churches which had been marked for demolition were in the end saved (though all too many were destroyed). Citizens' reactions also helped to adapt the plan to human needs. Some modifications were approved in advance by law, others were carried out illegally, thus inaugurating the practice of building "outside the plan", hoping for subsequent legalisation.

Gradually, the new capital city took shape. It remained for years a rough, tough place to live, with elements of a frontier town. The roads were unmade, causing dust to rise in clouds on a windy day in summer, and mud to clog the axles in winter. Ladies going out to parties in the evenings would ride on donkeys, or walk with big Turkish boots, to avoid the worst of the mud. Floods helped to spread fevers, which proved fatal to many of the Bavarians and some eminent Greeks. Justice was also rough. Property owners were liable to find their properties requisitioned for public use.

In 1844 Thackeray concluded that it was a farce to make this place into a kingly capital. But others responded to the excitement of a new adventure. Visiting in 1841, Hans Andersen spent an agreeable month and mingled with the society of the little town: Hansen, Dr Ulrichs, Ross, the Danish consul Travers, and the court chaplain Lüth. The road up to Athens through the olive grove was now a fine highway, not the bog it had been when he last came. ("It was very dusty, but it was, to be sure, classical dust.") He found French and German newspapers, cafés as good as in Vienna or Berlin, and a performance of Italian opera—one act from *Belisario* and one from *The Barber of Seville*. "Imagine for yourself a town built in a hurry, as if for a big market, and that the market is in full swing—and there you have the new Athens." Hansen told him that there were really no artisans: there were farmers, soldiers and robbers, who now and then picked up a hammer, watched for a while and thus turned themselves into smiths or bricklayers. He was teaching the students to draw, and they were showing remarkable comprehension in this as in foreign languages. The only thing to mar Andersen's enjoyment was that his penis gave him constant trouble.

One of the causes of tension was the new science of archaeology. The philhellenic Bavarians and the ancestor-loving Greeks saw archaeology as an essential tool in the recovery and presentation of ancient Greece to modern Europe, but also in the construction of the political and cultural identity of the modern Hellenic state. As we have seen, the site that above all others attracted their attention was the Acropolis. The purification of the site, and its incorporation into the new state's idea of itself, began even before Athens became the capital city.

There were at least two possible ways of looking at the Acropolis: as the central feature of a new, European capital city, to be landscaped, built on and beautified; and as the symbolic centre of reborn Hellenism, to be sanctified and purged of foreign elements. The first was a romantic architect's dream, the second a nationalist dream in tune with the times, leading by a natural progression to the site, half holy place, half tourist's paradise, that exists today. A third way, to treat the place as a multicultural museum of its own history, preserving the classical ruins, the Christian relics, the Florentine tower, and the Turkish mosque, simply did not occur to the planners and archaeologists. Their interest was severely focused on the ancient.

The first approach was actually tried, by Karl Friedrich Schinkel, the teacher of Schaubert and Kleanthes. He was invited by Otho's elder brother, the Crown Prince Maximilian, to redesign the Acropolis, to house a Royal Palace. The conceit may seem strange today, and Schinkel's plan was certainly bold. It provided for a long colonnaded palace to the south of the Parthenon, and a hippodrome on the other side, in the space between Parthenon and Erectheum. There were gardens and colonnades, and a great statue of Athena. Everything was used and incorporated in a grand architect's scheme. His dramatic architectural drawings are much reproduced and shown on the walls of smart Athenian hotels. Schinkel never visited Greece, so it is not surprising that there was something unreal about his approach. His scheme would have run into practical obstacles, over water supply, and the prior excavation of the building site. Klenze, who knew the ground, called it a "charming Midsummer Night's Dream of a great architect", which seems about right.

The Schinkel scheme was never adopted. King Ludwig, who still pulled the strings, ruled firmly that the monuments of antiquity should have priority and that nothing new should be built on the Acropolis. When he visited Athens in the winter of 1835-6, he and Otho chose a site for the Royal Palace, not where Kleanthes and Schaubert or Klenze had put it, but where it now stands, overlooking Constitution Square, with good views towards the Acropolis, the ruined temple of Olympian Zeus, and Lycabettus. The German F. von Gärtner was chosen as architect.

The Plaka

The core of the city was the area now known as Plaka, with its narrow winding streets, old churches, and Turkish and Roman monuments. Then, as now, it was the quarter of Athens with the most picturesque character. With the development of new Athens following Klenze's city plan, Plaka was converted into the "old town", a place of winding, narrow streets and old houses facing in towards courtyards. Under the early development schemes it was largely preserved. It therefore attracted residents such as General Church and George Finlay, who had two houses built there.

The Plaka proper was the small area near the monument of Lysicrates, marked apparently by a stone slab (*plaka*) at the junction of Tripodon, Adrianou and Kydathinaion streets. The broader area now known as the Plaka, stretching down on the northern and eastern sides of the Acropolis, as far as the boundary of the Agora in the west, Monastiraki Square in the north, and Philellinon Street in the east, was known as Alikokko until the early twentieth century, and was one of the divisions into which the Ottoman city was divided. With the coming of independence, the area more or less maintained its Ottoman character and shape, including the bazaar areas which developed in the second half of the Ottoman period, until they were wiped out by a great fire in 1884. This opened up Hadrian's Library and the Roman Agora for excavation, and pushed the main commercial centre of the city northwards to the area around Athinas Street.

The Plaka is still the best quarter of Athens for a stroll through history, and much more pleasant for this purpose than it was some years ago. It is the only quarter of Athens in which buildings and monuments from every stage of the city's history are concentrated within a few hundred square yards, the classical (the monument of Lysicrates), the Roman (the Roman Agora, the Library of Hadrian and the Tower of the Winds), the Turkish (the Fetije Mosque and the Tsistaraki Mosque on Monastiraki Square), together with a profusion of Byzantine churches from various periods, old vernacular housing and neoclassical nineteenth- and twentieth-century houses. The area is dotted with cafés and tavernas, and punctuated by small museums, of folk art, musical instruments, pottery and antiquities, most of them set in fine old houses. Some of the lower Plaka area, especially Adrianou Street, has surrendered to tourism. Its frontage, beneath some good solid old houses, consists of one tourist shop after another, selling gold and silver jewellery, obscene postcards of satyrs with enormous phalluses, books on sex life in ancient Greece, calendars of cats and kittens, dolls, and imitation ancient Greek pots.

The way for the tourist or resident to appreciate the richness of Plaka is to walk with a good book in hand, such as David Rupp's *Athenian Walks*, or Jim Antoniou's *Plaka*—if it comes back into print.

Some of the more exotic and interesting areas in which to stroll and shop are to be found on the lower edges of the Plaka. Just above Monastiraki Square, up against the west side of the Library of Hadrian, African street traders sell every imaginable form of dark glasses, incense, trinkets and gaudy mobile phone covers. Above the Library are the wicker shops from which you could economically equip an apartment with chairs, or buy a cheap suitcase that would split apart on the quayside at Patras. In Pandrosou Street in the old days you could buy leather sandals or shoes for a few drachmas, or have a tall pair of black Cretan boots made up for you. Hephaestou Street, as the name suggests, was full of metal work. Now it consists mainly of shops selling army surplus and every variety and colour of bead. In Avyssinia Square, off Hephaestou, is the antique flea market, particularly ripe for bargains in the period of new building in the 1960s, when old houses were being cleared daily prior to destruction. Further east in the little streets between the cathedral and the Acropolis are ecclesiastical shops where priests can buy vestments and plate for their churches, and visitors can commission reproductions of old Byzantine icons of much better quality than they would find in the tourist shops.

The Anaphiotika

In upper Plaka, above the din and clatter of commerce, the quarter known as the Anaphiotika hangs as high above the old town as it is possible to live. Looking down from the belvedere on the Acropolis, you can distinguish a group of small, huddled white-washed houses on the north-east slope, right up against the almost vertical wall of the rock. It is one of the more fascinating survivals of old Athens.

Anaphi is a small island a few miles east of Santorini in the Cyclades. The men of the Cyclades, and Anaphi in particular, were master builders. They were drawn to Athens by the building boom of the Othonian period, finding work on the Royal Palace and other public projects, living rough on the northeastern margins of the city. As the city plan was pushed outwards and rents increased within the area of planned building, the Anafiots looked for new quarters. Legend has it that they saw in the precipitous slopes of the Acropolis an image of their steep Cycladic homeland. Two men were the first to build themselves houses, above the then building line of the Plaka, taking advantage of the customary Greek law which provides that a house built illegally and topped with its roof within the night will escape demolition once day breaks.

The original Kleanthes-Schaubert town plan had left the northern slopes of the Acropolis outside the area designated for building, for later archaeological excavation. But the state lacked the money to conduct widespread excavations, and the pressures to build were too strong to be resisted. A small number of sites were designated for excavation between Adrianou and Hephaestou Street. Outside these restricted sites the state permitted construction in the Plaka area on the condition that in twenty years time, should it require a plot for archaeological purposes, the newly erected house must be demolished at the owner's expense. The Anaphiotika settlement thus grew up in the 1860s in a state of uncertainty, with the threat of eviction and demolition hanging over every house. The same applied to the wider Plaka area. In the event, only the Agora was requisitioned for excavation, late in the day. But the archaeologists' dream of getting at the underlying ruins remained until well into the second half of the twentieth century.

The Anaphiotika grew between two churches, St George of the Rock and St Symeon which the men of Anaphi found on the slope and restored and adapted. Between these markers about a hundred modest whitewashed stone and plaster houses were built, adapted to the curves and crannies of the steep slope. They lacked utilities. The kitchens and toilets were out in the yards. The people of Anaphi made use of the narrow streets to extend the outdoor living space of their households. They were like guest workers, who acquired a settled place in the life of the city but remained marginalized, in their own separate quarter, and regarded by respectable Athenian society as a blot on the face of the Acropolis. The story of their precarious existence, and the tensions between them and the municipal and archaeological authorities has been told by Roxane Kaftantzoglou in her book *Under the Shadow of the Acropolis,* based on interviews with the inhabitants in the late 1990s.

The Anaphiotika quarter was a poor vernacular settlement on the margins of the most sacred site of the new nation, the Acropolis. It flew in the face of developing ideas about the nature and proper management of this site. The archaeologists and planners wanted the Acropolis to be a permanent, sacred space and object of respect, separated from everyday life. At an early date access to the site was controlled, and patrolled by guards, as it had been for different reasons in Ottoman times. By extension, the areas around the Acropolis should be kept free of people and their day to day activities. The sheep seen grazing beneath the Acropolis in early photographs were an exotic deviation.

Sociologists see this process, in their characteristic language, as a disciplinary practice in the discourse of modernity, a tidying-up of real life in order to create a disciplined Hellenic society and space. The early planners were embarrassed by huts and shanties north of the Acropolis and wanted to remove them. Successive plans for an archaeological park round the Acropolis, following that of Ross, saw it in terms of landscaped space with tree plantings and the occasional preserved Byzantine church. Most of the literary and architectural establishment was unsympathetic to the Anaphiotika until the late twentieth century. The élite kept pressing the government to remove the settlement and make way for archaeology.

Dimitrios Vikelas wrote in 1897 that remnants of the old Turkish town and more recent hovels piled up more recently on the flanks of the rock spoiled the view of the Acropolis, but assured his readers that they were already condemned and that the plans were ready to clear the slope of the accumulated rubbish and unsightly buildings. But somehow the settlement survived. It seems to have remained essentially a Cycladic island settlement until around the time of the First World War, after which the composition of the inhabitants began to change. But throughout they showed a fierce independence and resistance to attempts by the Municipality or the archaeologists to dispossess them. As late as the 1970s plans were still being made to expropriate the houses. In the end, most of them were preserved by decision of the city council, though the inner section was demolished to make room for a path around the Acropolis.

What seems to have affronted the planners was not only that the Anaphiotika somehow contradicted and insulted the sacred Acropolis, but that the settlement was new ("nothing to do with the old town") and illegal. Up to the 1960s, while some had started to admire the houses' vernacular style and the plasticity of their architecture, architects were still talking of the filthy state of the area, its disrepair, the smells and the bad water, and archaeologists of the need to clear the area and dig. But the inhabitants managed to see off the planners (or some of them did—others allowed themselves to be bought out in the 1970s) and the Anaphiotika quarter has now become a part of picturesque old Athens which people want to see preserved. Photographers capture the geraniums and carnations flowering in old tin cans, the cats scurrying across tiny courtyards or sunning themselves on walls, the fugitive charm of the old.

Constitution Square

Constitution Square (Syntagma), which featured in the early city plans, is at the centre of the civic life of the modern city. It is here that people have gathered to hear of wars and rumours of wars, coups d'état have taken place, riots and demonstrations have started, political leaders have addressed mass rallies.

On the northern side stands the monumental Hotel Grande Bretagne, a house before it was a hotel, from early days one of the features of Athens, and currently refurbished in luxurious style for the 2004 Olympic Games. Advertisements in neon light up the lower, western side of the square, from which Ermou Street leads down to Monastiraki. On the eastern, upper, side of the square stands the Royal Palace of which the two kings laid the foundation stone in 1835, the same year that Otho married Amalia, daughter of the Grand Duke of Oldenburg. It was transformed into the present parliament building in the 1930s. In front of it is the monument of the unknown soldier, a late addition (1929-30). It is directly below the west front of the building, and its setting, in the form of a wall inscribed with the battle honours of Greece, cuts across the lower part of the façade. The sculpture itself, of a reclining nude figure in relief designed by Kostas Dimitriades, was controversial. Two Evzones stand guard, wearing their traditional kilts, leggings and clogs. Every so often they change the guard, making their slow loping march.

The Royal Palace/Parliament Building has had a bad press from travellers and domestic critics, but it served its purpose as a large (too large?) and dignified symbol, first of the monarchy and then of the democratic system. The centre of the square is an agreeable spot, reordered to accommodate the entry to the new metro. There is a marble plaza, with benches and trees. At Christmas the Municipality erects an enormous Christmas tree. The square with its café tables is shared by tourists, office workers, pigeons and homeless dogs.

The autocratic king and his queen moved into their new palace in August 1843. Less than a month later a military uprising took place in front of the palace. One of the leading spirits was General Makriyiannis, who had become disillusioned with Otho and his Bavarians. The rebellious soldiers demanded a constitution and the convoking of a National Assembly. This was the first and far from the last military coup to take place in Athens, where for much of the last hundred and seventy years politics has been conducted in the streets.

Otho described in a dramatic letter to his father King Ludwig how he was confronted by the entire cavalry and infantry of the garrison, marching on the palace with the cry "Long live the Constitution." The artillery joined them and trained a gun on the main palace gate. Otho negotiated with the leaders of the rebellion from the balcony. Under their guns, and their refusal to accept his prevarications, he was forced to accede to their demands. In a humiliating gesture, he appeared on the balcony together with the new ministers whom he had been told to appoint.

In Otho's account the people of Athens have a walk-on part, standing in front of the palace, cheering the new ministers and the king. Not for the last time the moving force for change were the officers of the army. The concessions made by Otho, which he tried to claw back, were not enough. Twenty years later in the face of a further uprising he was forced to abdicate and leave the country.

Power Politics

Otho's turbulent reign foreshadowed most of the experiences of modern Athens: construction, growth, financial crisis, military uprising, naval blockade and foreign occupation. The blockade was ordered in 1850 by the unpopular British Ambassador Sir Thomas Wyse, on Palmerston's instructions, in order to exact satisfaction for various Greek slights to British interests. The most important of these was the unsatisfied claim for compensation by a Portuguese vice-consul of Maltese Jewish origins, Don Pacifico, a British citizen, whose house had been sacked by an anti-Semitic crowd at Easter 1847. That year, apparently because a French Rothschild was in Athens and they feared disturbances, the police had forbidden the usual seasonal practice of burning an effigy of Judas, and the crowd took it out on Don Pacifico.

Since the Greek government failed to respond immediately to Wyse's demands, Admiral Parker and the British Mediterranean fleet seized the Greek fleet and blockaded Piraeus. The effect was an immediate rise in Otho's popularity.

The British (Wyse again) and French went even further during the Crimean war. The Turks had withdrawn troops from Europe to face their Russian attackers. With Otho's enthusiastic support, Greece tried to exploit the situation in early 1854 by infiltrating armed bands across the frontier with Ottoman Turkey, into Thessaly and Epirus. This was too much for Britain and France. Their troops occupied Piraeus from May 1854 to February 1857 and insisted on a declaration of strict neutrality from Greece. After the first shock, there were incidents of fraternization between Greeks and occupying forces, illustrating the ambivalent relationship between the Greeks and the "Powers" and giving currency to the picture of Greece as a "toy kingdom" which writers such as E. F. Benson later propagated. Officers of the army of occupation attended Otho's court balls, where Queen Amalia captivated the white-haired French admiral and the English colonel.

In fact, the British officers got on better with the court than with the British Legation. There was an "incident" when the officers of the 91st Regiment of Foot, quartered in Piraeus, refused to invite the staff of the legation to a luncheon party on the occasion of their steeple chase event, because they felt slighted by Wyse. The storm tinkled in the elegant nineteenth-century teacups!

When the unfortunate Otho departed into exile, the Greeks set about finding a new king, or rather the Powers did so for them,

The Throne of Greece, the Throne of Greece,
From which King Otho has been flung

wrote *Punch*:

Though Thrones are rarely marked "to let"
A tenant will be hard to get.

But a tenant was found, by England, and endorsed by the Great Powers: Prince William Sonderberg-Glucksberg, second son of King

Christian of Denmark and brother of Alexandra, who married Edward VII. Willy ascended the throne of Greece as King George I of the Hellenes in October 1863. He enjoyed a long and on the whole successful career, ended by an assassin's bullet in Thessaloniki in 1913.

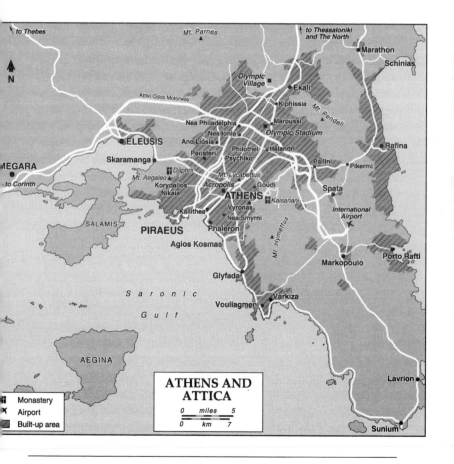

ATHENS AND ATTICA

CHAPTER TEN

Athens Capital City

The Crown Prince, born to the purple, moved us to tears when in the most Hellenic possible way he named our dear city of Athens "Capital of the free part of Hellenic territory".

Professor Spyridon Lambros, "The Crown Prince's Speech",
Estia, 15 January 1895

A trio or trilogy of public buildings, the University, Academy and National Library, help to define Athens as the new capital of a modern European nation. They face Panepistimiou (University) Street and back onto Academias Street. Other public buildings with similar claims include the Old Parliament building on Stadiou Street, the new Parliament, formerly the Royal Palace, on the corner of Constitution Square, and the cathedral.

Athens as capital was the political centre of a nation state modelled on western ideas and founded on an assumption of continuity with ancient Greece. The Acropolis represented this continuity in marble, the purified Greek language aspired to represent it in words, the buildings of Athens expressed it in architectural form.

Most of the inhabitants of Athens were newcomers. The population in the early 1830s was around 10,000. The numbers roughly doubled every twenty years, to a figure of more than 120,000 in the mid-1890s, so that as the century moved towards its close the native Athenians and their children were probably only one in three or four.

This population was made up of layers. There were the original Athenians. There was the small but influential set of Bavarians who had come with the king, including for a time the resented army of Bavarian mercenaries. There was a political class of Greeks, men influential in their own regions, who began to spend time in Athens in politics, business or at court. There were educated Greeks of the diaspora who were attracted by the idea of the new kingdom and wanted to make their way in it—the so-called "heterochthons" who found themselves an object of resentment to the "autochthons" or natives. There was a small foreign community, consisting in the early years of a few veterans of the war, Finlay, Church and others, the Italian hotel-keeper, Danish architects and German academics such as Ross, later expanded by scholars at the foreign schools of archaeology. And there were the Greeks who flocked to the capital city in search of employment or education. All of these, including the Athenian natives, were finding their bearings in a new environment. It must have been like a frontier town with high pretensions to civility.

The University

The three buildings on Panepistimiou Street represent the claims of the new capital to embody the ideology and education of the nation. Ancient Athens had been the school of Hellas. Modern Athens needed the institutions and buildings to be the same. The Bavarians were the mediators between the Greeks and Europe and the enforcers of an Athens-centred national ideology.

It took until the end of the nineteenth century for the great trilogy of buildings to be completed. The university came first, physically and institutionally. Formally known as the National Capodistrian University, it was established in 1837 and operated in the early years (1837-41) in a large Venetian house, extended by Kleanthes, in the Plaka, on the northern slopes of the Acropolis. This is now a museum, chiefly interesting for the building itself and the exotic collection of early medical equipment from the university medical faculty. The present university building, designed by the Dane Christian Hansen, was completed in 1842.

What did the university, with its four faculties of theology, philosophy, law and medicine, produce? Graduate unemployment. Accounts of nineteenth-century Athens are full of descriptions of the masses of students and ex-students of the law faculty, swelling the ranks of would-be politicians. The anonymous author of the little classic *Military Life in Greece* (1870) who came to Athens from Turkish lands in order to join the glorious Greek armed forces (and gave a wonderfully wry description of the reality as opposed to the dream) spent some time in the company of students in Athens in the 1850s. According to his account, there were between 3,500 and 4,000 of them, roughly one in ten of the population. His description brings out the rhythms of student life in digs, showing how students from all parts of Greek lands met each other through the mediation of Athens and its university.

The French author Edmond About wrote acerbically in 1855, "In the first years which followed the foundation of the university, all the youth studied law: when the courts of law were fully occupied, they fell back upon medicine. Now, the country possesses an army of judges and lawyers, and an army of doctors, without speaking of an army of officers." Towards the end of the century the French monarchist Charles Maurras described the two thousand students of philosophy, law or medicine, all of them aspiring public servants or parliamentary deputies, as a "people of barristers, priests and doctors [who] will never find in the entire East a sufficiently large number of people to preach to, of clients to cure and to advise." He feared that the state might finally have to work and pay for them, and that the reduction of the state to the function of provider and nurse would lead fatally to civil ruin. The state was still playing the role of provider, nurse and employer of last resort in the late twentieth century.

It was easy to laugh at the pretensions of the overeducated. But the university and the institutions of the new capital helped to mould a sense of what Athens and the new Greece meant for the nation and the outside world, and to spread that message outside the kingdom, through the teachers whom Athens sent out into the areas of unredeemed Hellenism, including distant parts of Asia Minor.

What did these people do all the time? The author of *Military Life in Greece* provides one answer. The hero-narrator, attracted by the glitter and promise of the independent Greek kingdom, comes to Athens to join the cavalry. After various setbacks, he decides to get to know the capital city better while awaiting an appointment. His down to earth protector and adviser Barba Nikolos advises him:

> *Here is what to do... In the morning go across to the dairy shop opposite to drink your milk; then until lunch time spend your time down here,*

*in the Lovely Greece (Oraia Ellas) café, with the newspapers and your
friends: the best people go there. Come back here at lunch time for
lunch—I always have good clean food here. Have your siesta here, and
in the evening go to Patisia, to the Columns, to Pafsilypos, to the Cave
of the Nymphs, to the Cucumber, wherever you like. There are plenty of
nice walks here. You can go down to Piraeus, or to Munichia for the
baths, or even to Kiphissia one day...*

There was no lack of cafés, nor of newspapers, in Athens in the middle
years of the century.

Symbols of State

The university was followed by the Academy, the name evoking western
European models, themselves founded on the idea of Plato's Academy.
It was designed by the Dane Theophil Hansen, brother of Christian,
completed in 1859, and later renovated by Ernst Ziller. The trilogy was
completed by the National Library, another of Theophil Hansen's
designs, built in 1887-91. The funding for this institution came from a
national "benefactor", the Cephalonian financier Panagis Vallianos. His
statue stands in front of the library between the two curving marble
steps leading up to the front entrance. The National Library has become

something of a scandal through overcrowding and lack of investment by the state, but at last there are reports of plans for revival.

These three buildings, with their neoclassical façades, are a fine sight, even across the busy traffic lanes of Panepistimiou Street. As an ensemble, they assert the civilized credentials of the modern state, and the Greek foundations of European civilization. This is achieved through the friezes and sculptures that decorate the buildings and their forecourts. Here, in front of the Academy, are Plato and Socrates. Here, in front of the university, are Korais, the scholar of the Enlightenment, and Capodistria, the learned first president of the Greek state. Here is Gregory V, the patriarch who was dragged from his throne and murdered on the outbreak of the Greek War of Independence, and plays a symbolic role as national martyr and link between the Orthodox religion and the nation (setting aside the irony that the Church hierarchy, used to rendering unto Caesar what belonged to Caesar, disapproved of the revolution).

Foreign enlightenment was also recognized, with the statue of Gladstone by Georgios Vitalis, which was put up in 1886 in front of the university. Athens is full of reminders of foreigners, from Byron and Canning in sculpture to the hundreds of foreign street names. Within a few hundred yards of the university, one finds Gambetta Street, Gladstone Street, Canning Square, and Edward Lo Street. (Who was Edward Lo (LO being my transliteration back into English of the Greek $\Lambda\Omega$)? The answer is an Anglo-Irish diplomat and Philhellene named Law who was chairman of the International Financial Committee, which regulated Greek finances at the end of the century. He was married to a Greek lady who was sister of the unfortunate General Hatzianestis, the commander of the Greek forces in Asia Minor in 1922, who believed his legs were made of glass and was executed along with five politicians as responsible for the Asia Minor disaster.) Even two of the three parallel streets which join Constitution with Omonia Square were named after Roosevelt and Churchill, but later reverted to their traditional names Akademias and Stadiou, just as the street of the university was renamed after Eleftherios Venizelos but reverted to Panepistimiou. But Gladstone is the only foreigner to have won a place in this area of national ideological space in front of the university.

The reason is his services to Hellenism over a long career. He was passionately interested in Homer, and no mean Homeric scholar. He followed the affairs of the Orthodox Church with close attention, and got into trouble back home for kissing the hand of a Greek bishop during his mission to the Ionian Isles in the 1850s. He denounced the spirit of interference in other country's affairs that led Palmerston to bully Greece over the case of Don Pacifico. He helped secure the fertile lands of Thessaly for Greece in 1881. He wrote pamphlets about Greek affairs, Homer and the Orthodox faith, with titles ranging from "The Hellenic Factor in the Eastern Question" to "The Slicing of Hector". He was a sharp critic of Ottoman rule, with his famous denunciation of the Turks at the time of the Bulgarian massacres in the 1880s ("bag and baggage"). He could sympathize with the problems of a young, still unformed state that the European powers seemed determined to keep in a position of dependency. He recognized that it is "in and by freedom only that preparation for fuller freedom can be made."

A short walk from the trilogy, in the company perhaps of David Rupp (*Athenian Walks*), can include many of the nineteenth-century buildings, which represent aspects of Athens as capital. Only a hundred yards or so from the Academy, on the corner of Omirou Street, is the headquarters of the Archaeological Society, symbolic of the way archaeology was used in the interests of the idea of the state and nation. In Klafthmonos Square, opposite and below the university, is an old house of the 1830s, which was one of Otho's early residences and is now the Museum of the City of Athens, containing furniture and pictures of the Othonian period. A block south of the square, along Stadiou Street, between Klafthmonos and Constitution Squares, is the Old Parliament building, now the National Historical Museum.

The Old Parliament illustrates the difficulty, which we have already noted, of getting anything done quickly in Athens. After Otho was forced to grant a constitution in 1843, the new Assembly met at first in a house, and later in the university, pending the construction of a proper building to accommodate it. The parliament building was started in 1858 and completed only in 1871. The design was by the French architect François Boulanger, who sketched out an impressive structure designed to contain two houses of parliament, a senate and a lower house. But as a result of the change of régime of 1863, and the accession of George, the constitution was revised, the senate was abolished, and the design had to be changed.

The resulting chamber is a heavy, clumsy building. In front of it is the flamboyant equestrian statue of Theodore Kolokotronis, the hero of the War of Independence. Against the east wall stands the neat figure of Harilaos Tricoupis, prime minister of Greece throughout most of the 1880s and the early 1890s, a crucial period of modernization and westernization. Tricoupis was Gladstonian in his comprehensive grasp of politics, economics, literature and philosophy, but lacked his durability. He wore himself out in the service of his country, and finally left Greece in 1895 following a crushing electoral defeat. His many services to Athens included the cleaning up, through a particularly tough chief of police, of the Psyrri area, a place of immigrants, small workshops and criminal gangs and racketeers.

Tricoupis died in the south of France during the holding of the 1896 Olympic Games, a venture about which he had doubts owing to the parlous financial state of the country. There is a statue of his long-standing opponent, the populist politician Theodore Deliyiannis, on the other side of the Old Parliament building. Though an older man, Deliyiannis outlived Tricoupis by nearly ten years. He died in 1904, stabbed outside the parliament by a dissatisfied gambler who resented the closing of the gambling saloons of Athens by Deliyiannis's government.

The monarchy stood at the centre of the new state (the constitution, when it was granted, took the form of a "royal democracy") and announced its central presence through the massive new Royal Palace. Many people thought it was larger and more expensive than it needed to be. Finance was represented by the National Bank of Greece, the most important banking institution of the nineteenth century, and the country's major commercial bank today. In the 1840s and 1850s respectively the Bank acquired two neoclassical houses, the Domnazou mansion and the Hotel Anglia on the upper side of Kotzias Square, and adapted them as its headquarters. On the opposite side of the square the city of Athens acquired a worthy town hall only in 1870. Its most intriguing contents are a set of puppets representing all the mayors of Athens.

Cathedrals and Churches

The new capital also required a cathedral. One of the early acts of the Greek state was to sever the dependence of the Greek Orthodox church on the Ecumenical Patriarchate in Constantinople and establish an "autocephalous" Church of Greece. (The two institutions were still quarrelling over turf in 2003.) This new institution required a cathedral worthy of its status as the national Church, and seat of the Archbishop of Athens and All Greece. As we have seen, those that remained of the numerous Byzantine churches which dotted the old town were originally parish churches of modest dimensions. None of them was fitted to serve as cathedral. By 1840, when the new Protestant church was already half built, people were becoming restive. General Makriyiannis referred to the Church of St Eirene, temporarily serving as cathedral, as a "hut" and criticized Otho for his neglect of church building as compared with his palace.

This was a little unfair. It was important to find the right site and the right design. The Athens Council argued strongly for placing it in the old town, rather than in a more distant and isolated position near the university. The king officially laid the first stone in 1842 on Christmas Day. From there to completion was a slow business. Theophil Hansen made the initial design. In 1846 Otho announced a competition to modify it, following the Greek-Byzantine order. The winning design, by Zezos, was not completed by the time of his death in 1857. The cathedral, dedicated to the Annunciation, was finally completed only in 1862, to designs by Boulanger. Stylistically it looks a mess, resembling a degraded form of Westminster cathedral rather than St Sophia. But, as Eleni Bastea has pointed out, the point was not so much direct visual descent from a Byzantine model as meaning and association. Here was a large, purpose-built cathedral church which proclaimed the religious affiliation of the nation and recalled in its imagery Greece's achievement of independence.

The foreigners also required their own places, sacred and secular. As early as 1836 the British resident Bracebridge reported that a Protestant cemetery had been planned and completed near the Ilissos river, to replace the Church of St George (the Theseion) where Protestants had been buried in the Turkish period. The British, Danish, Dutch, Bavarian, Prussian and Swedish governments all contributed. The cemetery remained in this position until the early twentieth century, when it was moved to the Athens First Cemetery further from the centre of town. The English community also bought ground for a Protestant church. The British minister Edmund Lyons, George Finlay, and the newly-arrived chaplain Henry Leeves, representing the British and Foreign Bible Society, formed a committee of management and raised money from the British government and private sources. The foundation stone was laid in 1838 and the church was built on what is now Philellinon Street to a Gothic design by Henry Acland, revised by the archaeologist and architect C. R. Cockerell and Christian Hansen. (It is remarkable how few buildings in Athens were the work of one designer.)

St Paul's Anglican-Episcopal Church continues to be a lively centre of mission and worship, enlivened by one of the very few organs in Athens besides the fine modern instrument at the Megaron concert hall. The church is a museum of the British and Protestant connection with Athens, from the stained glass windows commemorating the Dilessi murders, the memorial windows to General Church, the tablet marking where the philhellene Frank Hastings' heart was immured, through to the newly installed memorial tablet to Brigadier Stephen Saunders. Less familiar names are also commemorated: the son and daughter-in-law of Henry Leeves, who were murdered by villagers in Euboea in 1854; the minor composer Clement Harris, a pupil of Brahms, who joined the Greek forces as a volunteer in the 1897 war with Turkey, and died at Pente Pigadia in Epirus.

The Roman Catholic community was different. There were virtually no Greek Protestants (and attempts by Protestant missionaries to proselytize led to trouble). There was a substantial community of Greek Catholics, concentrated mainly on certain islands of the Cyclades, especially Naxos and Syros, the seat of the Catholic archbishop. The Catholics of Athens worshipped at first in a church improvised within the Ottoman *teke* near the Roman Agora. When this was threatened by planned excavations in the Agora in the early 1850s, the community decided to build their own cathedral. The chosen site was on Panepistimiou Street, which had been considered as a possible site for the Orthodox cathedral. A committee was established including the French, Austrian and Bavarian ambassadors, and this body launched an appeal for funds. It proved tough going. The foundation stone was laid in 1853 and the building completed only in 1887, to a design by Lysandros Kaftantzoglou, which was a simplified, blander version of the original plan by Klenze.

Architects and Benefactors

The physical aspects of the consolidation of Athens as capital are well described in Bastea's book *The Creation of Modern Athens* (2000). Alongside the public buildings there was a rapid growth in private housing, of various levels of modesty and grandeur, to meet the requirements of an expanding European city with an increasingly demanding public, both native and foreign. The city developed through a kind of dialogue between government and individuals who commissioned work, planners, architects and engineers who designed and built, and the public. The role of the Greek benefactors was as crucial in enabling this process, as was that of the planners and architects in establishing the shape and form of city and buildings.

The planners and architects, as we have seen, were trained in western Europe, primarily in Germany and Scandinavia. There was no native tradition or school from which they could have come, since the Greek vernacular did not provide what the new state needed. There was thus no way in which a Greek architect of the first generation of the independent state could have picked up the techniques of his profession within Greek lands. Kleanthes was Greek, born in Macedonia, but he and Schaubert, the authors of the first city plan, were trained in Berlin under Schinkel, and steeped in the neoclassical. The brothers Christian and Theophil Hansen, who designed respectively the university and the Academy, were Danish, trained at the Royal Academy of Fine Arts at Copenhagen. Gärtner (the Royal Palace) and Ziller (Schliemann's house, the Iliou Melathron, the Cadet School, the German Archaeological Institute, and a raft of public and private houses) were German. Boulanger (the cathedral and the Old Parliament) was French, Kaftantzoglou (the Polytechnic) was Greek and trained in Italy, Kalkos (Town Hall) a Greek who studied in Munich. This remarkable group of people were responsible for the dozens of buildings which made Athens a substantial city. These men established practices and traditions of planning and architecture that have been transmitted to the present day in the achievements of men such as Pikionis and Constantine Doxiades, the creator of the science of "oikistics" or "ekistics".

A roll call of the buildings erected through the generosity of the benefactors includes virtually all the notable public buildings of Athens: the university, the National Library (the brothers Vallianos); the Academy (Baron Simon Sinas); the Evangelismos Hospital (Andreas Syngros); the National Metsovian Polytechnic (George Averoff); the Evelpidon Cadet School (Averoff); the Zappeion (Evangelis Zappas) the Panathenaic Stadium (Averoff); and many others. Typically the large-scale benefactor was a Greek born somewhere in the outlying parts of Greek lands, who had made his fortune in one of the great commercial centres of the eastern Mediterranean, and having earned more money than he could easily spend was looking for a patriotic cause to support. Averoff came from the attractive Vlach mountain village of Metsovo in Epirus, and became a cotton king in Egypt. Baron Sinas was a super-rich banker from Vienna; Andreas Syngros from Constantinople. Zappas, after an adventurous early life including service in the War of Independence, made his money in Romania. They were men of substance, and one of them, Syngros, left a memoir illuminating the relations of such entrepreneurs and financiers with Greek political life. By the 1870s, when Athens had proved itself as capital and centre of Hellenism, they were ready to look with favour on projects to fund there, while also supporting their local Greek communities in Egypt, Turkey, Romania and elsewhere. Athens would not be the Athens we know without these men, who, often better than governments, were able to carry large-scale projects through to completion. The tradition is still alive in the charitable giving of large bodies such as the Onassis, Niarchos and Leventis Foundations.

From Otho to George I

Athens took shape in Otho's reign. The departure of Otho and the arrival of George I marked no great disjunction in the development of the city. But George was to reign for fifty years, and in that time much happened to Athens. He was a more worldly-wise figure than Otho. He paid more attention to the advice of Greeks, and he avoided the mistake of Otho in remaining childless. George was related to the better half of Europe's royalty. Early in his reign he travelled to Russia and returned with a bride, Olga, daughter of Grand Duke Constantine. The two were prolific. Among their many children were Constantine, Crown Prince and Prince of Sparta; George, who became High Commissioner of the Great Powers in Crete and married, unsuccessfully, Princess Marie Bonaparte; and Andrew, who married the charming but eccentric Alice and was father of the Duke of Edinburgh. The royal children were baptized in the Orthodox faith. The future of the dynasty was assured.

Athens was confirmed in George's reign as the ideological and economic centre of the Greek state. The move of the capital from Nauplion had already established Athens as politically dominant. It was the seat of government and of the monarchy. This brought with it a diplomatic corps, media, banking, the army, the Church, and an expanding public service offering elastic possibilities of employment. However, it was a fragile centre, its control over the rest of the country periodically contested whether by local barons or by brigands. Though the royal government had armed forces and gendarmes at its disposal, it did not enjoy a monopoly of the use of force. Gradually, however, the writ of central government was established, by a combination of force and patronage. The key was to engage and incorporate the regional chieftains and grandees in the Athens establishment. This was achieved, and the great names of the independence struggle continued to feature, into the second and third generation, in the ranks of the ministries, assemblies and court.

The capital aspired also to economic predominance. At the time of independence Athens was not a natural centre of commerce or communications. The country consisted of coastal regions and islands connected with each other or with the great ports of the Mediterranean, and mountain villages and towns, which were often virtual enclaves. Athens produced little. The port of Piraeus, which after the War of Independence amounted to nothing beyond a dilapidated customs shack, began to develop to serve the needs of Athens in imports, but for decades was far outstripped by the island port of Syros in the Cyclades, which in the mid-nineteenth century became the centre of Greek shipping and commerce. It was only late in the century that Piraeus overtook it.

Under the impetus of central government a network of roads was constructed and Athens came to serve as a metropolis, drawing in produce from a much wider area than Attica. The modernization scheme of Tricoupis included the construction of railways and harbours, and the Corinth canal, which opened in 1893. It was the watershed in the development of a modern economy, even though the Tricoupis experiment ended in national bankruptcy and Greece's default on its loans.

Tricoupis' modernizing thrust was accompanied by a late nineteenth-century flowering of culture. The leading figure of the "generation of the '80s" was a young man named Kostis Palamas, a prolific poet and public servant—for many years he served as Secretary of Athens University—who had the knack of touching a public nerve through his choice of subject and power of expression. Like most of the livelier writers of this time, he championed the demotic movement. In reaction against the increasing archaism of the institutionalized language of state business and education, he and his friends insisted on a language closer to the speech and everyday life of the people as their means of expression in poetry and story. His sculpture can be seen in front of the Municipal Cultural Centre in Academias Street, his face with broad moustache, his head resting on his hand in pensive mode.

Literary "generations" in Greece seem to come in fifty-year cycles: the next was the generation of the '30s, of Theotokas, Seferis and the modernists. Almost all those who made their mark in literary Athens in the 1880s were admirers of Tricoupis. A group of the younger men gathered around Professor Nikolaos Politis, the father of Greek folklore studies, in discussions of Greece's destiny and cultural identity. Folklore was an important constituent part of the debates which raged over Greece's national identity and cultural roots, since it could be mined for evidence of continuities at the popular level between ancient and modern.

Not all the prominent figures on the cultural and literary scene were Athenians. Yannis Psycharis, the extreme demoticist author of the travelogue *My Journey* (1888) was a professor in France, and Alexandros Pallis, the translator of the Gospels into demotic Greek, was a member of the commercial diaspora in Britain. But Athens was the arena of the literary and cultural debate, the site of literary cafés, small magazines, and publishing houses. It was an open society, not too difficult for outsiders to penetrate. Just as businessmen and financiers, such as Syngros, came from the diaspora to settle in Athens, so did literary men such as Emmanuel Roides, author of the satirical novel *Pope Joan*, and Dimitrios Vikelas, author of the best-selling novel of the War of Independence *Loukis Laras*. Both of them were born in Syros.

Heart of Hellenism

By a certain point in the first half of George's reign it could be seen that Athens was not just the capital of a small European state, but also the political and cultural heart of Hellenism, in reality, even if Constantinople remained the centre of dreams. Athens was the political home of the Great Idea of redeeming the Greek populations of the Ottoman empire. First articulated in 1844 by Prime Minister Kolettis, this conception was a thread running through Greek politics from that time until the early 1920s. Its logic demanded a trunk to the Greek state to which outlying limbs could be attached; and a head, or heart, for the trunk. This was Athens.

As early as the 1860s observers were referring to Athens as the core and heart of Hellenism. Historians have found various events to symbolize this status: most strikingly, the repatriation of the remains of Patriarch Gregory V, in 1871, fifty years after his death at the outbreak of the Greek Revolution. Following his hanging, the patriarch's mutilated body was thrown into the Bosporus. It was recovered, and eventually taken to Odessa for burial. By 1871 the Greek state felt confident enough to ask for it. The preliminary negotiations with the Porte were difficult. The Turks, fearing outbursts of Greek national feeling, were unwilling to allow the dead patriarch to transit the Bosporus except under the most discreet conditions.

The American Ambassador Charles Tuckerman arrived in Athens in time for the return of the patriarch's remains, and left a description of the solemn procession, lasting two hours, from the railway station to the cathedral. The king and queen followed the coffin. The remains were interred with due solemnity. They can still be seen in the cathedral, opposite a casket containing the bones of the sixteenth-century Athenian saint Philothei. The cathedral was the right resting place for an "ethnarch" who had assumed a commanding position in the nation's memory.

In the secular field, the Olympic Games of 1896 confirmed the primacy of Athens. In a speech in preparation for the Games the Crown Prince Constantine raised tears to the eyes of his listeners by referring to Athens as "capital of the free part of Hellenic territory". The unmissable inference was that at some future date the city should be capital of the whole of Hellenism, including the enslaved brothers and sisters within Ottoman lands. This identified the Crown with the Great Idea and asserted the now unchallenged position of Athens. But there remained a gap between the Greeks' view of themselves and their destiny, and that held by the outside world.

Cultured Tourists

The Athens of King George was attracting increasing numbers of tourist visitors, most of them persons of means and substance. One can trace the phenomenon through successive editions of Baedeker and Murray's *Handbooks for Travellers in Greece*, which set out the amenities available to tourists from the west, and gave useful guidance on how to travel in reasonable comfort about the country, and how conveniently to see the sights of Athens and Attica. It is clear from these books that the antiquities remained the main attraction. But one can tell also from the detailed attention given by Baedeker to varieties of game birds in Attica, that there were other amusements for well-off travellers.

In the 1870s tourism was for the most part still an activity of individuals and families. The group (not yet mass) tourism associated with Thomas Cook grew in the 1880s and 1890s. High cultural tourism, by sea, was pioneered by the French in the 1890s with their *croisières des savants*, stopping off for visits at Delphi, Delos and Athens, and hearing lectures by eminent scholars such as the director of the French School in Athens. These were the forerunners of the British Hellenic Travel Club of the first half of the twentieth century, itself a forerunner of Swan Hellenic cruises.

Though foreigners, as Byron discovered, tended to run down the Greeks, there was one constituency of specialists who needed Athens and Greece. These were the archaeologists and scholars of Hellenism. Greece and Athens were their raw material. As the Greek state asserted its rights of ownership and management over its own soil, it was no longer possible for foreigners, in the spirit of Elgin, Chateaubriand and so many others, simply to appropriate antiquities (though it was, and still is, possible to acquire them illegally from clandestine diggers and traders in antiquities). The development of a science of archaeology and the realization of the importance of material remains in explaining the culture of the Greeks led the scholarly community to want their own bases in Athens. The French, characteristically, were first in the field, establishing the French School in 1846. They were followed by the Germans, with their Archaeological Institute, the Americans with their School of Classical Studies, and the British, who belatedly set up their school in 1886. Others followed.

These schools were an acknowledgment that something had changed. The days of the amateur traveller and expropriator were over. Archaeologists had now to negotiate their presence and permits to work with a sovereign power. The pioneering agreement between Greece and the Germans for the excavation of ancient Olympia, which took place in the 1870s, contained provisions prohibiting the wholesale export of excavated works of art and other found objects.

The schools immediately became part of the intellectual life of the city of Athens, and still are. They are also potentially an important lobby on behalf of Hellenism and Greek interests in the world. Physically, they have made their mark also. Their mere presence has helped to preserve an important part of central Athens from development. The British and American Schools are havens of peace and greenery, the German Institute a handsome neoclassical building by Ziller.

In late nineteenth-century Athens tourists put up at one of the comfortable central hotels, such as the Grande Bretagne. One can tell from Baedeker and Murray that travel was still a matter of individual initiative and negotiation between tourist and the dragoman or guide, who could be found through the big hotels. Later, in the early twentieth century, well-informed visitors would ask Mr. Ghiolman, the prince of travel agents, to arrange their itineraries for them. Ghiolman seemed to anticipate his clients' wishes in an uncanny way, and Virginia Woolf, H. D. F. Kitto and many others are warm in his praises.

For the visitor to Athens, the chief attraction outside the city was Marathon, easily managed in a day's excursion. The visitors could have an agreeable day's ride across country, visit the battlefield, Herodotus in hand, and inspect the tomb of the Athenian dead. Or they could visit Sunium, or Daphni monastery and Eleusis. But even such excursions could expose travellers to risks on the road, and in times of insecurity it was customary to ask the Greek authorities to provide an escort of gendarmes. Things went disastrously wrong in 1870, when a group of British and Italian visitors set off early on an expedition to Marathon. On the way back they were ambushed by a party of brigands and held to ransom. After days in which they were moved from one part of Attica to another, while negotiations dragged on, they were killed by the brigands near the village of Dilessi. The incident caused a scandal. It exposed the fragility of Greece's institutions, bringing into the public domain an aspect of Greek life that Greeks preferred to remain hidden.

But by the time of the Olympic Games in 1896, law and order, the foundations of civilized life, were secured in Athens and Attica. The Games confirmed the stature of Athens in the eyes not only of the world outside, but of the Greeks themselves, who were continually seeking reassurance of the level of European civilization they had attained.

CHAPTER ELEVEN

Olympic Athens

"The flavour of the Athenian soil—the feeling of helping to bridge the gap between old and new—the indefinable poetic charm of knowing one's self thus linked with the past, a successor to the great heroic figures of olden times—the splendid sportsmanship of the whole affair—there is but one first time in everything, and that first time was gloriously, and in a manner ever to be remembered, the privilege of the American team of 1896."

Ellery Clark, member of the US team who won the high jump and long jump, in *Reminiscences of an Athlete: Twenty Years on Track and Field,* 1911

As you look southwards towards the sea from the top of Lycabettus you can see a large white marble structure against a background of dark green pine trees on Ardittos hill. This is the Panathenaic Stadium, forever associated with the revival of the Olympic Games. It faces the southeast corner of the Zappeion gardens and the bottom of Herod Atticus Street and the Presidential Palace. A few hundred yards to the west lies the temple of Olympian Zeus. Usually there are groups of tourists poking about on the broad pavement that joins the stadium to the street, their coaches parked by the broad avenue. There is a statue of a rather severe-looking Victorian gentleman on the pavement.

Here in classical times, and until the last century, flowed the Ilissos river. Generations of schoolboys knew of it because of a passage in Plato's dialogue *Phaedrus.* In the early nineteenth century it was no more than a small gravelly channel. Baedeker comments that it was a streamlet "barely more than a stride in width", which dried up in the summer completely, but could on occasion swell to a torrent. For the 1896 Olympic Games an extra temporary bridge was thrown across the riverbed to help the large crowds find their way into the stadium.

Our image of the Ilissos, formed by Plato, is a romantic one, of an idyllic brook surrounded with greenery, where the nymph Oreithyia, daughter of Erectheus, was gathering wild flowers when Boreas, the god of the north wind, seized her and carried her off. Socrates and his pupils rested on the turf under the plane trees by the stream, listening to the buzzing song of the cicadas, cooled by the sea breeze, and started to talk philosophy. Modern commentators have tried to undermine this picture, arguing that even in classical times the river was insignificant. But a river does not have to be significant to be agreeable. In any case, the romance cannot now be recaptured because the Ilissos is no more. In the 1950s the riverbed was covered over with the concrete of the modern city (King Constantine Avenue), and can no longer be seen. Some of the attraction of the entrance to the stadium is therefore now gone.

From the broad pavement of King Constantine Avenue you look right into the heart of the stadium, a handsome structure lying between two hills that have been joined by an embankment at the southern end to form the curve at one end of the race track. The northern end is open to the street. The track is flanked by marble rows of seats. Across the street, at the bottom of Herod Atticus Street, facing the stadium, is a well-known modern sculpture of a discus thrower, not in the classical pose of Myron's discobolus, but seemingly on the point of releasing the discus which he holds out above his head. In 1896, near this spot, a large rotunda was erected, which contained a panorama of the siege of Paris in 1870, a form of popular entertainment that was to be sidelined by the new art form of cinema.

The stern-looking nineteenth-century figure on the pavement near the entrance to the stadium is a marble statue of George Averoff, the Greek cotton magnate from Metsovo who made his fortune in Alexandria and became one of Greece's greatest public benefactors. It was Averoff who generously paid for the restoration and marbling of the Panathenaic Stadium, without which the Games could hardly have taken place in Athens. The statue was unveiled on the eve of the first revived Olympic Games.

Standing in the stadium today, one would find it difficult to say whether this was an ancient or a nineteenth-century building. In fact, it is a modern reconstruction, on the site of the ancient Athenian stadium where the Panathenaic Games were held. This was built in the fourth century BC in the time of Lycurgus, before which, apparently, competitive games took place in the Agora. In the second century AD Herod Atticus, an even more notable benefactor than Averoff, gloriously restored the stadium in Pentelic marble. His other benefactions include the theatre of Herod Atticus beneath the southern wall of the Acropolis, the main site of open-air events in the annual Athens Festival. Herod Atticus was a rich man by chance—his father had stumbled on a fortune of treasure buried at his family property in Kiphissia. With the decline of Athens and the end of pagan sports festivals, the stadium fell into disrepair, marble was carted away for building purposes, and grass covered over the remains.

The new planners and builders of Athens in the 1830s found little trace of the ancient structure. They found simply a natural stadium in the grassy hollow between the hills of Ardittos. But they knew that the ancient stadium lay beneath the earth. The site, an agreeable place for picnics and jolly dances on feast days, started being used for athletic sports in the 1870. A patriotic Greek from Romania named Evangelis Zappas, a former participant in the War of Independence, gave money for the construction of an exhibition hall where he envisaged the holding of industrial and agricultural shows, together with associated "Olympic" sports. This was the origin of the Zappeion exhibition hall. The surrounding park gradually filled with statuary of Greek literary and political figures.

At this stage in the late 1890s the Zappeion was relatively new and raw. Later it acquired more greenery. Henry Miller wrote in *The Colossus of Maroussi* that the Zappeion of 1939 remained in his memory like no other park he had known, as the "quintessence of park". He went there on his first night in Athens, during a heat wave, and was enchanted—by the dust, the heat, the poverty, the bareness, the containedness of the people, and the water everywhere in little tumblers standing between the quiet, peaceful couples. Miller was weaving for himself out of the magic of a quiet summer night an unreal tapestry of the holy innocence of the Greeks. Between the wars the Zappeion was the place where you would see nurses and nannies taking the children of the prosperous for their daily promenades. Later it contained broadcasting facilities of the Greek Radio and Television,

ERT. I went there on 13 December 1967, the day King Constantine launched his counter-coup against the military regime, and found the entrance barred by the army.

All this was far in the future. In the 1860s King George decided to have the stadium excavated at his own expense. The excavation was carried out by the German architect Ernst Ziller, who, we have seen, designed many of Athens' most distinctive buildings including the Cadet School, the Royal Theatre, and the Crown Prince's palace (which is now the Palace of the President of the Republic). As a result of Ziller's work, by about 1870 the shape and structure of the ancient stadium were known, and the idea of reconstructing it became feasible. The planned Olympic Games gave the opportunity.

Olympics Revived

Baron Pierre de Coubertin was a French educational reformer and sports enthusiast who took from England and the United States the ideas of fair play and amateurism, and grafted onto these the brilliant concept of an international, eventually global, sporting contest. In 1894 he organized an international congress in Paris to endorse his ideas. Coubertin borrowed the ancient title and some of the ancient symbolism for his Olympic Games, but built his idea on the foundation of the predominant sports of the later nineteenth century in their modern forms. The Paris Congress resolved that there should be Olympic Games every four years, moving from city to city.

Coubertin wanted Olympic Games to be held in Paris, to coincide with the Paris Universal Exhibition of 1900. That left a vacancy for games in 1896, if they could be organized in time. London was a possible host city, canvassed by a number of the delegates at the Congress, but was not particularly interested, nor was it favoured by Coubertin. Hungary wanted the Games. But Coubertin had other ideas, the vehicle for which was a middle-aged Greek scholar resident in Paris, named Dimitrios Vikelas.

Vikelas had made a tidy fortune in trade, working in his uncles' shipping office in London. The nervous illness of his wife Kalliope caused him to move to Paris, where she attended a clinic and he lived a productive life of scholarship and public affairs, translating Shakespeare, writing pamphlets on Greece's position in the world, and paying frequent visits to Athens. He wrote a novel about the Greek War of Independence, *Loukis Laras* (1879), which immediately became a classic and is still read by Greek schoolchildren.

The role Vikelas carved out for himself was to explain Greece to the French, British and Germans, and to explain western Europe and its culture to the Greeks. It must have struck the tiny sporting establishment in Athens that he would be the ideal person to represent Greece at Coubertin's Congress. With a certain show of reluctance, owing to his ignorance of sport, Vikelas allowed himself to be drafted as the representative of the recently established Panhellenic Gymnastic Association, effectively the representative of Greece herself. He not only attended the Congress, but he found himself chairing the subcommittee which dealt with the Olympic idea, and by agreement with Coubertin proposed Athens as the first host city. The proposal was enthusiastically endorsed by the Congress, and Vikelas was elected the first President of the International Olympic Committee (IOC).

Vikelas had proposed Athens on his own initiative. It remained for the Greek government and the city of Athens to agree. The offer of the first revived Games was flattering, but there was no way anyone could have predicted at that stage what a vast enterprise was being born. And the Greek government, under the austere Tricoupis, was none too keen on hosting an expensive affair, with no certainty of success. The government was more than usually strapped for cash. The currant trade, the backbone of Greece's export economy, had collapsed spectacularly in the early 1890s, and in October 1893 Tricoupis was obliged to tell parliament that the country was bankrupt. Not surprisingly, he refused all government financial support for the Olympic enterprise. The most he would promise, in the face of Coubertin's insistent lobbying, was benevolent neutrality.

To the Greek press and many of the public, the government seemed to be, literally, spoilsports. The general feeling was that this was an honour for Greece, and was owed to Greece. Vikelas said that once the question of Athens had been put on the table, it was a challenge that simply could not be refused. The Crown Prince, a staunch supporter of the Olympic proposal, took the same line. Both he and Vikelas argued that although the amenities in Athens might fall short of some other European cities, Greece would make up for this by the

Attic sun and sky and the hospitality of the people—which indeed turned out to be the case, although the weather in April 1896 was unusually bad.

The Crown Prince sent a representative to Alexandria to beard the benevolent Averoff in his home quarters. Averoff delivered. He endorsed plans by a young architect, Anastasios Metaxas, for the rebuilding of the stadium, and he funded the enterprise. Metaxas was a good choice. He later designed the house which is now the Benaki Museum, and the house on Loukianou (Lucian) Street which was the house of Prime Minister Venizelos and, after his death, was bought by the British government and became the British Embassy.

A reasonably up-to-date stadium was a necessary condition of the Games taking place successfully. But providing this in the cladding of an ancient marble stadium gave a wonderful stimulus to the imagination of athletes, spectators and journalists, an achievement reflected in the coverage of the Games. The stadium in 1896, after the first phase of Metaxas' work, looked more or less as it does today. But he did not have time or money to complete the marble cladding, which was installed only up to the first horizontal corridor. Above that were wooden benches painted white to blend with the marble. Still higher, above the level of the seating, spectators could sit on the grassy hill.

It was an ideal setting, but technically deficient. The curve at the end of the track was too sharp, causing the runners in the middle distance races, especially the 400 metres, to slow up as they rounded the bend. There was also criticism of the cinder track, which was judged to be too soft. But as Constantine had predicted, the atmosphere and hospitality made up for these defects.

The Panathenaic Stadium was the main focus of the 1896 games, but as will be the case in 2004, events were scattered around the city. The fencing took place in the Zappeion hall, the shooting in a newly built shooting range at Kallithea, and the cycling events in a new velodrome in Phaleron. Swimming took place in the sea, in the harbour of Zea, where today the flying dolphin hydrofoils start for the islands of the Saronic gulf. The marathon race started at Marathon and ended in the stadium.

American Triumph

In March/April 1896 teams converged on Athens from across the Atlantic and from many countries of Europe: Hungary, France, Germany, Sweden, Italy, and a few from Britain. The most adventurous and longest journey was that of the American team, consisting of athletes from Princeton University and the Boston Athletic Club (many of them from Harvard). They found a city in a fever of sports enthusiasm, with children competing on every square and plot of wasteland, and salesmen peddling everything from drinks and snacks to artistic events in the evenings. The Americans won the hearts of the Athenians, for their open, friendly manners and their strange war cries, the RA RA RAs with which they encouraged each other, and which so impressed the king that he called for a repeat performance.

The first day of the Olympic Games saw the largest crowd ever assembled in the history of the Greek state converge on the stadium for the opening ceremony. The men wore dark suits and hats, the ladies long dresses and hats. An observer described the various outfits of the ladies, their varied coiffures, the movement of their fans amid the black mass of several thousand spectators, the brilliant uniforms and the plumes of the officers, the striking colours of the floating flags, the lively semi-circle of spectators who, without tickets, occupied the top of the hills surrounding the stadium. Much of the organization was in the hands of the military, whose smart uniforms were seen everywhere. The subsequent course of the Olympic movement was present in embryonic form that day, in Palamas's *Olympic Hymn* and the flags of the winners' nations run up the flagpoles near the entrance to the stadium.

The first event of the revived Olympic cycle was a heat of the 100 metres, won by an American. It was a sign of what was to come. The American team dominated the track and field events. James Connolly, later a successful author of nautical yarns, took the first gold medal, for the triple jump. He was followed by Robert Garrett of Princeton, later a successful investment banker and collector of oriental manuscripts, who won the discus against strong Greek competition. The legend has it that Garrett had constructed a discus following what he thought were ancient Greek models, but found it too heavy to throw and abandoned the project. But on the eve of the games he picked up a discarded Greek

discus in the stadium and threw it a few times without difficulty. He decided then and there to enter for the event, and beat the favoured Greek contestants. The winning discus can be seen at Princeton University to this day.

In the view of the athletes such as Robert Garrett and Ellery Clark, and not just of the nostalgia-mongers of later generations, these first Olympic Games of 1896 were the expression of a vanished age of good sportsmanship and fun. Clark spoke of the "privilege" of being there at the start. It was a privilege that most of Britain's best athletes missed.

As with some other European ventures, the British seem to have thought that they did not need the Olympics as much as the Olympics needed them, and missed the bus.

The Marathon

All the contemporary sources agree on the sportsmanship of the Greek spectators. In the early stages they were frustrated by the failure of the Greek athletes to carry off medals. But all came right on the final day of sport, with the marathon race. This was the invention of a French antiquarian friend of Coubertin, Michel Bréal, who offered a silver cup for the winner of a race along the route from Marathon to Athens, following the precedent allegedly set in 490 BC.

As with much ancient history, it is difficult to disentangle facts from legends. Herodotus in his gripping account of the battle, in which the Athenians with their plucky Plataean allies defeated the superior forces of the Persian invaders, has one Philippides (or Pheidippides), a professional runner, running from Athens to Sparta in advance of the battle to seek Spartan aid: a course of approximately 245 kilometres (153 miles) which he seems to have covered in less than 48 hours. There is a modern "Spartathlon" covering the same course, for which the record of 20 hours 25 minutes was set by a Greek runner, Yannis Kouros, in 1984. Later writers have Pheidippides or Philippides racing back after the battle to announce to the Athenians in the market place, "We have won," and expiring on the spot. That seems to be legend. But certainly the Athenian troops made good time in marching back from the Marathon plain to the city after the battle, in order to forestall the Persians, who had taken to their ships and were sailing round Cape Sunium to attack what they hoped was an undefended city. The Athenians got back in time and placed themselves south of the city, between Athens and Phaleron. Seeing them the Persians turned their ships and sailed for home.

Whether this was Pheidippides' run, or the forced march of the Athenian infantry, the course from Marathon to Athens became the modern marathon, a race of approximately 26 miles from the site of the battle to the stadium. The course started near sea level and rose to the south of Mount Pendeli before descending gently past Ambelokipi into the city.

Long-distance running was beginning to stake a claim in European and American athletic circles, but few of the entrants for the Athens marathon were known to have covered this distance. The Greeks had, however: they held two trials for the race. One of those who scraped into the group of finalists was a young farmer called Spyridon Louis. Legend surrounds his performance on 10 April, but it really does seem to be the case that he stopped at one of the staging points and drank a glass of wine. Louis adopted a steady pace, unfazed by the speed of the early leaders, Lermusiaux of France and Flack of Australia. He ran steadily on, eventually overtaking all the rest.

There being no means of remote communication, it was through runners or riders that news of the progress of the race could be brought. It was therefore only a few minutes before the finish that rumours started to sweep the stadium, first that the Australian was leading, then that Louis was in the lead. Soon after, a small figure in white vest

appeared—though Giorgio de Chirico remembers him as being completely black—at the entrance of the stadium and ran steadily down the final straight, accompanied by the Crown Prince and his brother. The whole stadium erupted in shouts and cheers. The men threw their hats in the air. Even the impassive King George waved his hat. Louis had won for Greece and a legend was born. He led the final parade wearing the traditional Greek kilt or *foustanella*. He did not run again, but late in his life he was to be seen leading the Greek team in the opening ceremony of the Berlin 1936 Olympics, a sprightly sixty-year-old. His victory caused great joy, and did much to justify the whole Olympic adventure to the Greek people.

There is an annual Athens marathon, though it has not achieved the renown of the London, New York or Boston events. The race, however, is bound to be the main focus of the 2004 Olympics, and once again it will be the ancient stadium that attracts the crowds for the finish of the race. Ten million people will be hoping that another national hero, like Louis, will pull it off for Greece.

From 1896 to 2004

In the Athens of the 1890s the dust still rose in clouds from unsurfaced streets. The pavements were still cracked, uneven and dangerous, the roads potholed. The smells of downtown Athens were offensive, some of the streets as described by Roides were like open sewers, and bloody carcasses hung outside butchers' shops and brushed against pedestrians as they tried to pass. Smartly dressed officers crowded the streets and talked in the cafés about the unfair pressures of the Great Powers which prevented the just union of Crete with the mother country, and the imperious necessity of smiting the Turks.

But the foreign visitors could remain largely unaware of these features, and of the poverty and violence which were features of the tougher areas of immigrants from the country, and which led to a sharp increase in the numbers of murders and violent crimes in the later years of the century. The 1896 Games would not have taken place in Athens had the city not been seen as capable of hosting them, with the facilities required by foreign visitors with demanding standards. The 1894 edition of Baedeker wrote that so far as external conditions were concerned, a stay in Athens compared with a stay in Naples or Palermo, offering "all the conveniences which most travellers find necessary for comfort". The Greeks saw the Games as a challenging opportunity to show that Athens belonged to the ranks of civilized cities, and Greece to the ranks of civilized European nations. They proved to themselves that they had met this challenge with conspicuous success, in the pages of a special edition entitled *Greece at the Olympic Games of 1896*, published by the newspaper *Acropolis*. Public figures from the worlds of education, literature and public life, and some foreigners, all bore witness to the fact that the Games were a large-scale event carried out successfully in an atmosphere of perfect order and hospitality.

Apart from the marathon, the archery and some other formal events, the Panathenaic Stadium will play no part in 2004.

Technically it is out of date. The main focus of the 2004 Olympics will be on the sports complex at Maroussi, the northern suburb between Athens and Kiphissia which used to be well-known for its potters. Here a modern stadium of the 1980s is being adorned with a new steel-and-glass arching roof by a distinguished Spanish architect, Santiago Calatrava. Here will be the press centre. Not so far away will be the Olympic village, nestling under the flank of Mount Parnes. Events other than track and field will be spread among a number of sports complexes built for the occasion: an equestrian centre at Markopoulo in eastern Attica, a multi-sports complex in Phaleron, a yachting marina at Agios Kosmas near Glyfada, a weight-lifting centre at Nikaia (tailor-made for the sport at which Greek athletes have dominated international competition), and, more controversially, a rowing and canoeing centre at Schinias, a wetland near a sandy beach not far from the site of the battle of Marathon. The organizers had bad luck with the weather at the trials at Schinias in August 2003. The northeasterly *meltemi* blew strongly and two boats sank. They pray that this was a worst case scenario, not a foretaste of 2004.

For two weeks in August 2004 Athens will be host to the sports stars of the world, the sporting bureaucracy of the IOC, and a very large number of fans. August is the month in which Athens is normally deserted and traffic can flow. It is the best month for the contrarian to stay in the city and get some work done.

For the Athenians what matters about the Olympics is less the temporary disruption than the lasting effect they have on the life and amenities of the city. That too, like everything else about the Olympics, is a matter of controversy. The principle endorsed by the government and the organizing committee is that whatever is built will be done so in a sustainable way and will contribute to the amenities. The critics say this is not the case: an unrepeatable opportunity is being lost, and unrecoverable spaces such as the Marathon wetlands are being destroyed. It will take some time to be able to discern who is right. But at the least, the city's basic infrastructure is being improved, through the Attica ring road, the improvements to the Phaleron coast, and the light railways or trams being constructed from the centre of town to Glyfada and from the airport into town.

Meanwhile the Olympics have provided a good subject for speculation, about the desirability of the enterprise, the ability of the organizers to carry it off, the expense and the scandals attached to the procurement and construction processes. Some of these debates recall those of 1896. The government presents the Games as a national project, requiring national consensus. Most of the Greeks probably see them rather as Vikelas saw them in 1896, as a necessary challenge that could not be refused. On that occasion they helped to put Athens on the conceptual map of Europe, as a city with amenities, capable of organizing a major event, and a repository of certain values of civilization. In 2004 it could be asked whether Athens or Greece still needs to prove all these things. But most people in Greece would agree that the games are in some sense, as in 1896, a test of the maturity and competence of the Greek state.

The Great Idea

The maturity and competence that appeared to be vindicated by the 1896 Olympic Games were cruelly exposed a year later.

Nationalism was at the heart of the Great Idea. In the same years that Athens was presenting herself to Europe as a European capital, members of the Greek officer corps began to bypass the political process, seeing themselves as the only guarantee of honest, nationalistic policies. In 1894 a group of them had broken up the offices of the newspaper *Acropolis* as a warning against liberal, unpatriotic views. A few weeks later a group of officers founded a secret "National Society". It was designed to keep governments on the right track, and it helped to lead to war against Turkey. In April 1897 the Greek army, commanded by Crown Prince Constantine, attacked the Turks in Thessaly. It was decisively defeated and retreated in chaos. The course of the war showed how Athens was now the mirror of the nation's political and military fortunes.

It was clear in early April 1897 that there was going to be a war. Stephen Crane, author of *The Red Badge of Courage*, a great book which grew from his imagination and not from experience, came to Athens to see what a real war was like. He found unprecedented scenes of enthusiasm and patriotic ardour as the Greeks mobilized. Hundreds of young men volunteered to enlist in the army. In the streets enthusiastic crowds cheered the army, the volunteers, and the politicians who went along with the war fever. Crane let himself be carried away. He described the war as not a king's war, not a parliament's war, but a people's war.

By the time Crane came back from the front line, accompanying the Greek troops in their humiliating retreat from Thessaly, the mood had changed completely. As the first rumours of defeat reached the capital, people began to take to the streets, looking for some person or thing to blame. It could not be the Greek armed forces. It had to be their incompetent leaders, and at the top the Royal Family, who, as a disillusioned soldier told Crane, were not even Greeks, but foreigners. On 28 and 29 April 1897 thousands of men made the centre of Athens unsafe. They broke into the establishments in Ermou Street selling small arms, and helped themselves. They demonstrated outside the Royal Palace. For the first time in George's long reign (33 years by then) the throne was in real danger. The crowds included hundreds of would-be volunteers, Greeks from abroad who had come to help the country and were still waiting to enlist. Ships of the protecting powers rode to anchor in Phaleron bay. The British Ambassador told the king that HMS *Nile* was ready to take him and his family if the need should arise.

William Miller, who was present, commented that for a time Athens had no other thoughts than for the war and its consequences. Constitution Square became the equivalent of the ancient Agora, the meeting place where people of all backgrounds came together in front of the Palace to gossip, cheer detachments of soldiers, read the newspapers, and demonstrate their feelings. When a newspaper boy appeared with a new edition and shouted out the title, there was a rush for it. When news came from the front of a fresh disaster the people, including the staff, poured out of the hotels onto the square.

Defeat by Turkey was a national humiliation of the first order, with severe financial consequences for the Greek state. But the Royal Family weathered the storm, and the period of gloom and national self-questioning, which followed turned eventually to national renewal.

CHAPTER TWELVE

War, Migration, and Refugees

> *"The new Greece was born not in 1832 but in 1922, and the refugees were its new blood."*
>
> Spyros Markezinis

> *"Cold, snow, hunger."*
>
> Ioanna Tsatsos, 25 November 1941

Goudi lies on the east side of the city in the area between the Hilton Hotel and Mount Hymettus. In the early 1900s it was an area of military barracks and training grounds. Here in August 1909, tired of what they saw as the defeatism of the government over the national question of Crete, and intent on promoting their own professional interests, a group of young officers, spiritual followers of the National Society, carried out a coup d'état. They did not know what they wanted to do but they knew they wanted to be in charge. For months they controlled the activities of the government, which was still nominally in power. Then they summoned the Cretan revolutionary leader Eleftherios Venizelos to sort out the mess. That was the moment at which national renewal began.

Thirteen years later Goudi was the scene of a more tragic episode. In the wake of the defeat of the Greek army in Asia Minor in August 1922, another group of officers led another coup and established a revolutionary government, bringing to trial by court martial five politicians and one general whom they charged with high treason and personal responsibility for the disaster. The verdict was guilty. The six men were executed by firing squad at Goudi parade ground on 28 November 1922. This act of necessary revenge, in purgation of national humiliation, poisoned politics for a generation. Prince Andrew, a Lieutenant General with the Greek army in Asia Minor, was also arraigned, but escaped execution and was spirited away from Greece on a British warship.

Athens at War

Through the convulsions of the first two decades of the twentieth century, Athens remained recognizably the same city, the population increasing from 217,820 at the 1910 census to 292,991 in 1921. As prime minister, Venizelos inaugurated a radical reform of state finances and of the armed services, a new constitutional settlement, and a Balkan alliance, which led to the expulsion of Turkey from her European provinces in the Balkan Wars of 1912-13. The territory and population of Greece were almost doubled.

As in 1897, the city became a public stage on which the events of the war were played out: the mobilization, the requisitioning of motor vehicles and carts and animals, the demonstrations of joy when Greek successes were announced. The exuberance was checked by the assassination of King George in the fiftieth year of his reign by a madman in Thessaloniki, recently occupied by the Greek army. At the funeral of the king in March 1913 the people poured into the streets, and paid good money for places on balconies or at windows on the route of the funeral procession.

These last years before the Great War can be seen in retrospect as the end of an epoch, as was recognized by Ellen Bosanquet in her threnody on the Athens that was departing. There were still market gardens and vineyards at Ambelokipi, Pangrati and Kypseli, though these peripheral areas were beginning to be built up. (They are now of course part of the central city.) But developments in communications and transport signalled the coming of a new age. The press reported collisions between the hissing and clanking trams, electrified by now, and the milk carts, which were taking over from the wandering milkman who steered his flock of goats from district to district. With the newfangled telephone it was possible to order milk and other products for delivery to the home.

The First World War saw Greece divided between Venizelists, standing for alliance with the entente powers, and Royalists, favouring a neutrality hard to distinguish from sympathy for Germany. This meant turbulent years for Athens, in which the city was dominated first by Venizelists, then by Royalists when Venizelos set up a provisional government in Thessaloniki, then once more by Venizelists when he reoccupied the capital, installed there through the help of France and Britain. At one stage the two allies actually bombarded and occupied the Royalist capital. The foreign legations, and Schools of Archaeology, became centres of intelligence, giving rise to engaging memoirs by Compton Mackenzie and a variety of academic warriors.

Venizelos finally brought Greece into the war on the side of the entente, and the Greek army took part in the allies' campaign against the Bulgarians and Germans in Macedonia. It ended in victory. The reward was a mandate from the Big Four at the Paris peace conference to occupy Smyrna and the surrounding zone in Asia Minor, an area where the Greek population was strong. The years from 1919 to 1922 were an extension of the war years. First under Venizelos, then under Royalist governments, Greece's armed forces struggled to hold down Asia Minor in the face of economic pressures and lack of enthusiasm on the part of her allies.

In August 1922 Kemal Ataturk's Turkish nationalist army launched an attack on the Greek forces in the interior of Asia Minor, which quickly broke the Greek front and turned the Greek forces to retreat. As they fell back towards Smyrna, the modern Izmir, civilian refugees followed them towards the sea. Smyrna was occupied and burnt to the ground. Hundreds of thousands of Greeks left Asia Minor as refugees, many taking with them only a handful of possessions. They were followed within the next year by the remaining Greek population of Asia Minor and Eastern Thrace, exchanged for the more than 300,000 Muslim population of Greece under the terms of the Lausanne Convention of January 1923. This novel form of regulation of minority questions in effect recognized the existing state of affairs after the Turkish victory. In all, nearly one and a half million Greek refugees had to be resettled in Greece: approximately one for every three native members of the population, which was measured at almost five million in the 1928 census. A large proportion of them were disembarked at Piraeus. The census figures tell the story, rising from 292,991 in 1921 to 642,000 in 1926. If Piraeus is included, the population approached one million in the 1920s.

Refugee Crisis

Hans Morgenthau, who was sent as President of the Refugee Settlement Commission, established by the League of Nations and Greece in 1923, witnessed a shipload of refugees land at Thessaloniki:

> …*seven thousand people crowded in a ship that would have been taxed to normal capacity with two thousand… packed like sardines upon the deck, a squirming, writhing mass of human misery. They had been at sea for four days. There had not been space to permit them to lie down to sleep; there had been no food to eat; there was not access to any toilet facilities. For those four days and nights many had stood upon the open deck, drenched by an autumn rain, pierced by the cold night wind, and blistered by the noonday sun. They came ashore in rags, hungry, sick, covered with vermin, hollow eyed, exhaling the horrible odour of human filth—bowed with despair.*

The effects on Athens were devastating. Most of the refugees were temporarily parked in the big towns, Athens, Piraeus and Thessaloniki, though finally the main resettlement effort was to take place in the north of Greece, where refuges were put into new villages which

consolidated the Hellenic character of Macedonia. Those who came to Athens, arriving at Piraeus by ship, were housed in tents on open ground, around the columns of the temple of Olympian Zeus, in warehouses, schools and university buildings, and even in theatres, a family to each box. Refugees built themselves huts and shanties out of whatever planks and tin cans they could find and wherever they could find an accommodating spot, on waste ground and on the outskirts of the town. Because so many of the young men had been killed or sent into the interior of Anatolia in "labour battalions", women outnumbered men.

Survival was the first problem. Many died over the first winter of 1922-3. After the initial phase of chaos, misery and death, came the necessity of adaptation to a new society which was superficially like their own but different in important ways, and by and large hostile to the refugees, who were seen as alien, and troublesome economic competitors. The Greek historian George Mavrogordatos defined the three dimensions of the refugees' condition in inter-war Greek society as (1) economic deprivation, (2) downward social mobility, and (3) status deprivation, segregation, and discrimination.

Life at first had an improvised character. The streets of Athens took on a new look and sound as the refugees appeared in their tattered costumes from Asia Minor, pushing their peddlers' handcarts, trying to sell odds and ends, speaking strange forms of Greek or not yet speaking Greek at all, for many of the Greek Christian refugees were Turkish speakers. Morgenthau described how the less fortunate tens of thousands were camped out upon the bare hills around Athens, now bleak and cold with approaching winter, huddled in tents pieced together out of burlap bags, or in huts extemporized out of the ubiquitous five-gallon Standard Oil cans. Shoes made of discarded tyres became standard footwear, and tin cans served for cooking utensils.

It was as if the Greek communities of Asia Minor had been splintered into fragments, some of which were lost for ever, others coming to rest in Greece and seeking to be reunited with their fellows. The Old Palace on Constitution Square became a centre for administration of relief, and distribution of bread. Lists of names were posted here so as to reunite separated families. Dynamic leaders of some refugee communities negotiated with Greek officials at the

Agriculture Ministry and Ministry of the Public Welfare for facilities needed for new settlements—tents, houses, utilities, later schools and churches—and tried to form communities with hard working, like-thinking families.

As the humanitarian relief effort developed under the auspices of the League of Nations, the urban refugees gradually found more permanent homes. For those who had not succeeded, as most did, in finding or creating lodging through their own resources the government created whole new neighbourhoods, with utility housing, on empty space between Piraeus and the city of Athens and elsewhere on the fringes of the city. These quarters, Kokkinia, Kaisariani, Nea Ionia, Nea Smyrni, Vyronas and others, were laid out on grid plans, with basic housing designed for one or two families, earth roads, and simple utilities. The prefix "Nea" or new is often the sign of a refugee community, since the refugees recreated the names of their former towns and villages in the new environment. As well as these quarters, which are now firmly a part of the Greater Athens area, smaller settlements are dotted around Attica, from Anavysso and Phokaia on the coast near Sunium, where refugees from Cappadocia and Bithynia settled, to Rafina and Eleusis.

It was not until well after the Second World War that the urban settlements were linked to the mains sewerage systems. Uprooted, dislocated and planted in a largely uncomprehending society, the refugees developed their own ways of life, recreating a sense of community through the memories of their homes in Asia Minor and preserving an identity distinct from that of the Greeks among whom they had been placed. They continued to refer to themselves as "refugees" (*prosphyges*) and as people from Asia Minor. With the ingenuity and pride of outsiders, they made the best of their basic housing, extending downwards by excavating basements (which then served as flood traps during the annual autumn rains), keeping the streets clean, whitewashing the walls, growing flowers in tin cans, as on Cycladic islands. In the years of depression life was very difficult. The men found work in Piraeus factories, as street vendors or in the construction trade; the young women in factories and workshops, making shirts, or in domestic service.

Identity and Change: Yerania and Kaisariani

In the early 1970s, fifty years after the Asia Minor disaster of 1922, a young anthropologist from Oxford, Renée Hirschon, came to live in Yerania, a part of Kokkinia near Piraeus, and lived and talked with refugee families. She found that the communities had kept their identities and their pride. She described the look of the refugee neighbourhoods:

> In contrast with the ubiquitous modernity of angular cement, marble, and glass structures which increasingly suffocate the city, low houses appeared with tiled roofs and walls painted in pastel shades of blue, deep ochres, greens, and pink. Jasmine and honeysuckle twined around gates and walls, pots of geranium and sweet basil lined wooden balconies. Streets were clean and pavements marked with fresh lines of whitewash.
>
> A morning's view would reveal housewives returning from the local bakery with armfuls of bread, hanging washing in one another's yards, airing bed-linen on lines hung between lamp-posts. On certain mornings a bustle of activity at street corners showed women carrying bins of rubbish to the dustman's cart which moved ponderously down the main road, a hand-bell ringing out. While passing through in the late afternoon, you could see people sitting on pavements with a small coffee-cup beside them, chatting as strollers paused to exchange greetings.

Hirschon found that the initially attractive impression of these well-kept, colourful dwellings and the sociable atmosphere soon gave way to questions. The washing hanging between the lamp-posts and the children playing in the streets were signs of high population densities. Most of the houses turned out to be subdivided between several households, living on top of each other in conditions that generated tensions. The streets were rutted. The pungent odour and hum of a pump betrayed that a household's cesspool was being drained by a private contractor. Nonetheless the sociability and neatness were real, signs of the toughness, pride and adaptability of people who drew on their memories and sense of otherness to recreate their lives.

Today this sense of difference has been diminished, to different degrees in different quarters, by time and economic progress. One of the more attractive of the former refugee areas is the quarter of

Kaisariani, a mere ten minutes bus ride from Vasilissis Sophias Avenue. Here shops reveal the rise of prosperity in what is now a mixed area of middle- and working-class society. It has kept its working ethos, as the choice of newspapers hanging outside the kiosks, and the political graffiti and posters show. But among the bakers, greengrocers and grocers, the little shops selling trinkets and cheap magazines, are banks and smart ladies' clothes stores. Only a few low, single-storey refugee houses of the 1920s remain, with their tiled roofs, crouching between the five- and six-floor apartment blocks. Around Anagennisis (Renaissance) Square, the main square of the quarter, the smarter old houses, with two floors, have been listed for preservation. Most are now cafés and fish restaurants. Looking back up the main street, the eye stops at the blank mountainside, a grey-blue wall on which detail has been annihilated by the strength of the morning light of the sky behind.

A few minutes walk uphill from the bus terminus is a large cemetery, nestling among the pine trees, with rows of solid, well-kept white marble tombs, some bearing photographs of the departed. It lacks the splendour and sculptural elaboration of the First Cemetery but still speaks of the crucial role that permanence and memory hold in this society, many of whose parents and grand parents were uprooted from their homelands. When I was last there, three tawny dogs lay dozing in the sunny entrance, among the flower stalls, the marble funerary workshop, and the notices of the local authority ("Burial is for three years. Be sure to contact the ephor of the cemetery before this period expires..."). The cemetery has a quiet but purposeful feeling, as ladies in black and men in suits tend their relatives' graves, lighting lamps, renewing flowers, while the cemetery workers trim the ground cover plants under the cypress trees or repair a crumbling grave. Every few yards there are little standpipes for watering the flowers and paths during the dry months of summer. Across the road, around the Monastery of St John the Theologian, a clutch of battered beehives stands among the long spring grass in the pine trees.

A thirty-minute walk up hill beyond the cemetery brings you to the famous Monastery of Kaisariani, one of the enchanting places of Athens. The monastery is high enough to be clear of Athens' noise and pollution and to have extensive views back over the city to the

Acropolis and beyond. Here you can imagine yourself near Plato's Ilissos, which springs from nearby, or in a Sophoclean grove with nightingales. The gardens and arboretum, and wooded hills good for walking, are within fifteen minutes of central Athens.

Changing Cityscape: the Inter-war Years

"Few cities have changed more than modern Athens," wrote the historian William Miller in 1928. He had lived through the transformations since the late nineteenth century and the days of the horse-drawn trams. The agents of change he identified were the arrival of the refugees, the increase in population, and the advent of the motor car. It may seem to us that inter-war Athens, with only 5,000 cars, must have been paradise for the pedestrian. Not so for Miller. He recalled how in 1832 Sir Pulteney Malcolm, the British commander of the fleet stationed at Malta, had introduced the first two-wheeled carts, to transport building materials for the house he was having built at the village of Patisia (the house still exists, and is now a Home for Incurables.) The first four wheelers followed two years later. The automobile first appeared around the turn of the century. By 1914 and the outbreak of war there were about 226 motor cars. The royal princes were pioneers in motoring. Alexander, who briefly became king and came to a sad end, bitten by his own pet monkey, was notoriously keen on fast cars.

By the late 1920s the centre of the city was noisy with the hooting of klaxons and the grinding of the electric trams, and there were blockages at the main junctions. The apartment block was beginning to appear in central Athens, which hitherto had been a city of low-rise individual houses with their gardens. Miller noted several big blocks of flats with common entrances, something new for the Athenians.

By this time the focal points in the city had shifted. In the early days of King Otho, the smart area to live was Adrianou Street in the Plaka, and the main commercial hub was Ermou Street. Ermou was the street by which travellers from Piraeus entered Athens. It was the seat of the Council of State, the place of the first bric-a-brac dealer and the first western dressmaker, and the place to get your hair cut. The famous Lovely Greece (*Oraia Ellas*) café on the corner of Aeolou and Ermou was the centre of gossip and social life, and political agitation.

By the end of the century Ermou had given way to the broad streets connecting Constitution and Omonia Squares. Zacharatos café on the corner of Syntagma had taken the place of the *Oraia Ellas*. Stadiou Street, which had housed the professional classes, doctors, professors and lawyers, and had no shops, became the commercial and banking district of town. The old Royal Stables between Panepistimiou and Stadiou fell into disuse and this prime area was redeveloped between the wars as part of the business quarter.

Distinguished neoclassical houses now lined Vasilissis Sophias Avenue, and the elegant Kolonaki area, which had developed in the late nineteenth century, grew in importance. As the city expanded, some people chose to live outside, commuting from Kiphissia, Maroussi, the new "garden city" Psychiko, or from Old Phaleron and Glyfada.

A number of athletic clubs had sprung up in the 1890s, before the Olympic Games. Now new leisure pursuits were introduced. A golf course opened near Agios Kosmas and Glyfada in 1923, a new racecourse at the bottom of Syngrou Avenue at Phaleron in 1925. Planting schemes around the city, encouraged by the "philodasic" society (lovers of forests), were greening Lycabettus, Philopappus, the approaches to the Acropolis and the hills next to the stadium.

The growing population required more water. Athens is short of natural water supplies, springs having existed only on the Acropolis and a few other points. The emperor Hadrian, among his many other benefactions, provided Athens with a regular supply of water by an aqueduct which brought water from springs in the foothills of Mount Parnes, ending on the western flank of Lycabettus, at the cistern (*dexameni*) that has given its name to an attractive square. Successive local administrations since the 1830s had patched this up. By the 1880s it was clear that a more radical solution was needed, and Tricoupis's administration explored various schemes, including bringing water from Lake Stymphalia in the Peloponnese. It was only in 1925 that a contract was signed with an American company for creating an artificial lake in the hills near Marathon by means of a dam, and bringing water to Athens by tunnel and aqueduct. This is still a resource for the city of more than four million, but is now supplemented by water from mainland Greece northwest of Delphi. In Miller's time water was seen as a precious commodity. Today it flows freely.

Drinking water also has become abundant. In the nineteenth century it was brought down to Athens in barrels from the springs of Maroussi, Kiphissia and Kaisariani. Spyridon Louis, the marathon winner, acquired the concession to supply Maroussi water to the Athenians. Today every kiosk sells plastic bottles of chilled water.

The streets of Athens between the wars were controlled by a British-trained police force. Specialist foreign missions had a long history. They were one of the means by which Greek governments sought to accelerate development and to consolidate ties with favoured western countries. The Venizelos government had gone in for them in a big way before the First World War, inviting a French mission to reform the army, a British mission to train the navy, and an Italian mission for the gendarmerie. The three-man British police mission was invited by Venizelos in 1918, "for the purpose of introducing London police methods", and found itself responsible for training a city police force to replace the gendarmerie in policing the five main cities of Greece.

According to Miller, when the new "Towns' Police" was extended to central Athens in January 1925

an immediate improvement in the regulation of traffic was noticed: private cars were parked at fixed places, the stations of the motor-service reorganised, lists of fares and of the maximum number of passengers put up in the motor-omnibuses, and those vehicles regularly cleaned and disinfected, and smoking and spitting prohibited in a classical notice which contained two obsolete infinitives. In the early days citizens used to form groups to admire the manner in which one policeman held up the traffic. Smartness, fairness, politeness, punctuality, the use of force only as a last resort, and—greatest of all virtues in a Greek official—abstention from politics were inculcated, and the public obeyed the police because it was realised that there was one rule for everyone and that Sir Frederick Halliday's policemen were no respecters of persons. This was conspicuously shown during the General Election of 1926, when the police kept order.

Political Instability
Athens was not immune from the larger political, social and economic currents of the inter-war period. Immediately after the Asia Minor

disaster King Constantine departed into exile, dying the next year at Palermo. His son George, who succeeded him, followed him soon into exile and a Republic was declared. Under the republican regime, faced with the grave problems of settling and integrating the refugees, much of the country's energy was dissipated in political factionalism, enmity between Venizelists and populists, and interventions of the army. This was a period of coups and counter-coups, of largely forgotten dictators with names like Pangalos and Kondylis, whose expressions can be recaptured on early newsreels.

The swing of the pendulum brought King George back to Greece in 1935. Soon afterwards democratic institutions were put to bed when the former Royalist staff officer and inveterate political schemer Ioannis Metaxas took over the government of the country as dictator. Athens became the scene of youth rallies and healthy-looking national dances in the Panathenaic Stadium. This Greek-style fascism was particularly arduous for the communists, who were driven underground, their leaders imprisoned in the prison fortress of Nauplion, the little seaside town where Metaxas himself had served in the garrison as a young officer in the 1890s.

As economic conditions deteriorated with the slump of the 1930s, the refugee quarters became recruiting grounds for the Communist Party of Greece (KKE). One reason was the slowness and incompleteness of the resettlement process. Until after the Second World War some thousands of refugee families still lived in sheds and shantytowns. In the early days the refugees saw Venizelos as their only protection against an indifferent or hostile world. As time passed and their basic problems of economic and social integration remained unsolved, many turned to the communists. A map showing the voting pattern of Athens clearly shows a sharp distinction between the bourgeois central areas around Kolonaki and the outlying bastions of Venizelism, into which the communist vote made headway in the early 1930s. This phenomenon was concealed under the dictatorship of Metaxas when the Communist Party was forced underground. But it was to have important effects later, during the war.

German Occupation and Famine

Italian forces occupied Albania in April 1940. On 28 October the Italian Ambassador called on Metaxas with an ultimatum, to expire in three hours, demanding that Italy be allowed to occupy strategic positions on Greek territory. Metaxas said no. His and the country's defiance is commemorated every year as Ochi Day, the day when Greece said No. Once again Athens witnessed enlistment, the cheering of soldiers departing for the Albanian front, the anguish of casualty lists, the glory of Greece's short-lived successes against the Italian forces. But on 6 April 1941, impatient at the Italian failure to wrap up the campaign against Greece, the Germans intervened. German forces swept down from Yugoslavia into northern Greece. It took them only seven weeks to push the allied forces aside, forcing them to evacuate the Greek mainland.

On Sunday 27 May 1941 members of the German community of Athens, who had gathered at the German Archaeological Institute as a place of refuge during the Nazi forces' drive down on Athens, looked across to the Acropolis and saw the red flag of the Reich flying from the belvedere in the eastern corner of the citadel. The German military had arrived. The flag was hauled down from the Acropolis in a heroic gesture of resistance by the young Manolis Glezos during the night of 31 May. Hoisted again by the Nazi occupiers, it flew until 12 October 1944 when the Germans departed for the north, a few hours before allied forces drove in from Patras to liberate the city. As ever, it was the Acropolis that symbolized the state, enslaved or free, of the city and of the Greek nation.

The economy of Greece, and still more of Athens, was dependent on imported foodstuffs. The cessation of imports, and the shortage of draught animals, tractors, fodder, seed and fertilizers combined to create conditions of famine, and were aggravated by the brutally selfish policies of the occupying power. The big cities suffered more than the country, where food could more easily be procured. The poorer areas of Athens and Piraeus, especially the refugee quarters, suffered most. It was not long before there were shortages of basic foodstuffs. Bread, rice, oil and sugar were rationed. Inflation ate away the value of the currency.

Those who had gold, which eventually became the only useful means of exchange besides barter, could manage. Others began to starve. Queues developed in the streets. Fuel also ran short and eventually buses ceased to operate and the population walked. As factories were requisitioned and turned over to supplying the Reich, more and more people were deprived of work.

The winter of 1941-2 was unusually cold and famine set in. Official distributions provided only 350 calories *per capita* per day on average. The watery bean soup distributed in communal feeding centres may have added a further 140 calories. With occasional purchases of bread and vegetables and fruit when available on the market, the average energy per head per day was still not more than 800 calories, 2,000 being the minimum for bare subsistence. Death became commonplace and the people inured to it. One estimate is that 40,000 died in the year beginning October 1941.

In his book *Inside Hitler's Greece* (1993) Mark Mazower chronicles the effects in language that recalls Thucydides' description of the plague of the fifth century BC:

Desperate to earn money, people turned to peddling goods or begging. At the docks in Piraeus, a crowd of odd-job men occupied the quayside… Street vendors sold dirty-looking pieces of carob cake, figs and other fruit, or matches, cigarettes, old clothes. Beggars lay on the pavement. In the centre of Omonia Square, stretched out on the blankets above the warm air vents of the Metro, there were people of all ages, holding out their hands to passers-by… For many, the only means of survival was to gather wild grass and other weeds from the countryside around the city. These were then boiled, if there was fuel available, and eaten without oil. But these grasses had virtually no nutritional value… Children searched through rubbish bins for scraps of food, or waited near the service entrances of large hotels. Others clustered around the doors of restaurants. Some German officers tormented urchins by throwing them scraps from balconies and watching them fight among themselves… Though malnutrition enfeebled the body and made work increasingly exhausting, working families had little choice if they wished to stay alive but to continue as though nothing was happening… Because coal and wood had become very expensive, and sometimes unavailable, houses were not properly heated, and people succumbed to colds, flu and TB. After several weeks of malnutrition, people weakened quickly. Vitamin deficiency caused tumours and boils to appear on their hands and feet, and, unless cured, these spread on to the body and the face. Around half the families in the poor quarters showed these symptoms by the beginning of 1942.

The final stage before death was a state of physical and mental exhaustion. This was the point at which people simply collapsed, and were unable to raise themselves up again.

The strongest impression to come through in the first-hand records and diaries of the period is of the cold and the hunger. "Cold, snow, hunger," wrote Ioanna Tsatsos in her journal entry for 25 November 1941, "What will happen with the children's hunger?" On the last day of the year she described her journey home from the office to her home in Kydathinaion Street:

I walked home through the icy night. It was thick darkness. Here and there could be heard something like crying, like a plaint. I could imagine skeletal hands stretching out seeking something, which I was totally unable to give them. Not the least shred of hope can make its way in. The Germans are triumphing everywhere. And this hunger, like a mass extermination of the race, is killing us all.

Ioanna Tsatsos was the sister of the poet George Seferis and wife of Constantine Tsatsos, a friend and debating partner of Seferis, later to become president of Greece after Constantine Karamanlis returned from exile in 1974 to take over the reins of government. He became a hero to the students when he defied orders by observing 28 October, the day Greece said No to the Italians, as a holiday. She worked under the aegis of Archbishop Damaskinos on relief, distributing food to children and to the families of the executed and imprisoned. The Archbishop emerges as a hero of the war for his courage in confronting the occupiers, in providing relief, and in defending the Jewish community from destruction.

The Tsatsos couple were relatively fortunate, possessing goods which could be sold in return for food. She sold the children's bicycle for one gold pound and bought some stringy beans and yellow chickpeas. But when the supply of food dried up, everyone faced the same plight. Her diary records the steady and appalling attrition of the best young men, executed by the Germans for possession of arms or explosives, sabotage in the factories, or help in spiriting away to the Middle East British officers who had been left behind, and the despair of the widows and mothers who came to her for comfort. Throughout this time, their house was a meeting place for Tsatsos' friends who would gather to discuss the war, the resistance, and how to rebuild Greece after the nightmare came to an end. Karamanlis was one of them.

The famine was discriminating. Perhaps because they put their children's interests first, adults aged over forty suffered most, and especially men. The war therefore created widows and orphans. With death so common in the winter of 1941, the usual funeral ceremonies were disorganized, and as Thucydides had recorded of Athenians during the plague, people buried the dead as best they could. For many families, a proper burial was too difficult or too expensive to arrange. Some simply buried their dead wherever they could, in the frozen earth or in mass graves in the cemeteries. With hunger omnipresent, tempers frayed to breaking point. Some became listless or irritable. Others, as during the plague, indulged in a frantic pursuit of pleasure.

Liberation

Liberation came in October 1944. The German army withdrew, leaving political chaos. The Greek government in exile returned, led by George Papandreou, with the British army. The Athenians poured into the streets in a delirium of joy. The Greek flag rose again on the Acropolis, watched with emotion by thousands of Athenians including Ioanna Tsatsos. For a moment, happiness reigned. An image noted by Seferis in his diary more than a year and a half later caught the liberation of the spirit after the nightmare of occupation and war. He watched in the Archaeological Museum the unearthing of the statues which had been buried for the duration: statues, still sunken in the earth, naked from the waist up, planted at random; the arm of some colossal god; a naked woman showing only her smiling buttocks. "It was a chorus of the resurrected, a second coming of bodies that gave you a crazy joy."

But before this joy, there was the confrontation between the allied forces and the communists, and renewed bloodshed in the *Dekemvriana*, or the events of December 1944. The place from which to look at these events is Kolonaki, where the British, still the dominant power in Greece, had their embassy.

CHAPTER THIRTEEN

Lycabettus, Kolonaki, British Embassy

"The first big pink house on the left."
Advice to Sir Rex Leeper, British Ambassador to the Greeks,
on how to find the British Embassy when he entered Athens on
the liberation of the city in October 1944

Looking from Mount Lycabettus down towards Phaleron and the sea,
you see Kolonaki spread out immediately below you.

Until well into the reign of King George, this was scrubby hillside
pastured by sheep. Early and mid-nineteenth-century photographs
taken from the Acropolis show the bare hillside beyond the Royal
Palace, with a zigzag path up it. The quarter grew in the late
nineteenth century, stretching from the north side of Vasilissis Sophias
Avenue up the flank of Lycabettus. The British and American Schools,
which today are overshadowed by the Evangelismos Hospital and
hemmed in by blocks of flats, were built in empty countryside in the
1880s. Some students in the early days complained at the distance
from the middle of town. Even at the turn of the century there was
empty space in Kolonaki.

An absurd "diplomatic incident" took place in the 1880s on the
lower slopes of Lycabettus. Arthur Nicolson, a young and promising
diplomat, was posted from Constantinople to Athens in March 1884,
to take temporary charge of the British Legation. Nicolson did not
understand the Greeks. Trying to run the legation on the pay of a First
Secretary, he was bored, in debt, and tired of diplomatic life and
humdrum official work. His views on the economic policies of the
Tricoupis government were critical and did not make him popular.

One day Nicolson went for a walk up the side of Lycabettus through the pine trees. A Greek gendarme named Calpouzos, whose task was to prevent strollers from desecrating the pine wood by dropping cigarette ends, accosted him. He seized him by the arm and hit him over the shoulder with a stick. According to Nicolson's son Harold, his father explained in the demotic tongue that he was the British Chargé d'Affaires (but Harold Nicolson acknowledges that his father did not know Greek). The gendarme struck him again, violently, on the back of the neck. After an unsuccessful intervention by two Greek bystanders who tried to obtain the gendarme's name and number, Nicolson suffered a third assault, and retired. The gendarme threw stones at his retreating figure.

The person of a diplomat should be inviolable. Nicolson went at once to Prime Minister Tricoupis and complained. Within hours the offending gendarme was brought under escort to the legation and identified. An official note of apology was delivered by the Greek government. The king sent his aide-de-camp to express regret. Nicolson was assured that the gendarme would be dismissed. There the matter should have ended, and apparently Nicolson was prepared to let it.

Unfortunately, however, the German minister urged him to demand more public expiation. Stupidly, Nicolson agreed. He insisted that Calpouzos should be publicly dismissed and that an Order of the Day be read to the gendarmerie stating why. But when the Order of the Day was published, it seemed to place the blame for the incident on Nicolson. At this point Nicolson, in his son's words, lost his temper. He insisted that the Greek government issue a new Order of the Day, to be read out to the gendarmes in Constitution Square, after which the band was to play the British National Anthem in the presence of the British consul. The Greek Cabinet eventually agreed to this.

The whole affair might have been devised to show the Greeks in the most humiliating possible manner the unequal nature of their relationship with Britain. It infuriated the Greek press and parliament, and left Nicolson rightly ashamed of himself. The satirical poet Souris wrote a piece excoriating British pomposity. A few months later Calpouzos committed a murder and was found to be insane. He had apparently been suffering from cerebral inflammation at the time of the assault. By then Nicolson had left Athens, much to his relief. He went on to become Ambassador to Russia and Permanent Under Secretary at the Foreign Office. His urbane son Harold, after trying diplomacy himself, became a successful author. His account of this episode, published in 1930, is a nice morality story on the tendency of power to corrupt. Nowadays British diplomats do not have such power.

Hillside Neighbourhood

The urge to change and improve has not spared Lycabettus. In the 1880s the architect Ernst Ziller worked up a plan for turning it into a pleasant place of recreation, to be called the "airy sanatorium". Twenty years later, in the last work he ever published, Dimitrios Vikelas conceived the idea of turning the hill into a memorial park to the heroes of the War of Independence, removing the chapel of St George and installing a large shrine-cum-museum on the top. Luckily, no one paid any attention to this proposal. The whitewashed chapel and the blue-and-white Greek flag fluttering on the summit above the dark green pines are all that is needed. Then in the 1920s someone developed a scheme for a cog railway from the university area, tunnelling up and under the Frog's Mouth crag beside Lycabettus to the top of the hill, which was to be developed. This plan was also abandoned. The existing funicular railway built in the 1960s is discreet and has not damaged the looks of the hill.

Lycabettus looks very well as it is, and is at its best at Easter. After the priest emerges from the chapel on top of the hill at midnight to proclaim that Christ is Risen, and the flame is passed from one candle to another in the hands of the faithful, a watcher from down below in the city can see the path from the summit picked out by tiny points of light, as the people wind their way down the hill back to their homes.

The streets running northwards up the flank of the hill here are named after ancient Greek authors: Plutarch (the street of the British Embassy), Lucian, Herodotus. They turn to steps as the hill gets steeper. The transverse streets running west-east, Aristippou, Kleomenous, Deinokratous, Xenokratous, are named after two ancient philosophers, an architect and a sculptor. Here in Xenokratous, across the street from Philippou's taverna, is a simple stone tablet, in memory of Panagiotis Kanellopoulos (1902-86), who lived at no. 15 from 1952 until the end of his life.

Kanellopoulos was one of Kolonaki's most distinguished, and nicest, residents, a scholar, writer, politician and all-round renaissance man. He was born in Patras, but became an Athenian, and wrote a charming short book about the city. Like many Greek politicians, he belonged to a political dynasty. His uncle was the brilliant, doomed conservative politician Dimitrios Gounaris, who was executed in September 1922 for his alleged responsibility for the Asia Minor disaster. By marriage he was linked to Constantine Karamanlis. He seemed to graduate seamlessly from being the brilliant young man of the resistance and the Greek government in exile during the war to being the grand old man of Greek politics. As prime minister, he was hauled out of bed on the night of 21 April 1967 and placed under preventive detention as the Colonels' coup d'état was set in train. The then British Ambassador called in his commercial attaché early in the morning and sent him to find out where Kanellopoulos was being held, so as to intervene with the new rulers for his release. It was during that period, when he was under house arrest in his apartment in Xenokratous Street, that I met him. Later, in 1980, he came to the British Embassy for a dinner in honour of Harold Macmillan, and the two old warriors reminisced about the events of December 1944 in which they both played an important role. Until late in his life Kanellopoulos used to dine at Philippou's taverna, "The Barrels", only a few yards from his home.

Only a hundred and fifty yards along the street from Kanellopoulos' house is the little square of Dexameni ("the cistern"), the site of Hadrian's reservoir. The square has a children's playground, a little open-air café under the trees, and on Fridays a modest farmers' market.

Dexameni is associated with the Nobel Prize-winning poet Odysseus Elytis, who lived nearby and whose bronze statue stands in the square. An earlier and still greater writer, Alexandros Papadiamantis, was once photographed here by the writer Pavlos Nirvanas, at a time when the square was almost deserted. Papadiamantis, who came from the island of Skiathos, was always uneasy in the big city. He told Nirvanas nervously that they were attracting attention to themselves. Official literary events meant nothing to him. At a literary party in his honour at the Parnassos literary society, attended by all Athens, he escaped to the house of a grocer friend, and asked his wife to make him a cup of camomile tea.

In other words, Papadiamantis was in Athens but not of it. Virtually all Greek writers have lived in the city at one time or another but not all have adopted it or been adopted by it. And some, or most, have another country, a place of nostalgia to return to, in reality or in the mind. For Seferis it was his homeland, the village of Skala by the sea near Smyrna in Asia Minor, for Papadiamantis the island of Skiathos where he lived and where his stories are set, for Kazantzakis Crete. For Vikelas it was no single place, certainly not Syros where he was born, but the restless journey itself. His most vivid metaphor is the image of life as a railway journey in which the traveller, his back to the engine, can only see the country already passed.

But there are writers who have possessed or been possessed by Athens and who seem specially associated with it. In particular, they are those who have taken part in the literary market place, the politics or the café life of literature. They include the poet Palamas; the essayist Emmanuel Roides; the historian of Athens Dimitrios Kambouroglou; the poet George Drosinis; and the novelist Giorgos Theotokas. Among foreigners Henry Miller and Kevin Andrews, another Kolonaki resident, were also, and joyously, possessed.

Kolonaki Square

Kolonaki Square is the site of the original "little column", after which the area takes its name. Here you can sit at some of the best cafés in Athens enjoying a coffee or a drink and listening to the chatter of the golden youth and the not so young of Athens. (One of the best of all, the old Byzantium, where the bold could if they wished smoke the Turkish narghile, is long gone.) The kiosks lining the square are festooned with every kind of newspaper and magazine, Greek and foreign. The centre of the square is paved, with benches under the judas trees where one can sit in the shade near a fountain, keeping an eye open to avoid pigeon droppings. You used to see in the tarmac of the road that very Greek oddity, metal bottle tops soldered into the asphalt just where they dropped from the bottles carried across the street on trays by the waiters of the Kolonaki cafés.

Here you are only two minutes walk from the wonderful Benaki Museum and the Goulandris Museum of Cycladic Art. For foreign culture, there is the British Council, the leading purveyor of English language teaching in Greece, on the lower side of the square. It came to believe in information technology rather than books, and decided to close its excellent library in the mid-1990s, but was pushed into reverse by a vigorous campaign by local expatriate book lovers.

Kolonaki and its environs house a disproportionate number of the Greek "establishment" of politicians, retired ambassadors and admirals, and senior people in business, the media and the academy. It is an embassy quarter, and houses many of the foreign diplomatic community. The British Embassy and the Ambassador's Residence lie five minutes east of the square. The residence is a handsome neoclassical building. The working part of the embassy, the chancery, is an ugly concrete structure erected in the bleak post-war period for modern architecture. It towers over the tiny nineteenth-century Byzantine-style Church of St Nicholas.

Embassy under Siege

The history of the British Embassy illustrates the ways in which institutions adapt to change and growth in the city. When Athens was established as capital city, and the court and diplomatic corps moved from Nauplion, British Minister Dawkins took temporary quarters in a house belonging to the Negrepontis family, which stood solitary on the Attic plain in the area north-northwest of the Acropolis which is now known as Metaxourgeio (silk factory). Dawkins took this house for a rent of 6,300 gold drachmas, higher than that paid by the king for his first, temporary palace. Surprisingly it is still standing, splendid but dilapidated and pockmarked with bullets from the civil war. Later, after spending a period in the Plaka area, the British moved to a nineteenth-century house in Klafthmonos Square, then known as the Square of the Mint. The house was designed by Kleanthes and called the Ambrosios Rallis house after its first occupant.

The Rallis house was well placed in the centre of town, not far from the trio of neoclassical public buildings. It was damaged by earthquakes in 1853. By 1899, when the British government finally bought it, it was losing some of its former glory, and by the 1920s it was regarded by its occupants as a liability. But for many years this house was the centre of British diplomatic activity in Greece, and therefore, given the relationships of power between Greece and Britain, a centre of power. Compton Mackenzie described the legation as it was when he arrived there early in the First World War to conduct intelligence work:

> *The British Legation in Athens completely fulfilled my notion of what a Legation should look like. I can imagine no residence more eloquent of its vocation. To turn aside from the garish whiteness of Stadium Street and pull up in the carriage before that mellow house overlooking a large garden shady with dark pine and the feathery light green foliage of false-pepper trees was an experience... There returns upon my senses as I write these words the smell of the warm stone mingled with an aromatic breath of pines, with acrid whiffs of dust, and the sweaty leather of the horses' harness. Smith, the Legation porter, hurried down the wide steps from the great front door to help with the bags... And then the big entrance hall of the Legation fills with numerous figures in leisurely light suits of well cut clothes, who have emerged from various doors and seem to be flitting like butterflies round the canvas bags which have been flung down in a heap on the marble floor.*

By the 1920s the Klafthmonos Square area had become the banking quarter and the embassy was surrounded by multi-storey buildings. In any case by then it was too small. The Foreign Office embarked on a frustrating search for a new building, considering many sites including the Megaron Maximou, now the prime minister's office, and the present Italian Embassy. The British even bought land in Psychiko, thinking of building away from the town centre. Finally they abandoned the search and decided to extend and improve the Rallis house.

At this point an Anglo-Greek lady named Helena Schilizzi enters the story. As a young lady, thrilled by the victories of Greece in the Balkan Wars, she met the widowed Greek prime minister Eleftherios Venizelos when he came to London in December 1912. It was the beginning of a love on her side that found its fulfilment nearly ten years later.

Venizelos left Greece immediately after he fell from power in November 1920 and married Helena the following year at the house of their close friends Lord and Lady Crosfield in Highgate, London. She accompanied him on his return to Greek politics, after the disaster in Asia Minor brought about a reversal in political fortunes.

Helena was rich. In 1928 she bought from the National Bank of Greece the land for a new house, a good sloping site on the lower slopes of Lycabettus with views towards Mount Hymettus and the sea. The chosen architect was Anastasios Metaxas, by now an old man, who had designed the reconstructed Panathenaic Stadium for the 1896 Olympic Games. He built an imposing structure well designed for official receptions. Helena wrote later that she actually wanted a small house; but "they" proved to her that it had to be big so that the friends and supporters of Venizelos could all meet there. That is how political affairs work in Greece.

Venizelos died in Paris on 18 March 1936. His body was brought by train to Brindisi and thence by ship to his native Crete, where he was buried. Returning from Crete to Athens to deal with her private affairs and with the house, Helena found the courtyard full of flowers brought in tribute to her husband. Within a month of the old man's death she had offered the house for sale to the British government, for £50,000. After rapid exchanges between the then minister, Sir Sidney Waterlow, and the Office of Works in Whitehall, the offer was accepted, Waterlow moved into the house, and the former legation was soon afterwards destroyed. The British were thus implanted on an ideal site in the heart of Kolonaki.

For a short time, after the allied armies liberated Athens in October 1944, the building was at the centre of Greece's political history. The Greek government of George Papandreou entered Athens, followed by Harold Macmillan, the Minister Resident for the Mediterranean, and the British Ambassador Rex Leeper. Leeper had been accredited to the king when he was already in exile, so it was his first visit to the embassy. He claimed later that the embassy was described to him as the "first big pink house on the left". The house was a pale cyclamen colour. Leeper took over from the Swiss custodians, who had taken charge during the German occupation after the Americans, the original caretakers, had entered the war. Within a few minutes the Union flag was flying from the roof. Every room on the ground floor was stacked with furniture to the ceiling.

Greece was in a state of near civil war. In early December fighting broke out between units of ELAS, the communist armed forces, and British forces under General Scobie. The British held an enclave in the centre of town, ELAS controlling the outlying areas. The British Embassy became the political headquarters of the legitimist cause, supporting the government of Papandreou against the communists. Leeper brought all the embassy staff into the building. For the next five weeks there were some fifty people sleeping there. Conditions were harsh. There was no heat, light or mains water. Macmillan noted that they had fortunately filled all the baths.

In the Ambassador's words, the embassy was not very conveniently situated for purposes of protection—a large house built on rising ground, and all the more conspicuous because it was pink and continued to fly the Union flag. It was seriously exposed only on the side facing Kiphissia Avenue (Vasilissis Sophias), but as the best bedrooms as well as the dining room and the Ambassador's study all faced that way, personnel had to move about with care. There was continual sniping from the poor suburbs in front of the house, the bullets smacking into the walls like balls hitting a fives court wall. Mrs. Leeper, the Ambassador's wife, managed the establishment as if it were a large hotel, making the best of army biscuits, bully beef and spam to feed the staff.

From London Churchill paid close attention to what was happening. He had taken a personal interest in Greece ever since the 1890s, when his liberal sympathies were aroused on behalf of the oppressed Cretans. His instructions to Scobie were uncompromising: the rebellion of ELAS must be put down by force. Without disputing this, Macmillan argued that for peace to last there must be a political settlement based on appointing Damaskinos, Archbishop of Athens and All Greece, as Regent. The underlying issue was about the monarchy: whether King George II should return to his country before or after a plebiscite. Virtually all the Greek political world believed that there should be a plebiscite first. Only the king, supported hitherto by

Churchill, disagreed. Churchill had extravagantly described the archbishop as a "pestilential priest, a survival from the Middle Ages".

Churchill flew out to Athens on Christmas Eve, with Anthony Eden, the Foreign Secretary. He wanted to see for himself, and to meet the archbishop and the prime minister, Papandreou. His arrival was a relief for the beleaguered Athenians of the Kolonaki enclave. It is astonishing how many of them still today claim as children to have actually seen Churchill from their balconies as he entered or left the British Embassy.

Churchill was in his element. He sat firmly in the line of fire in the Ambassador's study, conferring with his officials and with the archbishop, to whom he immediately took a liking. He addressed the plucky women camping out at the embassy. He wrote home to his wife describing the "intensely dramatic" conference at the Greek Foreign Ministry: "all those haggard faces round the table, and the Archbishop with his enormous hat, making him, I should think, seven feet high". He gave a press conference at the embassy to a deeply sceptical British and anti-colonial American press. The building was deadly cold. As a background to Churchill's robust defence of his policy, the room was penetrated by the sounds of battles in progress on Philopappus hill and in Iroon, the built-up area south of Omonia Square and northwest of the Acropolis.

Churchill returned to London on 29 December. He had achieved his object of getting the warring parties to talk. King George II issued a proclamation appointing the archbishop officially as Regent and accepting that there should be a plebiscite on the question of the monarchy as soon as conditions allowed it. ELAS laid down their arms.

Post-war Revival

The legacy of the German occupation was heavy. Prolonged malnutrition had reduced the resistance of the people, and deficiency diseases persisted: conjunctivitis, trachoma, scabies, tuberculosis, and in the countryside malaria. Red Cross officials spoke of the dignity and patience of the Greek people in their affliction. But the post-war years saw a slow recovery, massively aided by American and UN relief. American goods became part of the economy of Athens and of the most distant parts of the countryside. The ubiquitous tin of Californian squid was a characteristic sight in mountain village shops even in the 1960s.

The American writer Edmund Wilson undertook a trip to Britain, Italy and Greece for the *New Yorker* in the spring and summer of 1945, and reported his impressions in an acute though tendentious book, *Europe without Baedeker* (1947). Wilson arrived by US army transport and drove into Athens from Eleusis airport along the Sacred Way, observing the Acropolis which rose above the low roofs of Athens: "astonishing, dramatic, divine, with at the same time the look of a phantom". He found his bedroom in the Hotel Grande Bretagne riddled with bullet holes. (This was not surprising: the Grande Bretagne was in the thick of things, and overlooked the demonstration that had sparked off the confrontation between British troops and the communists in December 1944.) The waiters were unhelpful, whether sullen, discouraged or stunned by all that they had been through. But the city moved him, by contrast with Rome, as

> *a clean and well-swept city of small buildings, white, pale gray or dry yellow, that are almost never ornate in the Mediterranean manner, but rather simple and uniform, with a dignity of classical taste; and, among these, a few ancient monuments that are perhaps the things of the kind most worth seeing in the whole Western world. You understand for the*

first time that it is true that, in matters of architecture, the Romans merely imitated the Greeks, and you realize what a coarsening and deadening process this imitation was. The Parthenon itself, the Erectheum, the temple of the Wingless Victory keep a vitality, a splendor and a grace that I have never seen in any other ruins. They do not seem the bones of perished ages; they still transform the world where they shine—a world of square houses and shops that might otherwise seem chalky and meager but that, beside them, catches something of their distinction.

Wilson found that the American soldiers preferred Greece to Italy. The Greeks were quieter and less theatrical. There were fewer beggars in Athens and few prostitutes. Compared with Italian cities, Athens seemed orderly, prosaic and new, with a certain monotony of the streets, and a certain mediocrity attached to the city. As compared with Italy, Greece was a country where "nobody has anything at all." In Italy commodities were still being produced and sold—striped neckties, pink slips, lace brassières, perfume, candy and cakes. In Athens there was nothing. The women wore dreary cheap dresses and were without make-up. The men wore no ties. The best that could be got in one of the better restaurants was a slice of fish, a dish of cut-up tomatoes, a bottle of retsina and a slice of watermelon. However, the Athenians had saved their electric plant during the German evacuation and the city still looked cheerful at night, "twinkling among its hills under the dry clear summer sky."

Despite the deprivations, cultural life quickly revived. For the westward looking, sophisticated literary community of Kolonaki, Maroussi and Kiphissia, this was the period in which cultural ties between Greece and Britain were strongest. A galaxy of literary figures served after the war at the British Council in Athens. They were headed by the historian of Byzantium Steven Runciman, who described postwar Athens in a series of vivid letters to his mother, and included Patrick Leigh Fermor and the writer Rex Warner, whose translations of Thucydides I have used in this book. These men were friends of George Seferis, George Katsimbalis (Henry Miller's "Colossus of Maroussi") and Ghika, who married Rex Warner's former wife Barbara. For a time the leading little magazine of Athens was the *Anglo-Hellenic Review*, edited by George Katsimbalis, in which some of Seferis's work was first published. Others associated with this golden age were the poets John Lehmann and Bernard Spencer. Edmund Keeley has evoked the literary atmosphere of pre- and post-war Athens in his book *Inventing Paradise* (1999), which traces the friendship of Miller, Durrell, Seferis, and Katsimbalis. Later the city and its environs continued to attract the brighter literary stars in and outside the British Council firmament, including Robert Liddell, Francis King, John Fowles and Barry Unsworth.

The 1950s and 1960s, the period of recovery from the civil war, were good times for expatriates in Athens. Their pounds and dollars bought plentiful drachmas. The cost of living was low. The country was beautiful. The private car had not yet ruined Athens. It was easy to earn a living teaching English as a foreign language, even without qualifications. The demand among upwardly mobile Athenian families for English seemed insatiable. One could teach at the British Council (whose Athens operation is still its largest ELT venture worldwide) or at one of the Greek *phrontisteria* (an Aristophanic word for a private teaching institute) or privately, one to one. The money was good. The cost in inconvenience of waiting all morning at the Aliens' Bureau in Canning Square for renewal of a residence permit (which required one to show pink slips proving that one had changed foreign currency into drachmas) was tolerable. For those who were out of work and cash, there was always the last resort of blood donation, at about 400 drachmas, roughly £5, a time. It was a good life for teachers and for would-be, or genuine, artists and writers.

Power Shifts

After the war it was evident that the British Embassy needed more room. The present concrete chancery building was erected in the 1950s. Its defences were tested by some large-scale demonstrations over the Cyprus issue. But apart from the Cyprus question, where Britain was the colonial power with direct interest and responsibility, the weight of influence had moved in the late 1940s, with the Truman doctrine, to the United States.

The consequences of this power shift are still felt today. At one extreme, citing US complicity with the regime of the Colonels, the N17 terrorist group saw the US as the principal agent of a system of exploitation, political control and Greek dependency, and made American officials their main targets. At the level of popular feeling, a strong strand of anti-Americanism, a product of resentment at dependency, made itself felt at all levels of society. The US president is referred to as the *planetarchis*, or ruler of the planet. The US Embassy, Walter Gropius's modern building on Vasilissis Sophias, became the standard target of large demonstrations organised by the Communist Party. Violent scenes outside the US Embassy are still a familiar sight on television. At the level of real, as opposed to demonstrative politics, Greek governments and oppositions quickly recognized the shift in global power and influence and behaved towards the Americans accordingly. The proconsular position of recent US ambassadors, with their constant access to Greek foreign ministers, is a token of this.

An anti-American demonstration brings the story of the British Embassy more or less up to date. In March 1999 there was a series of well-attended demonstrations against the NATO bombing of Serbia and Kosovo. After the US, Tony Blair and Britain were seen as the main culprits. I was ambassador at the time. As the marchers proceeded along Vasilissis Sophias towards the American Embassy, a group of activists, who had clearly planned this in advance, charged left up Loukianou Street, pushing the police in front of them, aiming for the front gates of the British Residence. The police gave way. The assailants managed to climb over the railings, manhandling the courageous embassy guards who resisted them, and battered through the glazed surface of the heavy bronze front door. Once inside they went on the rampage, smashing the queen's portrait and some items of furniture and splashing red paint on a valuable tapestry in the hall. The Cretan footman Leonidas confronted the rioters and reminded them that this was the house of the great Venizelos, a part of Greece's as well as Britain's heritage. Shame on them if they damaged it! Whereupon the demonstrators left.

CHAPTER FOURTEEN

The Modern City

> *"What really gives the post-war cement city a lighter definition is some-thing invisible from either sea or air: an underground life that still belongs to the neighbourhoods, each bearing remnants of the village life that came to Athens during this century with the millions who moved there from the provinces and places abroad for a share of the action."*
> Edmund Keeley, *Inventing Paradise*, 1999

In the year 2002 a team of Greek architects put together a picture of Athens for the International Exhibition of Architecture of the Venice Biennale. They entitled their exhibition and commentary *Athens 2002: Absolute Realism*. It shows what the present generation of architects and specialists of planning and built space think of their city.

The thesis of the organizers, put crudely, is that old-fashioned architecture and town planning are dead. Athens has managed to escape the formalities, rules and traditions of European civilization (which ironically originated in Athens itself) and imposed its own rhythms, shapes and concepts, which are characterized by nasty words like caesura and separation, disruption, inversion, instantaneity and excess, voids, gaps, incompleteness and disproportion. Athens is portrayed as the closest thing in Europe to a third-world metropolis. (A poll of students from New York who were in Athens in summer 2003 found Athens much more like Istanbul than Barcelona or Rome.) Some architects believe that there is a curious, anarchic attraction in the way Athenians have shaped their urban environment in defiance of rational planning. They come close to proposing that whatever is, is right.

Let us translate the abstract nouns into real examples. "Caesura" is seen in the separation of the archaeological sites, or parks, from the commercial city. Unlike Rome or Paris, the historical layers of Athens are not integrated into the modern city, but are cut off from it. Tourists are "voluntary prisoners of a city centre that is closed to automobile traffic." Unlike Rome or Paris, where churches and cathedrals are a proud and equal part of the city's historical fabric, in Athens the little Byzantine churches and chapels have been submerged and overborne by the concrete and glass fabric of the modern city. The little Chapel of Holy Power (Agia Dynami) in Ermou Street, tucked beneath one corner of an office block, is only the most striking example, where no attempt has been made architecturally to reconcile the old and the new, the ecclesiastical and the capitalist. They simply coexist. The reason is simple. These churches date from a time when Athens was a small market town with parishes served by small local churches. It lacked the medieval and Renaissance development of the great cities of Europe.

Private and Public Spaces
The architects of the Venice Biennale see Athens as a city where the normal respect for the division of public and private space does not apply. Athenians invade public space. The outsides of their houses become encrusted with extensions, balconies, air conditioning units and antennae. The shops on the big streets leading into Athens from the seaside, Syngrou and Vouliagmenis Avenues, selling furniture, lighting and motor cars, are topped by enormous advertising panels for cars, cigarettes, drinks and all the products of consumer society. The show rooms blaze with lights in the evening. Squares, waste plots, strips of land beside the highway are occupied by gypsies, whose presence is accepted just as the refugees of 1923 were accepted in their tented encampments, and the inhabitants of Ano Liosia who took to tents after the severe earthquake of 1999. Central squares are colonized by dogs. Pavements are taken over by shops, as in Athinas or Solonos Street, the latter one of the most uncomfortable of central Athenian streets for pedestrians.

The incomplete is seen in the skeletons of buildings on building sites, the steel rods that stick up in weird sculptural forms from flat roofs of uncompleted buildings, a phenomenon found throughout Greece. The inhuman is found in the invasiveness of the great streets, Syngrou again, Piraeos and others, which slice through residential and commercial areas, bringing with them their clutter of underground passages and bridges.

All this is true, up to a point. It is the modern, often ugly, equivalent of the picturesque in nineteenth-century Constantinople or Cairo. It is also a very fine field for architectural theorists using long words. Their message is that the concept of the architect-designed building incorporated in a planned city is dead. If the Athenians are good at colonizing and humanizing their material surroundings, this surely is a sign of their ingenuity and their individuality in rejecting the communal. We cannot withstand these developments, it is argued, and we should find a way of incorporating them in a new architecture for the twenty-first century.

What the architects are saying is a reflection of what is lacking in Athens as compared with Paris, Rome, Prague, Madrid or other great cities of Europe. The greatest buildings of Athens are ruins of the fifth and fourth centuries BC. There are some lovely Byzantine churches. There are a few fine neoclassical public buildings, notably the Academy, the university and the National Library. There are good examples of nineteenth- and twentieth-century houses, though fewer than there should be because of the destruction of the 1950s and 1960s. And there are some good examples of modern architecture to show, from the Gropius American Embassy to the Hilton Hotel (controversial as both of these examples are). But there is not the consistency of a city with a continuous history of development,

reflecting the succeeding styles of the centuries. Athens' history is one of disjunction, and when the new start was made in 1834 there was not the existing fabric nor the traditions of public building, nor—a vital point—the public resources to create a great city. The nineteenth-century pioneers made a brave try. The twentieth-century followers were overwhelmed by events. The influx of refugees in the 1920s led necessarily to cheap, utility housing. The mass migration to the city of the post war period led to the wholesale destruction of the existing urban fabric at a time when new building was for the most part undistinguished. It is easy for Greeks to despair and conclude that the city is too complicated and difficult to be managed. But Athens is Athens, not Rome, and must be appreciated for what it is.

Shanties and Suburbs

As we have seen, Athens has grown in waves. The post-war history of the city has been one of explosive growth, expanding prosperity, and development of the suburbs.

This process started with the post-war boom associated with Constantine Karamanlis as Minister of Public Works and later, from 1955, as prime minister. The stabilization of the Greek currency and the end of the civil war led to a great influx of people into Athens, escaping the continuing insecurity and poverty of the countryside, and looking for work. One effect, for the haves, was the concentration of housing through the building boom associated with the system of *antiparochi*. Another was the absorption of the poor and marginal through illegal building known as *afthaireta*. Both the haves and the have-nots exploited and flouted the building laws.

The most obvious sign of unplanned development is the way in which Athens' housing creeps outwards and upwards, up the sides of the hills flanking the plain. The city is in a continuous state of flux. This can be observed all the way round, from Hymettus to Aegaleo. Migrants and the homeless build what they can and await retrospective legalization. Out at the margins of the city, and even within it, in previously empty or protected areas such as the Turkish Hills (Tourkovounia) you can see this process happening.

Typically, in the 1950s and 1960s a property company would make available a substantial piece of land outside the city plan, dividing it up into small plots and selling them at a modest price as agricultural land (they could not be sold as building land, since they were outside the city plan, i.e. they had no planning permission). The purchasers would then construct a house or shack on the land, erecting it overnight so as to avoid the attentions of the official bulldozers that might demolish illegal buildings. This explains the number of half-built skeletons to be seen in and around Athens, hollow concrete frames sprouting rusting metal prongs. Once erected, the houses and their owners entered into a long and complex process of adaptation, negotiation, integration, and eventual legalization. Because they were illegal they lay under the constant threat of demolition. Yet politicians and officials had an interest in keeping them thus dangling, rather than destroying them, and in gradually making available to them essential services—water, electricity, sewers, connection to the bus routes—as a means of political influence and patronage. As a general rule concessions were made to illegal settlers in the periods before elections. Normally demolition, the final sanction, was commuted for fines. As recently as summer 2003, with elections impending, new legislation was in preparation providing for the umpteenth time for the settlement of illegal settlers' status and relationship with the state.

This is a game in which the government, officials and the people are all involved. It seems to suit everybody. It is a way, within the economic constraints on public housing, of ensuring that everyone has a roof over his or her head, while some people make a lot of money. It may also have served as a means of political pressure and social control. In its crude way the system has worked, but at the cost of some jerry building, much of it on the flanks of the hills that surround Athens, and environmental problems owing to the reduction of water run off from the land surface, causing serious flooding.

In parallel with this continuous extension of the city's housing stock and its boundaries, the more attractive suburbs, in areas such as Kiphissia, Maroussi, Philothei and Psychiko, have become gentrified quarters for the prosperous, full of smart new architect-designed houses with swimming pools, gates and security. The smart areas extend further and further north. Alongside these residential developments, there has been a move of business to Maroussi, and the development of shopping malls and fast food outlets in what used to be the relatively tranquil suburbs of Maroussi and Kiphissia. Similar trends are observable in the coastal strip below Phaleron. Architects talk of this as an extension of the periphery and some have predicted the death of the centre of town, but this has not happened: indeed, the opposite may be taking place. Some architects dislike rich, self-enclosed plots with private houses, as being contrary to an idea of community. But they represent a rational choice of how to live. Meanwhile, communities remain, in smaller, more open neighbourhoods; and the inhabitants of the bourgeois suburbs create their own networks of contact. The technopolis or megalopolis has not yet arrived.

Legacy of the Colonels
The watershed period for post-war Athens was the years of military dictatorship from 1967 to 1974. Before 1967, while the signs of future problems were becoming plain to see—the growing use of the private motor car being the biggest—the city was still an agreeable place to live, so that urbanists such as Professor George Prevelakis could write of this period as almost a paradise. Most of the functions of a city were concentrated in a moderate circumference in the centre. Theatres, government offices, banks, cafés and restaurants, commercial enterprises, were all there. You could walk from one to another, or take a short bus ride. You could live in the centre, or outside, and still get to work within half an hour by bus (or increasingly, and there's the rub, by car). You could still get out of Athens and down to the sea at Phaleron or Glyfada or Vouliagmeni within an hour or so. Paradise—and yet the seeds of decay were present. A population with increasing wealth and desire for consumer products was buying cars as the prime symbols of status and means of escape from the city. And the system of *antiparochi* had already destroyed a large number of the city's older houses, putting in their place rows of apartment blocks which would enormously concentrate the density of population in the centre, creating pressure on means of transport. This created a vicious circle: people tried even harder to bypass the circulation problem by using their own cars, and thereby made the problem worse.

These tendencies continued under the Colonels' regime. In addition, the Colonels made matters worse by lifting the restrictions on height of buildings.

Two buildings symbolize the rule of the Colonels. The first is the buff-coloured War Museum just across the road from the British Embassy on the southern side of Vasilissis Sophias Avenue. It is a massive, chunky building, a badly arranged display redeemed by some superb items relating to the War of Independence, and by the series of attractive drawings of the Balkan Wars and the Asia Minor war by Thalia Flora-Karavia.

The second, representing the uprising of the young against the dictatorship, is the Athens Polytechnic. This is a fine neoclassical building by Lysandros Kaftantzoglou, north of Omonia Square on Patision (28 October) Street. It was funded by a bequest of Nicholas Stournaras, another benefactor from Metsovo (whence the name "National Metsovian Polytechnic"). The Polytechnic was the scene of the events that came to symbolize the brutality of the Colonels' regime and the resistance of the student body. Students occupied the building in November 1973, and flaunted their rejection of the military government, draping a large banner over the balcony proclaiming "NO TO THE JUNTA". On the night of 16/17 November tanks smashed their way into the Polytechnic grounds, and police and the army put down the student rising with decisive force, causing a number of deaths. 17 November thus came to symbolize the spirit of resistance to oppression, which is why the vicious terrorist group N17 took the date for its name.

Towards the Future

After the Colonels came the recovery and consolidation of Greece's democracy under Karamanlis, and entry into the European Union, seen by the Greeks as a life raft in the choppy and changeable waters of southeast Europe. The years since 1974 have been mixed for Athens, as some enlightened ministers battled with pollution, unplanned development, and the inexorable growth of the motor car culture, and won partial victories. There is hope in the growth also of civic consciousness, expressed through local conservation groups and residents' bodies, and the national *Elliniki Etairia* (Greek Society).

There is some hope also, and challenge, in the prospect of change as the concrete apartment blocks of the inter-war and post-war years come to the end of their lives and need to be replaced over the coming decades.

At present, the city is in a fever of preparation for the 2004 Olympic Games. New installations are rising, belatedly, from the dust and churned mud of building sites. Hundreds of angular cranes are poised over the city. Downtown buildings are covered with netting or *trompe l'oeil* tarpaulins, behind which they are being cleaned up. Squares are cordoned behind plastic sheeting for refurbishment, museums closed to the public. The Greeks have tested the patience of the IOC to the limits by their delays. They claim confidently that they will be ready on time, though the Calatrava roof for the stadium in particular is a complex and novel engineering feat, and there is no margin of time if something goes wrong during the installation.

But the changes under way in Athens go further than Olympic facilities. Other major infrastructure works are being put in place, taking the Olympics as the occasion. The National Road that sweeps down on Athens from the north has been linked by a northern ring road with the main road up to Athens from the Peloponnese. Every few months new sections of road are delivered, causing a mixture of relief and confusion. A new tram, or light railway, will link the centre of town with Piraeus and Phaleron and the yachting marina at Agios Kosmas. A new suburban railway will link Athens with a number of nearby regions, possibly opening up a culture of commuting.

The Culture Minister, Evangelos Venizelos, a massive man with an inexhaustible facility for talking, has said that the Olympics should reorient Athens towards the sea. He had in mind the major leisure re-development taking place in the coastal area between Phaleron and Piraeus, including the mouth of the Ilissos river. Apart from this, the developments that will mean most to the foreign visitor are those which fall under the heading of the "Unification of Archaeological Spaces". The Ministry of Culture has established a company under this name (Greek initials EAHA). Many different projects are grouped under this broad heading, which reflects an old dream of linking up the main classical sites and creating a single archaeological park in central Athens. If the theorists of *Absolute Realism* are to be confounded, it is by this project, which attempts to show that there is still a possibility of large-scale interventions in the public space of the city for the benefit of residents and visitors alike (though critics ask which residents, since every project causes inconvenience to some locals).

The major project under the Unification heading is an ambitious plan to link the sites running in a long band from the Panathenaic Stadium westwards through the precinct of the temple of Olympian Zeus to the surroundings of the Acropolis and thence through the Agora down to the Kerameikos cemetery. The first part of this project, the pedestrianization of Dionysios Areopagites Street south of the Acropolis, is complete and has transformed the southern aspect of the Acropolis and its approaches, banishing the coaches and cars. It has been well done, with sensitive landscaping, although some visitors complain about the cobblestones. Other sections, including the pedestrianization of Queen Olga Street between the stadium and the temple of Zeus, will be complete by the time this book appears. If the ministry has the tenacity to keep going and complete the project it will have transformed the centre of Athens and realized part of the dream of planners since the early days of Ross and Klenze.

Other projects have been brought under the heading of the Unification, with the Olympic Games as the pretext. The façades of many of the main buildings in the city centre are being cleaned up, the advertising, posters, neon lights, and excrescences removed. This requires persuasion in the case of privately owned buildings. Four new underground car parks are being built, at last, including the park behind the War Museum, which fills the "hole in the ground". And four of the city's most important squares, Constitution, Omonia, Monastiraki and Koumoundourou (also known as Freedom), are being reformed and landscaped.

Predictably, some of these projects have caused a storm. They were put out to open competition by EAHA. The winners of the Omonia competition came up with a spare, post-modernist scheme in which concrete predominated. Most people think it is horrid. The Municipality disliked the scheme and succeeded in modifying it, to the disgust of the architects. The chairman of EAHA publicly declared that the idea of open competition had been a mistake for which the people of Athens were now forced to pay. Many people mounted on high horses. The Monastiraki scheme also suffered interference when the archaeologists insisted on a blander surface, rejecting the coloured mosaic of tiles that the designers had introduced.

All this confirms the difficulty of getting things done in Athens, and the defective processes of consultation. But change is happening. Even the new Acropolis Museum, a project involving so many difficult issues of planning, archaeological conservation and international cultural politics, looks as if it is on the point of getting done.

This modern structure, designed by Bernard Tschumi and Michael Photiades, will rise from the ground, itself thick with archaeological deposits, to the south of the Acropolis. The architects had the difficult task of creating a design that would be worthy of the contents, including the Parthenon sculptures or Elgin Marbles, without itself competing with the Acropolis and the Parthenon (as the Hilton Hotel, the first modern building of its height and dimensions, was accused of doing in the 1950s). Again, the project, which won an open international competition, is controversial. It has divided the planning and archaeological communities, some of whom believe that the wrong site was chosen. The richness of the archaeological deposits surprised the planners, and the museum has been redesigned to leave them revealed beneath the structure. It has been held up by successive delays, the latest caused by a decision of the Council of State. But most people expect it to happen.

But even when (if?) the Acropolis Museum is built, there will be a void at its heart, because the greater part of the Parthenon sculptures, those which are in the British Museum, will not be in it. Not many Athenians would publicly question the museum on these grounds, still less on the grounds that these sculptures should not be returned. The return of the marbles is a generally accepted cause, at least in public discourse. And yet one cannot help wondering at the resources being put into a project which is thus compromised in advance by the British Museum's firm refusal to return the sculptures.

Yet the void will be symbolic of one essential aspect of the city of Athens and its antiquities: the way parts of its heritage have been assumed, taken over, and integrated in the spiritual and artistic life of the world. In this way the legacy of Athens will always be a part of our heritage. But the city of Athens, with its multiple identities and its modern life, is more than this legacy.

The adaptation of the city to the needs of its inhabitants and of visitors continues and will never stop, always posing the challenge of how the ancient and the modern should coexist. The building of the metro was a good example. It is a great facility, an easing of the stress of life in Athens, but it also brought to the surface new aspects of the ancient city. The metro, which opened in 2000, was many years in the conception and building. Its construction was a delicate undertaking because of the archaeological riches of subterranean Athens. The planners had to allow for intensive rescue excavations at the sites of the stations and ventilation shafts, and for the compelling requirements of the Archaeological Service. This was probably the most important rescue excavation of modern times, covering an area of sixteen acres lying within the modern city, in a necessarily short space of time.

Besides providing relief for Athenian commuters and shoppers, the result was literally a revelation, for some of the best of the objects revealed by the excavations have been exhibited in glass-fronted displays in the main metro stations. The visitor can inspect these while the Athenians hurry about their daily business. The display at Constitution Square combines a cross section of the ancient city, showing the system of water supply in terracotta pipes, with a selection of grave findings, toys, loom weights and other remains. Along one wall also there is a fine selection of nineteenth-century photos of Athens, enormously enlarged, showing the wide, half-empty boulevards, horse-drawn trams, men in hats, and in the background, Lycabettus bare of pine trees, a rocky country hillside. The visitor can now match his wanderings above ground with a subterranean tour.

Some of the best of the finds from the metro excavations were collected in an exhibition at the Goulandris Museum of Cycladic Art. Viewing this small exhibition, *The City Beneath the City*, and its catalogue, one can follow the topography of the ancient city. The small selection of about 500 of the 30,000 moveable objects which were unearthed, illustrates the cycle of Athenian history over a period of twenty-five centuries: day-to-day life, roads, buildings, water supply, the craftsmanship of the potter, burial practices, sculpture, public life and religion—in short, life and death. It is no surprise that most of the objects were found in graves. The children's graves contain terracotta birds, dolls and rattles. A dog's grave confirms that some Athenians were devoted to their pets.

The preparation for the Olympic Games goes on. In the Plaka area, they are starting to relay and light a section of the ancient Street of the Tripods, which led from the Agora to the theatre of Dionysus and was lined with the choregic monuments recording victories in the annual theatre festivals of the ancient city. One of these, as if by magic, has survived, and is a picturesque part of the Plaka today. This is the monument of Lysicrates, which seems to embody the tenacious survival of traces of the past in the present. A monument recording the victory of a certain Lysicrates around 334 BC, it survived to become a part of the Capuchin monastery erected in 1669 AD. Known as the "Lantern of Demosthenes", it became a prominent feature of the descriptions and drawings of western travellers. Byron used it as his study when he stayed with the Capuchin monks in 1810-11. The monastery burned down under Turkish occupation in 1826, but the monument was later restored with French help. Today, set on its own in the heart of the Plaka, it is a token of classical grace and balance in the city which, without constant attention to preserving what is good, could overwhelm and devour its own past.

Appendix A

Some Museums and Galleries and a Sculpture Park

Within half an hour you can walk from Constitution Square to all the major museums in Athens. But who would want to? The problem with the classic old Greek museums, such as the National Archaeological Museum at Athens, is that they consisted of collections of chunks of antiquity put together by expert archaeologists for people who knew quite a lot about the history of classical Greece already. The displays in many Greek museums, however great the contents, are jumbled and crowded and the lettering unhelpful. The museum as a place of exciting exploration and explanation has come to Greece only recently. But it has come. The little museum at Amphipolis in Macedonia is a model of how to present and explain the thousand-year history of a small but important town. In Athens the Benaki Museum is the best presented collection covering the whole history of Hellenism. The Museum of Cycladic Art is a model of presentation of a more limited collection.

Athens is itself an open-air museum. As well as the ruins of antiquity and the Byzantine churches, the streets and squares contain pointers to the history of the independent modern state in the form of statues and historical monuments. Many of these are relatively unknown. They can easily be missed by the visitor. I have therefore described the best of them below, in "A Stroll in the Athens Sculpture Park".

The following list of museums is not exhaustive. There are several, on theatre, film, epigraphy, philately, trains, and devoted to particular artists, which will appeal mainly to specialists. Diane Shugart's *Athens by Neighbourhood* is a good guide to them. I have given a few sentences to each interesting museum, and highlighted a few of the many things which have given me pleasure—whether the best-known object or an unknown gem.

Acropolis Museum
The Acropolis Museum, which has stood on the Acropolis since the 1870s, now has a second meaning, as the planned "New Acropolis

Museum", which has been designed to hold the Parthenon sculptures (Elgin Marbles). The old Acropolis Museum—essential viewing—is a low-lying single-storey building tucked discreetly behind the Parthenon. It contains the sculptures found on the Acropolis since 1834, including some masterpieces: the mourning Athina, the calf bearer, and a number of archaic sculptures of maidens discovered during the excavations of the 1880s, as well as most of those fragments from the Parthenon sculptures which have not ended up in the British Museum, including parts of the procession of horses and riders from the north side. The planned new museum, designed by Bernard Tschumi and Michael Photiades, will stand south of the Acropolis, south of the pedestrianized Dionysius the Areopagite Street, near the imposing Weiler building and the Acropolis metro station. From the museum there will be an extensive view of the south side of the Acropolis and the Parthenon, and it will be a ten-minute walk up to the Acropolis entrance. Assuming the museum goes ahead, the visitor will thus be able to see at the same time the sculptures and a part of the building from which they came; or, as a sympathetic British MP put it, "if the marbles are ever returned, visitors will be able to see the friezes looking out of their left eye and, looking up, see exactly where they would have been on the temple" (though this would only be so of the southern frieze). The snag is that the British Museum has no intention of repatriating the Parthenon sculptures, which nationalist rhetoric has made into the main point of the new museum, although there is a case to be made for the museum on other grounds too. And the British government has no intention of leaning on the British Museum. Needless to say, the project has been controversial in Greece as well as internationally, because of the need to secure the land for the museum, and because of the archaeological remains, mainly Roman and early Christian, which have been found on the site and which will be displayed as part of the museum. The government has given assurances that the new museum will be completed in time for the 2004 Olympic Games.

Do not miss: the grave sculpture of the Mourning Athena leaning on her spear, which has inspired much subsequent funerary art; the archaic statues of maidens (*Korai*); the calf bearer (*moschophoros*) carrying on his shoulders a calf for sacrifice. Do not miss the Parthenon

sculptures in the Duveen Gallery of the British Museum, either, whatever your views of the Elgin Marbles controversy.

Benaki Museum

Corner of Koumbari Street and Vasilissis Sophias Avenue, just below Kolonaki Square

This is one of the essential museums of Athens, a private Foundation, and the best displayed in its modern transformation (completed in 2002). The museum is the creation of Antonis Benakis (1873-1954), whose father, from Alexandria, played a prominent part in the liberal politics of Venizelism and who amassed a great collection. It was founded in 1930, in the former Benakis family home, a neoclassical house designed by Anastasios Metaxas. The collection covers the whole history of Hellenism over the centuries, including wonderful examples of Byzantine icons and of popular and folk arts and crafts. Reflecting Benakis's Egyptian background, it is strong in Egyptian, Coptic and early Christian art. It has the best museum shop in Greece, the perfect place to buy a reproduction silver bowl or embroidered textile as a present, and a fashionable top-floor restaurant with good views from the terrace. The museum has an (outhoused) historical archive, including the papers of Eleftherios Venizelos, and good photographic archive including early photography of Athens. Also outhoused is the Nikos Hadjikyriakos-Ghikas gallery, in Ghika's former house in Kriezotou Street.

The museum is a must, and the Ghika house is strongly recommended.

Byzantine and Christian Museum
22 Vasilissis Sophias Avenue
The Byzantine Museum was established in 1914, and housed for a time in the basement of the Athens Academy. In 1930 it was transferred to the Villa Ilissia, an Italian Renaissance-style villa south of Vasilissis Sophias Avenue, designed by Stamatios Kleanthes in 1848 for Sophie de Marbois-Lebrun, the eccentric Duchesse de Plaisance. Of mixed French and American parentage, she married one of Napoleon's generals, divorced him, and came to live in Greece around the time the independent state was established. The museum, which contains a fine collection of icons, has been in a state of transition for years, with much of its collection not on display; but fairly soon the new extension will be ready. This is built underground and will give a neutral background to items on display, lacking the colour of natural light. When the new museum opens, the villa will be used for temporary exhibitions. Meanwhile it houses those parts of the permanent collection that are on display, including sculpture, icons, textiles, ceramics, frescoes, ecclesiastical vestments and minor arts, and on the ground floor reconstructions of three Byzantine types of church.

Do not miss: the two-sided icon of the Crucifixion on one side and the Virgin Hodegetria ("Leader" or "Guide") on the other; and the thirteenth-century two-sided icon of St George on one side and two saints on the other. Both are in Gallery 7.

Goulandris Museum of Cycladic and Ancient Greek Art
Neophytou Douka 4, Kolonaki

This is the best place in the world to look at the curious white marble Cycladic female figures, with their thin heads, arching slightly backwards, and arms folded over the chest, which have had such an effect on twentieth-century sculptors including Henry Moore and Picasso. They vary greatly in size. Most of them come from graves in the Cyclades in the early Bronze Age (third millennium BC), and their religious function is debated. The museum also has a superb collection of pots and bowls from the classical period. It is professionally labelled and presented, and not too large. There is an extension in the fine Stathatos mansion, a nineteenth-century house by Ziller, on Vasilissis Sophias Avenue, and a pleasant café serving a light lunch. Do not miss: the Cycladic figurines.

Goulandris Natural History Museum
13 Levidou Street, Kiphissia

The Goulandris Natural History Museum in Kiphissia is the creation of the late Angelos Goulandris and his wife Niki, herself a distinguished botanical artist (no connection with the Goulandris Museum of Cycladic Art above). It was founded in 1964. The museum has a rich herbarium. It has established a biotope/wetland centre in Thessaloniki to help avert the loss of wetlands in Greece and the Mediterranean region. A new "Gaia Centre" for environmental research and education was inaugurated in 2000.

Gounaropoulos Museum
6 Gounaropoulou, Zographou

The house of Georgios Gounaropoulos, the modern artist, who lived and worked here from 1932 until his death in 1977. (Thus three of Greece's twentieth-century painters, Ghika, Gounaropoulos and Tsarouchis, have their own museums each in his own house or apartment.)

Jewish Museum
Nikis 39, Plaka

This museum presents the history of Greek Jewry since the early settlements of the Hellenistic period in Macedonia, Thessaly, Attica,

Crete, Samos, Rhodes and many other parts of Greece (St Paul preached in the synagogues of Corinth, Thessaloniki and Veroia.) The largely hellenized communities of Romaniote Jews in Ioannina and elsewhere were much outnumbered by the Sephardic Jews, driven out of the Iberian peninsula, who settled in Greek lands at the end of the fifteenth century. Much the largest Sephardic community was in Thessaloniki, where the Jews were the largest single element in a multi-ethnic population. They were destroyed in the Holocaust. Nearly 50,000 Jews were deported in 1943 to Auschwitz, of whom only 2,000 returned. The ancient Romaniote communities were also virtually annihilated. At the end of the war only about 10,000 of the pre-war community of nearly 80,000 remained alive in Greece. The museum tells this story, with moving personal histories, and displays the material culture and traditions of the Jewish communities.

Kanellopoulos Museum
Corner of Theorias and Panos Streets, Plaka
This agreeable small museum, housed in the Michaleas neoclassical house in the Plaka district, contains the ancient artefacts, sculpture, vases, jewellery etc, and Byzantine and post-Byzantine icons and folk art collected by Pavlos and Alexandra Kanellopoulos and donated to the Greek state. It makes a pleasant stopping point in a stroll around the higher slopes of the Plaka.

Lalaounis Museum of Jewellery
Karyatidon and Kalisperi 12
Ilias Lalaounis is Greece's master designer of jewellery, the creator of designs in gold and silver, many inspired by the natural world and by ancient and Byzantine motifs. The attractive museum is not far from the Acropolis metro station and the site of the new Acropolis Museum.

Museum of Greek Folk Art
Kydathinaion 17, and Monastiraki Square
Though this is on the edge of the Plaka, the building is a rather depressing physical setting for the museum. But do not be put off. It contains a good selection of silver and other metal work, woodwork, folk costumes, textiles and embroidery, Greek shadow theatre, and best

of all a reconstruction of a room from Mytilene covered with delightful wall paintings by the naif artist Theophilos Hatzimichael (1868-1934).

There is also a branch of the museum, the Museum of Greek Popular Art, in Monastiraki Square, containing ceramics and pottery. The setting, the eighteenth-century Tsistaraki Mosque, named after a Turkish governor, is as interesting as the contents, the best of which are pots by immigrant potters who came to Greece in the 1920s as refugees after the Asia Minor disaster.

Do not miss: the Theophilos paintings.

Museum of Greek Folk Music
Diogenous Street 1-3, Plaka
The museum contains an astonishing variety of musical instruments of every variety, stringed, wind and percussive, from all over Greece. Many of these are now found only in the museum, but parts of the tradition are alive and well. You will hear small groups formed around a clarinet and guitar or lute (or in the case of Crete, bowed Cretan lyre and lute) playing at weddings and festivals in country villages. Recordings of the various instruments and combinations, which you can listen to through earphones next to the glass cases, bring the museum alive.

Museum of the City of Athens
7 Paparigopoulou, Klafthmonos Square
This house, occupied from 1837-43 by King Otho and his new bride Amalia, was made by combining three private houses. The museum was founded by Lambros Eftaxias, great grandson of the first owner, and is also known as the Vourou-Eftaxia Museum. It has been restored in Othonian period style with many original furnishings and objects and nineteenth-century drawings. It contains a recreation of Amalia's parlour.

National Archaeological Museum
Patision Street
The National Archaeological Museum is one of the essential ports of call for those interested in the arts of classical and pre-classical Greece. It is also an important part of the history of the country. The museum

was designed by Lange, modified by Ernst Ziller, and built between 1866 and 1889. It contains an incomparable collection of sculpture, vases, bronzes and gold from all over Greece. Visitors over the years had to get used to unimaginative and crowded display and amateurish lettering on captions. But things are improving, and the first few galleries, containing the archaic *Kouroi* or young men, are now a pleasure to visit as well as an aesthetic feast. The museum was closed throughout 2003 for refurbishment, so perhaps we are in for a pleasant surprise when it opens again in time for the Olympic Games in 2004.

Do not miss: the Vaphio gold cups, found near Sparta, showing the catching of bulls in nets, and other fine gold work in the Mycenean display; the archaic marble sculpted figures, male (*kouros*) and female (*kore*), some of which astonish by their grandeur, serenity and simplicity; and the fifth-century BC bronze statue of Poseidon which was found in the sea off Cape Artemision in Euboea.

National Gallery: Alexandros Soutzos Museum
50 Vasileos Constantinou
The National Gallery, a building of the 1960s opposite the Hilton Hotel in the triangle of land between Vasilissis Sophias, Vasileos Constantinou, and Michalakopoulou Streets, should not be missed by those interested in the landscape and the social history of Greece. It is not too large to take in, and it contains many surprises for those who associate Greece only with Byzantine iconography. The national collection took a long time to find a home. As early as 1834 the new state was legislating about the conservation of art and ancient monuments and the housing of a national permanent collection, though no such collection existed. Gradually one was built up from donations, from the collections of Capodistria, Alexander Soutsos, a late nineteenth-century benefactor, Averoff and others, and hung in the National Technical University. The present permanent gallery was completed in two phases, in 1969 and 1976, and the collection rehung in 2000 after some years of absence from the walls. It contains some good examples of post-Byzantine work, but is essentially a collection spanning the eighteenth century to the present day. Greece's best-known painters are well represented: Nikiphoros Lytras, Gyzis,

Iakovides, who incidentally taught Giorgio de Chirico, Parthenis, Maleas, Ghika, Tsarouchis, Moralis and others.

Do not miss: the painters of the early twentieth century and between the wars, especially Ghika; and from the nineteenth century the evocative Iakovos Rizos (1849-1926), "On the Terrace (Athenian Evening)", 1897, oil on canvas.

National Historical Museum
Old Parliament Building, Kolokotroni Square
The National Historical Museum, essential for lovers of history in search of education, but not altogether easy viewing, is the collection of the Historical and Ethnological Society of Greece, founded in 1882 to safeguard and collect the nation's material treasures and documents. Like the National Gallery, it was originally housed in the National Technical University. Since 1960 it has been in the solid neoclassical building of the Old Parliament, which housed the Greek parliament from 1858 to 1934, when it was transferred to the Old Palace overlooking Constitution Square. The collection illustrates the development of Greece from 1453 to, in theory, the present day, but the period after the Balkan Wars is inevitably skimped. It is particularly strong on the War of Independence, on land and sea, on weaponry, and on national costumes. The display is traditional. The museum has a good archive of photographs.

Do not miss: the delightful collection of figureheads from Greek ships which took part in the War of Independence.

Naval Museum of Greece
Akti Themistokleous, Piraeus
This covers naval history from ancient to modern times, including the battle of Salamis and Greek naval exploits in the War of Independence. There is an open-air branch of the museum on the seafront at Old Phaleron, where you can see the historic battleship *Averoff*, which did good service in the Balkan Wars, and the trireme *Olympias*, a modern reconstruction of an ancient trireme constructed through the enthusiasm of Cambridge classicists and which successfully performed sea trials some years ago.

Numismatic Museum
12 Panepistimiou
For coin buffs this is a treasure. For others it is still interesting, because the museum is in the impressive Renaissance-style House of Troy (*Iliou Melathron*) designed by Ziller for Heinrich Schliemann in 1878-9.

Piraeus Archaeological Museum
Harilaou Trikoupi 38, above Zea
This is a good place to visit in between ferry boats. Particularly interesting are the standard measures used in the Salamis market to check that traders were offering fair value, and the bronze ram and stone anchors from the ancient Athenian navy.

Tsarouchis Museum
Ploutarchou Street 28, Maroussi
The twentieth-century painter Yannis Tsarouchis lived here. The house contains a fair selection of his work.

Venizelos Museum
Eleftherias Park, Vasilissis Sophias
The museum, at the upper end of the park, contains a varied selection of photos, documents and objects commemorating Eleftherios Venizelos. (There is another museum which does much the same in the Liberal Club on Christou Lada Street.) Near the museum is a building housing temporary exhibitions of modern art, the environment etc.

War Museum
Vasilissis Sophias Avenue
An oddity. The War Museum is the buff-coloured block of granite standing on the south side of Vassilissis Sophias Avenue, near the Byzantine Museum. To the south of it is the enormous hole in the ground now being filled in and turned into a car park. The War Museum, predictably, was erected in the time of the Colonels' regime (1967-74). It contains a jumble of exhibits from every period of Greek history, from classical antiquity to the Korean War. As a gesture to Hellenic political correctness, there is a room devoted to Cyprus. The museum is good for the fanatic, of arms and armour or of the esoteric

details of Greek military history. It is not so good for the general public. The labelling is amateurish and unhelpful to foreigners. But tucked away in the military jumble are some good paintings, prints and mementos of the War of Independence. And the museum has one great asset, a large collection of watercolour drawings and pastels of the Balkan Wars and of the Greek war in Asia Minor, by a lady called Thalia Flora-Karavia (1871-1960). These sketches, of campaigning at Emin Aga in February 1913, of the hospital improvised at Philippiada, of watering the horses, of bread ovens on campaign, of King Constantine and his staff, and of many other scenes, are a fine record of what it was like to be at war in 1912-13 and 1921.

Do not miss: drawings of scenes from the Balkan Wars and the 1921-22 Asia Minor campaign by Thalia Flora-Karavia.

A Stroll in the Athens Sculpture Park

There is no Athens sculpture park. But dotted around the city centre, on pavements, in squares, and in the parks are statues and sculptures illustrating the history of Greece since the time of independence. (The First Cemetery, described separately, contains a further monumental history of Greek taste and Athenian society. Another sculpture park is the garden of the KAT hospital in Kiphissia.) Here are some of the more interesting, with a map showing their position. A walk starting in front of the University, then following Stadiou Street to Constitution Square, then along Amalias and into the Zappeion park, emerging near the stadium, walking up Herod Atticus street, then along Vasilissis Sophias to the Hilton and a little further to the memorial statue of Ion Dragoumis and the statue of Venizelos in "Freedom Park", will take in a good selection. Those who want further examples and details will find some in David Rupp's *Athenian Walks*.

Some of these works of art and history have suffered terribly from vandalism, and at many periods their plinths and even the statues themselves have been daubed with paint and graffiti. The city has done a good job recently in cleaning them up, though there has been controversy over methods of cleaning, centring on the damage done to marble surfaces by high-pressure hoses.

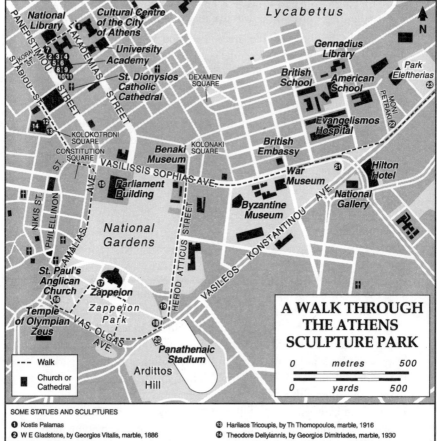

A WALK THROUGH THE ATHENS SCULPTURE PARK

- - - Walk
■ Church or Cathedral

| 0 | metres | 500 |
| 0 | yards | 500 |

SOME STATUES AND SCULPTURES

❶ Kostis Palamas
❷ W E Gladstone, by Georgios Vitalis, marble, 1886
❸ Rhigas Velestinlis, by Ioannis Kossos, marble, 1869-71
❹ Patriarch Gregory V, by Georgios Phytalis, marble, 1869-72
❺ Capodistria, by Georgios Bonanos
❻ Adamantios Korais, by Georgios Vroutos, marble, 1875
❼ Panagis Vallianos, by Georgios Bonanos, marble, 1899-1900
❽ Apollo, by Leonidas Drosos, marble, 1860s
❾ Athina, by Leonidas Drosos, marble, 1860s
❿ Plato, by Leonidas Drosos, marble, 1860s
⓫ Socrates, by Leonidas Drosos, marble, 1860s
⓬ Theodore Kolokotronis, Lazaros Sochos, bronze, 1904

⓭ Harilaos Tricoupis, by Th Thomopoulos, marble, 1916
⓮ Theodore Deliyiannis, by Georgios Dimitriades, marble, 1930
⓯ Monument of the Unknown Soldier, by Kostas Dimitriades, stone, 1932
⓰ Byron, by A Falguière, marble
⓱ The cousins Zappas: Evangelis Zappas by Ioannis Kossos, marble, 1864
⓲ 'The Discobolus', by Kostas Dimitriades, bronze, 1927
⓳ 'The Wood breaker', by Dimitrios Philippotis, marble, 1872-75
⓴ Georgios Averoff, by Georgios Vroutos, marble, 1896
㉑ 'The Runner', by Kostas Varotsos, plate glass, 1988
㉒ Ion Dragoumis, memorial obelisk
㉓ Eleftherios Venizelos, by Yiannis Pappas, bronze, 1969

Main Source: "Ta Glypta tis Athinas" ("The Sculpture of Athens"), Kathimerini, Epta Imeres (Seven Days), 25 October 1998

As a general rule of thumb, the older the better. Though some recent modernist works are impressive, for example Varotsos' *Runner* in front of the Hilton Hotel, many of the bronze busts of ancient poets and thinkers with which Mayor Avramopoulos, the predecessor of the present mayor, filled the squares and streets (see for example Amalias Avenue, on the pavement near the entrance to the National Gardens, and Kotzias Square) are pretty tacky.

The best places to see Athens's ancient sculpture are the great museums, and especially the National Archaeological Museum and the Acropolis Museum in Greece, and the British Museum. But the best place to see post-Byzantine sculpture and statuary is in the open air, especially in front of the three neoclassical buildings of central Athens, the National Library, the university and the Academy, and in the National Gardens, the Zappeion park, and the Champs de Mars (Pedion Areos). In the latter the giant equestrian figure of King Constantine embodies Greece's nationalist and imperialist ambitions of the period from 1897 to 1922.

The place to start is either behind or in front of the university. Behind the university, on the other side of Akadimias Street, is the Cultural Centre of the City of Athens. In front of it is an array of statuary of very variable quality. The one to look at is a marble statue of the poet Kostis Palamas, author of the *Olympic Hymn,* sitting with his head resting on his left hand. In front of the university, facing Panepistimiou Street, extending his right hand in a commanding gesture, is Gladstone, the Grand Old Man. The statue was sculpted by Georgios Vitalis and erected in 1886. Gladstone visited Athens only once, during his short and ill-starred period as Governor General of the British Protectorate of the Ionian Islands. It was mid-winter 1858, and the snow lay on the Acropolis. Gladstone met the king and senior officials and departed again. He commented, "The view—the ruins—and the sculptures, all these together are too much for one day," an unusual admission for so indefatigable a traveller. The Greeks were right in seeing Gladstone as one of the greatest of philhellenes.

Placed neatly on the forecourt of the three buildings are other statues of ancient and modern heroes, gods and goddesses and benefactors. In front of the university façade are the poet and revolutionary Rhigas Velestinlis and the Patriarch Gregory V, who was martyred by the Turks. On either side of the steps are Capodistrias, the first president of independent Greece, by Georgios Bonanos, and Korais, the scholar whose writings encouraged the Greeks to believe that they were a nation, again by Vroutos. In front of the double stairway leading to the National Library is the man who funded it, the shipowner Panagis Vallianos. The most imposing sculptures are those of the Academy, which has Apollo and Athena standing on columns on either side of the entrance, Plato and Socrates seated, and the financier-benefactor Baron Sinas in the hall, all by Leonidas Drosis.

Walk down to the parallel Stadiou Street and along towards Constitution Square. In front of the Old Parliament building, now the National Historical Museum, is the equestrian statue of Theodore Kolokotronis, hero of the War of Independence. Against the southeast side of the building stands Harilaos Tricoupis, the modernizing prime minister of the second half of the nineteenth century, who opposed the Olympic Games and died in the south of France during them; and on the other side of the building is his long-time opponent Theodore

Deliyiannis, prime minister during the Games and the 1897 war, who was murdered by a disappointed gambler on the steps of parliament in 1905.

On the upper side of Constitution Square, beneath the western façade of the Royal Palace, now the Parliament building, is Dimitriades's monument to the unknown soldier. People stop here to watch the Evzones changing the guard. Around the three marble walls enclosing the monument are inscribed all the battles of the history of the modern state, an impressive and evocative list. The central part of the square is also dotted with sculptures.

Walk along the eastern side of Amalias Avenue, passing the bronze busts, to the corner of Amalias and Vasilissis Olgas Avenue, which is to be pedestrianized as part of the Unification of the Archaeological Spaces. Here on the corner is a splendid statue of Hellas crowning

Byron with a wreath, by the French artist A. Falguière after a design by Chapu.

The Zappeion park is too full of statues for me to note them. They include the Zappas cousins themselves. If you walk through the park and emerge at the southeast end, at the bottom of Herod Atticus Street, opposite the Panathenaic Stadium, you will see two sporting images in stone, a discus thrower straining with effort, and a man chopping wood (a sculpture which pleased Giorgio de Chirico). Looking across the busy street of Ardittos/Vasileos Constantinou, you can see on the pavement between stadium and street Georgios Vroutos's statue of the benefactor George Averoff, who financed the reconstruction of the stadium.

If you now walk up Herod Atticus Street past the Megaron Maximou, the office of the prime minister, and the President's Palace, and turn right at the top onto Vasilissis Sophias, walking past the Byzantine and War Museums, you will soon see looming up the fine façade of the Hilton Hotel, and on the plot in front of it which divides traffic streams, the controversial sculpture known as *Dromeas* ("The Runner"). This giant sculpture by Kostas Varotsos, commissioned by the city of Athens, is one of the most striking objects to be seen in central Athens. It is constructed of greenish plate glass, built up in flat horizontal sheets in the form of an angular runner, some thirty feet tall, thrusting forward south-westwards towards the town centre and the Acropolis. It was first displayed in Omonia Square and then moved in 1994 to the present site. The Runner divides people sharply into admirers and detractors, the latter probably outnumbering the former. Many think that it is not in the right place; but it is not so easy to say where that should be.

A few yards further up Vasilissis Sophias to the northeast, on the pavement near Moni Petraki Street, is an obelisk marking the place where the writer and political philosopher Ion Dragoumis (1878-1920) was murdered. A modest memorial marking a tragic episode in Greek history, the column bears a moving short poem by Palamas. Ion Dragoumis was a brilliant member of one of the great political and intellectual families of Greece, son of Prime Minister Stephanos Dragoumis. As a career diplomat he served in the Greek consular service in Macedonia, Thrace, Bulgaria, Constantinople, and in the

Foreign Ministry in Athens in the early years of the twentieth century. He developed a powerful brand of nationalist thought, mixing demoticism with reaction against western liberalism. It may be his belief in the eastern roots of Hellenism which led the contemporary historians John Koliopoulos and Thanos Veremis to label him, I think unfairly, as "perhaps one of the most overestimated Greek men of letters". He entered parliament as an anti-Venizelist in 1915 and was exiled to Corsica in 1917. On 12 August 1920, two days after the signature of the Treaty of Sèvres, Venizelos was shot and wounded by two disaffected anti-Venizelist officers as he was about to embark on a train for Greece at the Gare de Lyon. When the news reached Athens, Venizelist crowds went on the rampage. Driving down to Athens from his home in Kiphissia, Dragoumis was stopped by security forces, taken out of his car and shot.

Penelope Delta, née Benakis, Venizelos' most uncritical fan, who herself had earlier fallen deeply in love with Dragoumis, drily noted in her diary for 12 August,

Attempt on Venizelos's life yesterday evening at the Gare de Lyon by two Greek officers of the reserve. Light wound on the shoulder which will not prevent him from leaving in a day or two, they say.
Great disturbances in the country.

Night—*they have murdered Dragoumis.*

Venizelos himself was luckier. He survived this and other attempts on his life. The most dramatic took place on 19 June 1933. He and his wife Helena had been dining with his friends the Benakis at their house in Kiphissia. Penelope Delta was present. Venizelos and Helena left for Athens in his Packard limousine at about 10.30 p.m., followed by an aide in a Ford. After they had passed through Maroussi, a Cadillac swung in behind them and shots were fired, disabling the Ford and killing its driver. The assassins then concentrated their fire on Venizelos' car. They wounded Helena several times in the buttocks and stomach, but somehow the bullets missed Venizelos himself. His chauffeur was wounded in the head and died a few days later. The Packard, riddled with bullet holes, can still be seen in the Venizelos Museum at the Liberal Club in Christou Lada Street.

A bronze statue of Venizelos, about twice life size, by the sculptor Yiannis Pappas, stands on a stone plinth on a patch of grass beside Vasilissis Sophias Avenue in Eleutherias (Freedom) Park, not far from the Megaron Mousikis. If you are lucky the graffiti may have been cleaned away from the plinth.

These two men, Dragoumis and Venizelos, conclude our walk around the monuments. Ion Dragoumis left his comment on Athens, and on his own state of mind, in a poem dated 26 June 1899, which he called "Life in Athens and Surroundings":

Whether I am bored or not bored
The world goes straight on
Like the road to Patisia.

Whether I am thinking or not thinking
The sun rises
Stones root and grow in the mountains
Honey on Hymettus
And priests at Penteli.

Whether I am alive or not alive
The moon shines
(When there are no clouds)
And the goats eat grass

And in Athens, the village
With so much dust
And so little water
I am bored, I think and I am alive.

Appendix B

Fun with Greek Words and Phrases

Glossary: lit. language thing, from glossa (γλῶσσα), tongue or language, also meaning a sole (the sort you eat)

I have tried to make the text of the book self-explanatory, but here is an explanation of some Greek words and words derived from Greek.

Adespota (Αδέσποτα) Without masters, as of ownerless dogs, from the root *despotes* (δεσπότης) meaning master, despot, tyrant.

Afthaireta (Αυθαίρετα) Lit. self-chosen, arbitrary, used of illegal housing developments.

Agia Triada (Αγία Τριάδα) Holy Trinity.

Anaphiotika (Αναφιώτικα) Lit. things from Anaphi, used to denote the houses of the people from Anaphi which cluster round the higher slopes of the Acropolis on the northeast side. Anaphi is an island in the Cyclades, from which construction workers came to Athens to find work in Otho's time.

Antiparochi (Αντιπαροχή) Lit. provision in exchange, used of housing development through exchange deal between owner of land, developer and buyer.

Archaiolatreia (Αρχαιολατρεία) Archaiolatry, ancestor-worship.

Autochthonoi (Αυτόχθονοι) Autochthons, native-born Greeks, distinguished in the early years of the Greek state from heterochthons or Greeks from abroad.

Autocephalous (Αυτοκέφαλος) As in Autocephalous Church of Greece: lit. having its own head, i.e. independent of the Ecumenical Patriarchate.

Dekemvriana (Δεκεμβριανά) *Ta Dekemvriana* are the events of December 1944 in Athens, including the confrontation between the communist ELAS and British forces.

Dexameni (Δεξαμενή) Reservoir or cistern, the reservoir at the Kolonaki end of Hadrian's aqueduct which gave its name to Dexameni Square.

Dimosion Sima (Δημόσιον Σήμα) The public burial ground in classical Athens.

Doseis (Δόσεις) Doses, i.e. instalments payable under a hire purchase agreement, or in buying property.

Ecumenical (Οικουμενικός) As in Ecumenical Patriarch: lit. universal, or catholic, from the word meaning the world or universe.

Ekdromi (Εκδρομή) Expedition, excursion, as in weekend trip to the country.

Elliniki Etairia (Ελληνική Εταιρεία) The Greek Society, the society for conservation and protection of the natural and built environment.

Epiphaneia (Επιφάνεια) Surface, appearance, epiphany: the title of a famous setting by Mikis Theodorakis of bitter-sweet poems by George Seferis.

Epitaphios (Επιτάφιος) The Good Friday service and procession in which a funerary bier is carried through the streets: the title of a setting by Theodorakis of poems by Yannis Ritsos.

Fastfoodadiko (Φαστφουντάδικο) Fast food outlet, by analogy with e.g. *ouzadiko*, a place to drink ouzo and eat *mezedes*, or little bites.

Heterochthonoi (Ετερόχθονοι) Heterochthons, Greeks from abroad, distinguished in legislation in the early years of the Greek state from *autochthonoi* or native Greeks.

Iera Odos (Ιερά Οδός) Sacred Way, the ancient route from Athens to Eleusis, and the modern road along roughly the same route.

Ieros Vrachos (Ιερός Βράχος) Sacred Rock: the Acropolis.

Katharevousa (Καθαρεύουσα) The purifying language, contrasted with the "demotic" language. The grammar and vocabulary of *katharevousa* were modelled on ancient Greek.

Kerameikos (Κεραμεικός) Lit. the potters' quarter, from the root word which gives us ceramics; by extension, the ancient cemetery near the potters' quarter.

Kolonaki (Κολονάκι) Little column, -aki being the diminutive ending; the little column having given its name to Kolonaki Square and surrounding area.

Kore (Κόρη) A maiden, as in the archaic sculptures of girls found in particular on the Acropolis.

Kouros (Κούρος) A young man, male equivalent of *kore*, as in the archaic sculptures found on the Acropolis.

Laiki (λαϊκή) People's, popular, as in *laiki agora*, the people's market.

Megali Idea (Μεγάλη Ιδέα) Great Idea, used of the political project developed in the 1840s of incorporating the Greeks of Asia Minor, the southern Balkans and the Aegean rim within the Greek state. The Asia Minor disaster of 1922 put an end to it.

Megaron Mousikis (Μέγαρον Μουσικής) The main Athens Concert Hall, a state-of-the-art modern hall, now being extended.

Metaxourgeio (Μεταξουργείο) Silk factory, an area of downtown Athens.

Mezedes (Μεζέδες) Small eats, such as pieces of octopus or squares of cheese and tomato served e.g. at an *ouzeri*; to be distinguished from Cypriot *mezedes*, which constitute a whole meal in themselves.

Mitropolis (Μητρόπολις) Cathedral, as in Mitropoleos Street, the street of the Cathedral.

Mona-Zyga (Μονά–Ζυγά) Odds and Evens, used to describe the system in force since the 1980s by which cars may enter the central "ring" area of Athens only on alternate working days, according to whether the number plate ends with an odd or an even number.

Nekrotapheio (Νεκροταφείο) Lit. burial place of corpses, a cemetery.

Nephos (νέφος) Cloud, used as shorthand for the cloud of pollution that affects Athens.

Oikogeneia (Οικογένεια) Family.

Omonoia (Ομόνοια) Concord, as in Omonoia Square (Place de la Concorde).

Oraia Ellas (Ωραία Ελλάς) "Lovely Greece", the well-known nineteenth-century café.

Ostrakon (Οστρακον) Potsherd, i.e. fragment of pottery, giving us the word ostracism, the democratic process by which Athenian citizens from time to time voted for the banishment of a leading citizen, each citizen inscribing the name of the man whom he would banish on an *ostrakon*.

Ouzeri (Ουζερί) A drinks establishment serving ouzo, beer and snacks.

Panepistimio (Πανεπιστήμιο) Lit. place for "all branches of learning", i.e. university, as in University Street.

Pantokrator (Παντοκράτωρ) Almighty, all-powerful, an attribute of the Christ whose image is painted in the dome of Byzantine churches such as the Daphni monastery church.

Parea (Παρέα) Company, one's friends (at say a taverna evening, or a weekend expedition).

Periptero (Περίπτερο) Kiosk, lit. with wings (*phtera*) around (*peri*).

Philodasic (Φιλοδασικό) Forest-loving, from *dasos*, a forest, as in Philodasic Society.

Phrontistirion (Φροντιστήριο) A private commercial teaching institute, used for cramming on exam subjects, and learning English as a foreign language; from the ancient Greek (same word) as used by Aristophanes of a *phrontistirion* patronized by Socrates.

Polykatoikia (Πολυκατοικία) An apartment block, lit. a many-homes place, from *poly*, many, and *katoikia*, home or dwelling place.

Prosphyges (Πρόσφυγες) Refugees.

Syntagma (Σύνταγμα) Constitution, as in Constitution Square; also regiment.

Tourkovouno (Τουρκοβουνό) Turkish mountain: the hilly outcrop north-northeast of Lycabettus.

Further Reading

About, Edmond, *Greece and the Greeks of the Present Day*. Edinburgh: Constable, 1855.

Alexiou, Margaret, *The Ritual Lament in Greek Tradition*. Cambridge: Cambridge University Press, 1974.

American School of Classical Studies at Athens (ASCS): Princeton. Series of illustrated booklets about the Agora of Athens, arising from the School's extensive excavations.

Andersen, Hans Christian, *Diaries*, Patricia L. Conroy and Sven H. Rossel (ed.) Seattle/London: 1990.

Andrews, Kevin, *Athens Alive*. Athens: Hermes Publications, 1979.

Andrews, Kevin, *Athens*. London/New York: Dent, 1967.

Antoniou, Jim, *Plaka*. Athens: Lycabettus Press, 1973.

Baedeker, Karl, *Greece: Handbook for Travellers*. London: Baedeker, 2nd edn., 1894.

Barber, Robin (ed.), *Athens: Blue Guide*. London: A&C Black, 1999.

Bastea, Eleni, *The Creation of Modern Athens: Planning the Myth*. Cambridge: Cambridge University Press, 2000.

Beard, Mary, *The Parthenon*. London: Profile Books, 2002.

Beaton, Roderick, *An Introduction to Modern Greek Literature*. 2nd edition (revd). Oxford: Oxford University Press, 1994.

Beaton, Roderick, *George Seferis: Waiting for the Angel*. New Haven/London: Yale University Press, 2003.

Benaki Museum, *Athens 1839-1900: a Photographic Record*. Athens: Benaki Museum, 1985. Expanded edn., ed. Fani Constantinou, 2003.

Biris, Kostas E., *Ai Athinai apo tou 19ou eis ton 20on Aiona (Athens from the Nineteenth to the Twentieth Century)*. Athens: Melissa, 1966, 1995.

Bosanquet, Ellen S., *The Tale of Athens*. London: Methuen, 1932.

Bosanquet, Mrs. R. C. (the same person), *Days in Attica*. London: Methuen, 1914.

Bouras, Haralambos *et al*, *Athinai apo tin Klasiki Epochi eos Simera (Athens from the Classical Period until Today)*. Athens: 2000.

Bower, Leonard and Bolitho, Gordon, *Otho I: King of Greece*. London: Selwyn & Blount, 1939.

Brewer, David, *The Flame of Freedom: the Greek War of Independence 1821-1833*. London: John Murray, 2001.

Byron, George Gordon, Lord, "Notes on the State of Greece", from the Preface to *Childe Harold*, Canto Two, in Lord Byron, *Selected Poems*. London: Penguin Books, 1996.

Cainadas, Elias, Margaris, Nikos S. and Theodorakakis, Marios, *Flowers of Athens, a Field Guide*. Athens: Patakis, 2000.

Calligas, Lizzie, *The Sacred Way*. Athens: Agra Publications, 1998.

Camp, John M., *The Archaeology of Athens*. New Haven/London: Yale University Press, 2001.

Chandler, R., *Travels in Asia Minor and Greece: or, An Account of a Tour, made at the Expense of the Society of Dilettanti*. 2 vols., 3rd edn., London: Booker & Priestley, 1817.

Chirico, Giorgio de, *The Memoirs of Giorgio de Chirico*. London: Peter Owen, 1971.

Clogg, Richard, *A Concise History of Greece*. 2nd edn., Cambridge: Cambridge University Press, 2002.

Constantinou, Fani and Kardamitsi-Adamou, M., *Athina Tote kai Tora* (Athens Then and Now). Athens: Olkos, 2003.

Dodwell, Edward, *A Classical and Topographical Tour through Greece in the Years 1801, 1805 and 1806*. 2 vols, London: Rodwell & Martin, 1819.

Drosinis, G., *Skorpia Phylla tis Zois mou (Scattered Leaves from my Life)*. 3 vols., Athens: Society for the Distribution of Useful Books (SDOV), 1982, 1983, 1985.

Duckworth, H. T. F., *Some Pages of Levantine History*. London: Alexander Moring, n.d.

Elytis, Odysseus, "Funerary Epigrams", John Chioles (trans.), in *Greece: a Traveler's Literary Companion*. Artemis Leontis (ed.), San Francisco: Whereabouts Press, 1997.

Finlay, George, *The Journals and Letters of George Finlay*. J. M. Hussey (ed.), 2 vols, Camberley: Porphyrogenitus, 1995.

Freud, Sigmund, "A Disturbance of Memory on the Acropolis", in *Complete Psychological Works of Sigmund Freud*. James Strachey (ed.), vol 22, London: Hogarth Press, 1964.

Garrett, Martin, *Greece: a Literary Companion*. London: John Murray, 1994.

Hall, Peter, *Cities in Civilization: Culture, Innovation and Urban Order.* London: Weidenfeld & Nicolson, 1998.

Haritatos, Manos *et al, I Athina ton Valkanikon Polemon 1912-1913 (The Athens of the Balkan Wars 1912-1913).* Athens: Cultural Centre, Municipality of Athens, and ELIA, 1993.

Hetherington, Paul, *Byzantine and Medieval Greece: Churches, Castles and Art.* London: John Murray, 1991.

Hinks, Roger, *The Gymnasium of the Mind: the Journals of Roger Hinks 1933-1963.* Wilton, Wilts.: Michael Murray, 1984.

Hirschon, Renée, *Heirs of the Greek Catastrophe: the Social Life of Asia Minor Refugees in Piraeus.* New York/Oxford: Berghahn Books, 1998.

Horton, George, *Modern Athens.* New York: Scribner's, 1901.

Kaftantzoglou, Roxane, *Sti Skia tou Ierou Vrachou: Topos kai Mnimi sta Anaphiotika (In the Shadow of the Holy Rock: Place and Memory in the Anaphiotika).* Athens: Ellinika Grammata, 2001.

Kanellopoulos, Panagiotis, *Athens.* Philip Sherrard (trans.), Munich: Knorr & Hirtle Verlag, 1964.

Kardamitsi-Adami, M., *Otan Ktizotan i Athina: Dimosia Ktiria 19ou Aiona (When Athens Was Being Built: Public Buildings of the 19th Century).* Athens: Libro, 1999.

Keeley, Edmund, *Inventing Paradise: the Greek Journey 1937-47.* New York: Farrar, Straus & Giroux, 1999.

Koliopoulos, John and Veremis, Thanos, *Greece, the Modern Sequel: from 1831 to the Present.* London: Hurst & Co., 2002.

Korres, Manolis, *The Stones of the Parthenon.* Athens: Melissa, 2000.

Koubis, Takis *et al, Athens 2002: Absolute Realism: 8th International Exhibition of Architecture, Venice Biennale 2002.* Athens: Hellenic Ministry of Culture, 2002.

Laborde, L.-E. de, *Athènes aux XVe, XVIe et XVIIe siècles.* 2 vols, Paris: J. Renouard, 1854.

Lancaster, Osbert, *Classical Landscape with Figures.* London: John Murray, 1947.

Lancaster, Osbert, *Sailing to Byzantium: an Architectural Companion.* London: John Murray, 1969.

Leontis, Artemis (ed.), *Greece: A Traveler's Literary Companion.* San Francisco: Whereabouts Press, 1997.

Leontis, Artemis, *Topographies of Hellenism: Mapping the Homeland.* Ithaca/London: Cornell University, 1995.

Lidderdale, H. A. (ed.), *Makriyiannis: the Memoirs of General Makriyiannis 1797-1864.* Oxford: Oxford University Press, 1966.

Llewellyn Smith, Michael, *The British Embassy, Athens.* Athens: British Embassy, 1998.

Llewellyn Smith, Michael, *Olympics in Athens, 1896.* London: Profile Books, 2004.

Lorenzatos, Zissimos, *The Drama of Quality: Selected Essays.* Liadain Sherrard (trans.), Limni: Denise Harvey, 2000; (includes essays on Papadiamantis and Pikionis).

Lucas, F. L. and Lucas, Prudence, *From Olympus to the Styx.* London: Cassell, 1934.

Lytton, 1st Earl, "Athens", in *After Paradise.* London: 1865.

Mackenzie, Compton, *First Athenian Memories.* London: Cassell, 1931.

Mackenzie, Molly, *Turkish Athens.* Reading: Ithaca Press, 1992.

Mahaffy, J. P., *Rambles and Studies in Greece.* 5th edn., London: Macmillan, 1907.

Mahaffy, J. P., "Greece in 1884", *The English Illustrated Magazine*, vol 1, 1884.

Matton, Lya and Matton, Raymond, *Athènes et ses monuments du XVIIe siècle à nos jours.* Athens: Institut Français d'Athènes, 1963.

Maurras, Charles, *Anthinea: d'Athènes à Florence.* 9th edn., Paris: Félix Juven, 1913.

Mazower, Mark, *Inside Hitler's Greece: the Experience of Occupation, 1941-44.* New Haven/ London: Yale University Press, 1993.

Melville, Herman, *Collected Poems.* Howard P. Vincent (ed.), Chicago: Packard & Co., 1947.

Melville, Herman, *Journals.* Evanston & Chicago: Northwestern University Press, 1989.

Micheli, Lisa, *I Athina se Tonous Elassones (Athens in Minor Tones).* Athens, 1987.

Micheli, Lisa, *Monastiraki: Athens's Old Market.* Athens: Oceanida, 1985.

Micheli, Lisa, *Plaka.* Athens: 1985.

Miller, Henry, *The Colossus of Maroussi*. New York: New Directions, 1941.

Miller, William, "The Early Years of Modern Athens." London: Anglo-Hellenic League, 1926.

Miller, William, *Greece*. London: Ernest Benn, 1928.

Miller, William, *Greek Life in Town and Country*. London: George Newnes, 1905.

Ministry of Culture and Museum of Cycladic Art, *The City beneath the City: Finds from Excavations for the Metropolitan Railway of Athens*. Athens: Kapon Editions, 2000.

Mommsen, Theodore, "The Venetians in Athens and the Destruction of the Parthenon in 1687", in *Medieval and Renaissance Studies*. New York: 1959.

Morgenthau, Henry, *I Was Sent to Athens*. New York: Doubleday, 1929.

Murray, John, *Handbook for Travellers in Greece*. 6th edn., London: John Murray, 1896.

Nestlehutt, Mark S., "Anglicans in Greece: The Episcopal Mission and the English Chaplaincy at Athens", in *Anglican and Episcopal History*, vol LXV, 1996.

Nicolson, Harold, *Sir Arthur Nicolson, Bart., First Lord Carnock: a Study in the Old Diplomacy*. London: Constable, 1930.

Panourgia, Neni, *Fragments of Death, Fables of Identity: An Athenian Autobiography*. Wisconsin: University of Wisconsin Press, 1995.

Papageorgiou-Venetas, Alexander, *Athina: ena Orama tou Klasikismou (Athens: a Vision of Classicism)*. Athens: 2001.

Papageorgiou-Venetas, Alexander, "The Ancient Heritage in Modern Metropolitan Life: Landscaping the Archaeological Sites of Athens", *Annales d'Esthétique*, vol 29-30, 1990-91.

Pausanias, *Guide to Greece*. Peter Levi (trans.), London: Penguin, 1971.

Petsalis-Diomedis, Thanasis, *Deka Tria Chronia (Thirteen Years)*. Athens: Hestia, 1964.

Plato, *The Last Days of Socrates*. Hugh Tredennick (trans.) London: Penguin Books, 1954.

Plutarch, "Pericles", *The Rise and Fall of Athens*. Ian Scott-Kilvert (trans.), London: ,

Prevelakis, Georges, *Athènes: urbanisme, culture et politique*. Paris: L'Harmattan, 2000. (There is also a Greek edition, entitled

Epistrophi stin Athina (Return to Athens). Athens: Hestia, 2001.)

Protestou, Errica, *Athens: a Guide to Recent Architecture*. London: Könemann, 1998.

Renan, Ernest, *The Memoirs of Ernest Renan (Souvenirs d'enfance et de jeunesse)*. J. Lewis May (ed.), London: Geoffrey Bles, 1935.

Ricketts, Charles, *Pages from a Diary in Greece*. Paul Delaney (ed.), Edinburgh: Tragara Press, 1978.

Roessel, David, *In Byron's Shadow: Modern Greece in the English and American Imagination*. Oxford: Oxford University Press, 2002.

Roides, Emmanuel, "Athinaikoi Peripatoi" ("Athenian Walks"), in *Apanta (Complete Works)*. Alkis Angelou (ed.), vol 5, Athens: 1894-1904.

Seferis, George, *A Poet's Journal, Days of 1945-1951*. A. Anagnostopoulos (trans.), Cambridge, Mass.: Harvard University Press, 1951.

Seferis, George, *On the Greek Style: Selected Essays on Poetry and Hellenism*. Rex Warner & Th. D. Frangopolous (trans.), New York: Little, Brown, 1966. (Contains essay on Makriyiannis.)

Shugart, Diane, *Athens by Neighborhood*. Athens: Ellinika Grammata, 2001.

Sicilianos, Demetrios, *Old and New Athens*. London: Putnam, 1960.

Skoubourdis, Artemis, *Athens: History, Art, Monuments*. Athens: 1996.

Skouzes, Panaghis, *Chronikon tis Sklavomenis Athinas (A Chronicle of Enslaved Athens)*. Athens: 1948. (Extracts in Andrews, *Athens Alive*.)

Smyth, Ethel, *A Three-legged Tour in Greece*. London: Heinemann, 1927.

St Clair, William, *Lord Elgin and the Marbles*. Oxford: Oxford University Press, 1998.

Stoneman, Richard, *A Literary Companion to Travel in Greece*. London: Penguin Books, 1984.

Stoneman, Richard, *Land of Lost Gods: the Search for Classical Greece*. London: Hutchinson, 1987.

Stuart, James and Revett, Nicholas, *The Antiquities of Athens Measured and Delineated*. 4 vols, London: John Murray, 1762-1816.

Symonds, John Addington, "Athens," in *Sketches and Studies in Italy and Greece*. 3rd series, London: 1898.

Thackeray, W. M., *Notes of a Journey from Cornhill to Grand Cairo*. Heathfield: Cockbird Press, 1991.

Theotokas, Giorgos, "The Funeral of Palamas" (1945) and "'Great Athens' and its Future," in *Pneumatiki Poreia (Spiritual Progress)*. Athens: Hestia, 1961.

Thucydides, *The Peloponnesian War*. Rex Warner (trans.), London: Penguin, 1954.

Tomkinson, John L., *Travellers' Greece: Memories of an Enchanted Land*. Athens: Anagnosis, 2002.

Tomkinson, John L., *Athens: the City*. Athens: Anagnosis, 2002.

Tomkinson, John L., *Athens: the Suburbs*. Athens: Anagnosis, 2002.

Tsatsos, Ioanna, *Phylla Katochis (Pages from the Occupation)*. Athens: Hestia, 1976.

Tsigakou, Fani-Maria, *The Rediscovery of Greece: Travellers and Painters of the Romantic Era*. London: Thames & Hudson, 1981.

Twain, Mark, *The Innocents Abroad*. New York/Oxford: Oxford University Press, 1996.

Vatopoulos, Nikos, *Facing Athens: the Façades of a Capital City*. Athens: Potamos, 2003.

Veniselos, Helena, *À l'ombre de Veniselos*. Paris: Editions Génin, 1955.

Vikelas, Dimitrios, "L'Athènes d'aujourd'hui", in *Apanta (Complete Works)*. Alkis Angelou (ed.), vol 8, Athens, 1997.

Vikelas, Dimitrios, "To Nekrotapheio ton Athinon" ("The Athens Cemetery"), in *Apanta (Complete Works)*. Alkis Angelou (ed.), vol 5, Athens, 1997.

Vitti, Mario (ed.), *I Stratiotiki Zoi en Elladi (Military Life in Greece)* 1st edn., Vraila, 1870. Athens: Hestia, 1993.

Warner, Rex, *Views of Attica and its Surroundings*. London: John Lehmann, 1950.

Wilson, Edmund, *Europe without Baedeker*. New York: Doubleday, 1967.

Wordsworth, Rev. Christopher, *Athens and Attica: Journal of a Residence There*. 2nd edn., London: John Murray, 1837.

Yalouri, Eleana, *The Acropolis: Global Fame, Local Claim*. Oxford/New York: Berg, 2001.

Yiannakopoulos, Georgios A. (ed.), *Refugee Greece: Photographs from the Archive of the Centre for Asia Minor Studies*. Athens: 1992.

Index of Literary & Historical Names

Index of Places & Landmarks

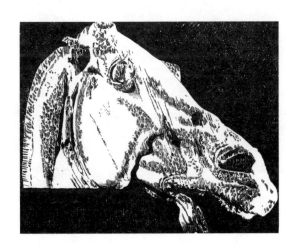